Acknowledgments

Writing a baking book has always been one of my dreams, and thanks to a fantastic team of people it has happened.

I am very grateful to the following people who have contributed so much to this book. Jo Turner for believing in me and making this all possible; Marley Flory for designing the book (Penguin edition), I love your style; Jess Redman for editing (Penguin edition), thank you for making it so easy; Adrian Lander for the beautiful photography, always a pleasure to work with you; my wonderful partner Tim Keenan, for all of your help with recipe testing, taste testing and assisting at the photo shoot; and finally my Mum and Dad, for allowing me to develop my baking skills as a child, make a mess of your kitchen and use the oven in the middle of summer—love you both.

BAKE

THE ESSENTIAL COMPANION

Alison Thompson

Photography by Adrian Lander

TUTTLE Publishing

Tokyo | Rutland, Vermont | Singapore

Contents

Introduction

I have loved baking for as long as I can remember. At the age of eleven I put together a cookbook full of my favorite recipes. I spent many weekends tapping out the carefully selected recipes on my mother's typewriter, then illustrated the book with drawings and bound it with a plaited piece of wool. I still have the book to this day and will continue to use it forever, as it is full of childhood memories and great recipes that work every time.

Bake is really an extension of that first book. Twenty years on there are, unsurprisingly, many more recipes, with varying levels of difficulty. The recipes included here are my absolute favorites, many of which I have been making for years. Others have kindly been given to me by friends and family; some were passed down from my great-grandmother, who was a wonderful cook. During the fifteen years I've been working as a chef and pastry chef, I have refined my baking skills—and in this book I share with you everything I know.

Baking is so satisfying; we learn new skills each time we try a new recipe. But best of all, baking brings us together, both in the kitchen and at the table—I love watching the smiles as people take their first mouthful and eat with joy.

I wish you every success with your baking and hope you find it as rewarding as I do.

Alison Thompson

Alison Thompson

Tips for Successful Baking

Read the recipe before you begin
Read through the entire recipe before you begin baking, ensuring that you have all the ingredients and equipment required, and the necessary time to complete the recipe without rushing.

Assemble ingredients and equipment before you begin
Always weigh and measure the necessary ingredients and prepare any equipment (e.g. line cake pans or baking sheets) before beginning a recipe.

Preheat the oven
Always preheat the oven to the specified temperature. Trying to bake in an oven that is not preheated will alter the cooking time, and will adversely affect the outcome of most recipes.

Weigh and measure accurately
For a recipe to work, the ingredients need to be measured as perfectly as possible. Take your time weighing and measuring to avoid mistakes.

Clean up as you go
Keep your work surface clean and organized. This will help avoid any mix-ups and allow you to work much faster.

Follow the recipe
The first time you make a recipe, follow it exactly. Afterwards you can make a note of any changes you might want to try next time.

Practice makes perfect
Baking is a skill that grows over a lifetime. The more you practice, the better and quicker you will become.

Basic Baking Techniques

Beating
Beating is a quick mixing process used to aerate a mixture. Unless otherwise specified, it should be done in the bowl of an electric mixer fitted with the paddle attachment, on medium to high speed. Some beating (such as creaming butter and sugar) can be done with hand-held electric beaters.

Prebaking (sometimes called blind baking)
Prebaking is the precooking of a pastry case, using weights to keep the pastry from rising. Ensure the pastry case has been well chilled before prebaking to prevent shrinking. Preheat the oven to the required temperature, then line the inside of the pastry case with aluminum foil or parchment baking paper. Fill the case to the top with ceramic prebaking beans (or use rice or dried pulses) and fold the aluminum foil or paper over the top of the beans. Bake until the edges of the pastry begin to color, then remove the weights and aluminum foil or paper. Return to the oven and cook until golden. Any cracks or holes in the case can be repaired with raw pastry then the case returned to the oven until set. (Note: Rice or pulses that have been used for prebaking are no longer able to be consumed—store them separately and use for prebaking only.)

Checking that baked items are cooked
As every oven is different, times and temperatures for baking can only ever be taken as a guide. It's important to know how to tell when products are cooked.

- When bread is ready it will be golden brown and firm to the touch, and when tapped it will sound hollow.

- When a cake is ready, a skewer inserted into the center will come out clean, and the cake will have come away from the sides of the pan. (Sponge cakes require a different technique: press gently in the center of the cake and if the sponge springs back, it is ready.)

Flouring a work surface

Many bread and pastry doughs must be rolled out on a surface that has been dusted with flour; this prevents sticking. A sieve or shaker is the best way to lightly and evenly dust your work surface with flour.

Folding

Folding is a gentle method of mixing ingredients and is usually used to combine beaten egg whites with another mixture. Folding is always done by hand, never with an electric mixer. Use a rubber spatula and drag it through the center of the mixture towards yourself, then give the bowl a quarter turn and repeat. Continue this process until the mixture is evenly combined.

Freezing

Some uncooked and cooked baked goods can be frozen. Always wrap items well in plastic wrap and label with the product name and date made.

- Cooked (un-iced) cakes can be frozen for up to 3 months.
- Bread and brioche can be frozen for up to 3 months.
- Uncooked puff, sweet and savory pastry can be frozen for up to 1 month.

Cakes and breads can be defrosted at room temperature (allow up to 8 hours for large items). Frozen raw pastries (such as puff, sweet and savory) are best defrosted in the refrigerator overnight.

Kneading

Although most kneading can be done in an electric mixer, you will still have to knead the dough or pastry by hand into a smooth shape for baking or rolling out.

If you do not have an electric mixer, most bread doughs can be mixed by hand in a large bowl, then kneaded until smooth and elastic on a lightly floured work surface.

To knead by hand, begin by shaping the dough into a ball on your work surface, then all in one motion use the heel of your hand to push the dough downwards and away from yourself. Fold the dough over itself back into a ball. Give the dough a quarter turn and repeat. Continue this process until the desired texture is achieved. (Kneading time is usually the same whether using a mixer or kneading by hand.)

Lining with parchment baking paper

Lining your pan will ensure the cake comes out easily, without sticking. To line the base of the pan, place your cake pan on a sheet of parchment baking paper and use a pencil to trace around the base. Using scissors, cut around the shape, cutting about 1 in (2.5 cm) outside the line. Snip around the edge of the paper at 1 in (2.5 cm) intervals, stopping at the drawn line. Spray the inside of the cake pan with vegetable oil or brush with melted butter, then press the cut-out parchment baking paper into the base, allowing the snipped tabs to fold up the sides of the pan. To line the sides of the pan, cut a strip of paper that is as wide as the height of the pan and long enough to wrap around the outside of the pan. Place the strip into the cake pan, pressing it against the sides, and use a little vegetable oil spray or melted butter to secure the join.

Lining with pastry

To line a pie dish or tart pan with pastry, first knead the pastry into a smooth ball. On a lightly floured work surface, roll out the pastry to the desired shape—it should be slightly larger than the dish to be lined and $\frac{1}{8}$ in (3 mm) in thickness. Wrap the pastry gently around the rolling pin, then carefully unroll the pastry over the dish. Press the pastry into the corners of the dish; if it tears, press it together to seal the holes. Use a sharp knife to trim excess pastry from around the top of the dish.

Piping

Piping is when a mixture is forced through a piping bag and out of a nozzle to create a particular shape or design. Whipped cream, choux pastry, icing and meringue are all commonly piped. To pipe, half-fill a piping bag with your mixture, then twist the top of the bag to remove any air. Apply even pressure from the top with one hand to force the ingredients out through the nozzle, and use your other hand to guide the bag (without applying pressure).

Placement in the oven

The center of the oven is the best place to bake. If you have to bake on two levels, rotate the baking sheets halfway through the cooking time to ensure an even result.

Proving (letting the dough rise)

Proving refers to the period during which a yeast dough is set aside to leaven (rise). The process takes place in two steps. After a yeast dough is mixed, it is placed in a bowl and covered with plastic wrap, then allowed to rise until doubled in size—this is the first proving. (Always oil the bowl to prevent the dough sticking.) The second proving occurs after the dough has been punched down and formed into the shape it is to be baked in.

The times specified for proving should be used as a guide only, as the amount of time needed will vary depending on room temperature—bread may take longer to rise if the room is cool. All of the recipes here ask you to put the dough in a warm place; choose a warm room in your house, or place the dough next to the oven.

TIP Here is a technique I often use for proving. The benefit of this method is that the dough has its first proving in the refrigerator overnight, saving you a couple of hours the next day—great if you want to enjoy fresh bread for breakfast.

Make the dough with cold water (it must be cold for this method to work). Place in a bowl or container large enough to allow plenty of room for rising, and cover tightly with a lid or plastic wrap. Refrigerate overnight (this is the first proving). The next day, remove the dough (or as much of it as you need) from the refrigerator and continue to follow the recipe as usual; the second proving will just take a bit longer because the dough is cold. The dough will keep for up to 3 days in the refrigerator, allowing you to bake fresh bread with little effort 3 days in a row.

Punching down (also called knocking back)

This process is performed after the first rising of a yeast dough. It requires you to punch (knock) the air out of the dough to return it to its original volume. To punch back the dough, press the dough down firmly with your hands, then turn it over and press down again—repeat three or four times.

Separating eggs

This is the process of separating the egg yolk from the egg white. Carefully crack the egg in half over a bowl, allowing the egg white to drain into the bowl while keeping the yolk in the shell. Very gently transfer the yolk back and forth from one half of the shell to the other, until all the egg white is in the bowl. Place the yolk in a separate bowl. (Note: If any yolk or shell falls into the egg white, use a large piece of egg shell to scoop it out.)

Sifting

It is essential to sift the dry ingredients for cakes and biscuits to aerate the mixture, remove lumps and make sure the various dry ingredients are well combined. To sift dry ingredients, place a large piece of parchment baking paper on your work surface, place the dry ingredients into a sieve and shake them through onto the parchment baking paper. Then lift up the parchment baking paper and pour the ingredients into the bowl. (Note: There is no need to sift flour for bread recipes.)

Splitting cakes into layers

To split a cake into even layers, a long serrated bread knife is required. Place the cake on a plate or board and use the knife to mark around the edge of the cake where you would like to cut it. To remove the first layer, cut $\frac{3}{8}$ in (1 cm) into the cake all the way around, then continue to turn the cake, cutting deeper and deeper, until you reach the center. Transfer the top layer to another plate and repeat the process to remove the next layer.

Straining

Straining is the process whereby liquids are poured or passed through a sieve to remove lumps.

Tempering chocolate

Tempering is the process of heating and cooling chocolate in a controlled way that allows uniform, small cocoa butter crystals to form. When chocolate is tempered correctly the chocolate will have a glossy appearance, snap when broken, and have a smooth feel in the mouth. Incorrectly tempered chocolate will have a matte finish and crumbly texture, and will melt easily when handled.

There are many ways to temper chocolate. Below is the method I like to use: it is quick, reliable and less messy than other techniques. Note that a cooking thermometer is required.

1 Chop the chocolate (minimum 9 oz/250 g) into small pieces and place two-thirds of it in a heatproof bowl.

2 One-third-fill a saucepan with water and bring to a boil, then remove from the heat. Place the bowl of chocolate on top (the base of the bowl should not touch the water) and allow the chocolate to melt and reach a temperature of 104–113°F (40–45°C). Remove the bowl from the saucepan of water and dry the bottom of the bowl to prevent any water drops from getting into the chocolate. (Alternatively, the chocolate can be melted in the microwave for 30 seconds at a time, stirring well between each burst.)

3 Add half of the remaining chocolate to the melted chocolate and stir well until melted. Keep adding the remaining chocolate a little at a time, stirring constantly, until the chocolate begins to melt more slowly. Stop adding chocolate at this stage and stir well. The desired temperature for the chocolate at this point is 90°F (32°C) for dark chocolate and 86°F (30°C) for milk or white chocolate. Keep stirring until the chocolate cools to this temperature. (If the chocolate gets too cold, place the bowl over the hot water again for a few seconds.)

4 To test if the chocolate is tempered, drizzle a small amount onto a spatula or piece of aluminum foil. The chocolate should set within 3–4 minutes (at room temperature) and have a smooth glossy appearance; it is now ready and must be used immediately.

Turning a cake out of the pan

Most cake recipes will suggest that the cooked cake be cooled in the pan for a period of time before turning out. This is because cakes are very fragile when hot.

When the cake has cooled slightly, place a wire rack upside down on top of the cake pan, then invert the cake onto the wire rack. Carefully lift up the cake pan to remove it, and peel off the parchment baking paper. Gently turn cake over and allow to cool completely on the wire rack.

Whipping

This technique is usually used for cream or egg whites. Use an electric mixer fitted with the whisk attachment, or use hand-held electric beaters. To avoid making a mess, start whipping at a low speed then gradually increase the speed. Recipes often state to whip cream or eggs until 'soft peaks' or 'firm peaks' form: soft peaks should not hold their shape, while firm peaks should hold their shape. (Note: Be careful not to overwhip: overwhipped cream will quickly turn to butter, and overwhipped egg whites will become lumpy and dry.)

Whisking

Move your whisk quickly and vigorously through the mixture, from left to right, until the mixture is smooth.

Zesting

Use a fine grater or a zester to remove the zest from the surface of citrus fruits such as lemons, limes and oranges. Be careful not to remove any of the bitter white pith.

Equipment and Utensils

Baking dishes

Baking dishes are used for baking pies, puddings and other desserts, and are usually made from glass or ceramic. I have used two sizes in this book: a 3 pt 3 fl oz (1.5 L) dish, and 8 fl oz (250 ml) dishes for individual serves.

Baking sheets

Baking sheets come in many shapes and sizes to suit different purposes and oven sizes. The most commonly used sheet size in this book is 12 in × 16 in (30 cm × 40 cm). In most cases it will not matter what size your baking sheet is as long as the items you are baking fit on the sheet.

Bowls

A graduated set of stainless-steel mixing bowls is useful for mixing different-sized mixtures. Microwave-safe plastic or glass bowls are essential for heating and melting ingredients in the microwave.

Brownie pan

A 8 in × 12 in (20 cm × 30 cm) brownie pan with straight sides is used for all brownies in this book. Always line your brownie pan with parchment baking paper, leaving some paper overhanging the sides so the cooked brownies can easily be lifted out.

Cake pans

Cake pans come in many sizes. The most commonly used pans in this book are a 8 in (20 cm) round cake pan and a 10 in (25 cm) round cake pan. Springform pans have removable sides, allowing the pan to be removed from the cake, rather than the cake from the pan; they are particularly useful for cakes with a topping that may fall off or be damaged if the cake was turned upside down. Using a pan that is a little larger or smaller than that specified will not affect the recipe too much. However, if your pan is considerably different, you may need to adjust the cooking time.

Cherry pitter

A cherry pitter is a small tool that allows you to remove the seed from a cherry while keeping the fruit intact. They are available from cookware shops.

Cutters

A graduated set of round cutters is essential for cutting out biscuits, scones and pastry. I have also used a gingerbread-man cutter in this book. Many other cutter shapes are available, allowing you to create biscuits to suit a theme or event. Cutters come in lots of different sizes—the smaller the cutter you choose, the more biscuits you will make.

To use a cutter, first dip it in flour (to prevent sticking) then shake off the excess. Press the cutter down firmly on the dough or pastry, and remove in one clean action.

Double boiler

A double boiler is used to gently heat or melt ingredients such as chocolate. You can buy double boilers from cookware shops. To make your own, one-third-fill a medium-sized saucepan with water and set a heatproof bowl on top. The bowl should fit neatly into the saucepan, without touching the water. Place the saucepan over medium heat and bring the water almost to a simmer (be careful not to boil the water, as this can quickly overheat your ingredients).

Dough scraper

A metal or plastic dough scraper is useful for cleaning the last of the dough from your bench and for portioning dough and pastry. The plastic versions sometimes have one edge rounded for scraping ingredients out of bowls.

Electric mixer

A freestanding electric mixer is an invaluable addition to the baker's kitchen. Choose a good-quality mixer that comes with three attachments: whisk, dough hook and paddle. If you do not have an electric mixer, hand-held electric beaters will suffice for tasks such as creaming butter and sugar, and whipping cream or egg whites. However, you will not be able to use them to mix dough or pastry; mix these by hand in a large bowl and then knead on a lightly floured surface. (Kneading time is the same whether using a mixer or kneading by hand.)

Food processor

An electric food processor is primarily used to grind, chop and mix ingredients. Choose a processor with a good-quality bowl and blade.

Hand-held electric beaters

Hand-held electric beaters can be used for creaming butter and sugar, and whipping cream and egg whites. Many cake batters can be made with electric beaters instead of a freestanding electric mixer.

Knives

There are three knives that I use regularly when baking. The first is a long serrated knife, used for splitting cakes into layers and slicing bread loaves. I also have a large chef's knife for chopping ingredients such as nuts, veg-

etables and chocolate. The last is a small paring knife, essential for smaller jobs such as scoring decorative designs in pastry and trimming fruit.

Loaf pan

Loaf pans are used for baking loaves of bread and brioche. For the recipes in this book I have used a 8½ in × 4½ in (22 cm × 11 cm) loaf pan. If your loaf pan is slightly larger or smaller it will not affect the recipe too much. However, if it is considerably different you may need to adjust the cooking time.

Measuring cups

I tend not to use measuring cups when baking, as weighing dry ingredients is far more accurate and it's easier to measure liquids in a measuring jug.

Measuring jug

I have two measuring jugs: one for measuring liquids up to 8 fl oz (250 ml), and a larger one that holds up to 34 fl oz (1 l). Using the smaller jug for small quantities gives a more accurate measurement. Always place your jug on a flat surface and check the measurement at eye level to ensure it is exact.

Measuring spoons

A graduated set of small spoons (¼ teaspoon, ½ teaspoon, 1 teaspoon and 1 tablespoon) is required to measure small amounts of liquid and dry ingredients. Be sure to use level spoonfuls for an accurate measurement (you can level dry ingredients with the back of a knife).

Microwave

A microwave is not essential but can be useful for tasks such as melting or softening butter, and melting chocolate. Be sure to use microwave-safe cookware, and check the food regularly. Chocolate should be stirred every 20–30 seconds to prevent burning.

Muffin trays

Six- or 12-hole muffin trays are required for baking muffins and cupcakes. Line them with paper cases to make cleaning easy. A standard muffin-tray hole is 3 in (7.5 cm) in diameter and 1½ in (4 cm) deep. If you are using jumbo or mini muffin trays, you'll need to adjust the cooking time.

Palette knives

Palette knives are used for spreading icings and cake fillings. They usually have a plastic or wooden handle and a long, flat, flexible metal blade with a rounded end. They are available in various sizes to suit different jobs. One large and one small palette knife is adequate.

Pastry brush

Pastry brushes are used for brushing baking pans and dishes with melted butter or oil, brushing glazes and syrups onto pastries and cakes, and brushing melted butter between layers of phyllo pastry. Choose a good-quality brush, and wash and dry it well after each use. If bristles begin to fall out, discard it and buy a new one.

Pie dish

A pie dish with a diameter of 10 in (25 cm) and depth of 2 in (5 cm) is used for the recipes in this book. Choose a dish made from glass or ceramic, with smooth, angled sides that allow you to easily remove slices of pie.

Piping bags

Piping bags are used for piping soft mixtures into shapes for baking or decoration. Disposable piping bags are the easiest option and can be bought at cookware shops. Reusable piping bags must be turned inside out and washed and dried thoroughly between each use. For smaller jobs, like piping chocolate for decoration, you can use a small plastic bag with the corner snipped off. For all larger jobs, like piping choux pastry or whipped cream, a piping bag is essential.

Piping nozzles

Piping nozzles are fitted into the base of piping bags. They come in different shapes and sizes, for different purposes.

Rolling pin

A rolling pin is a long, smooth cylinder used for rolling out pastry and dough. Choose a rolling pin at least 16 in (40 cm) in length. I prefer a wooden rolling pin, but choose whichever type you feel most comfortable using—whether it has handles or not is up to you.

Scales

Scales are the most accurate way to measure ingredients. A set of digital scales that measures in small increments (¼ oz/5 g or less) is the best choice. A set that can determine weights up to 4 lb 6 oz (2 kg) will be adequate and is quite inexpensive. Some models can also be set to measure in ounces.

Sieve

A mesh sieve is used for sifting and combining dry ingredients, and for straining liquids. It's good to have a couple of different sizes on hand for large and small quantities.

Silicon baking sheets

Used in place of parchment baking paper to line baking pans, these non-stick reusable sheets can save a lot of waste and money in the long run. They will last for years if looked after: wash after use with a soft sponge in soapy water and dry well. Never scrub these sheets with anything abrasive or use a knife on them. Be sure to buy them in the exact size needed to fit your baking pans, as they cannot be cut to size.

Spatulas

Spatulas are used for mixing ingredients and scraping down the sides of a bowl. It's handy to have at least a couple, in different sizes. Rubber or silicon is the best option. (Silicon spatulas are heat resistant and can be used to stir ingredients during cooking.) Unlike wooden spoons, spatulas are not porous and will not absorb flavors.

Tart pans and rings

The tart pans most commonly called for in this book are a 10 in (25 cm) round tart pan with a removable base, and individual 4 in (10 cm) tart pans, also with removable base. I sometimes use a 14 in × 4½ in (35 cm × 11 cm) rectangular tart pan with removable base. Tart pans with a removable base allow you to easily remove the tart from the pan once it's cooked. You may choose a tart pan with either straight or fluted sides; this will not affect the recipe.

I use a tart ring for deeper tarts. Tart rings have no base (so must be set on a baking sheet) and can easily be lifted straight up off the baked tart or quiche. The tart ring used in this book is 8½ in (22 cm) in diameter and 1½ in (4 cm) deep.

Tart pans and rings do not need to be greased, due to the large amount of butter in the pastry.

Thermometers

A small probe cooking thermometer with a digital readout is the best choice for checking the temperature of chocolate when tempering. A sugar thermometer is required for cooking sugar syrups. Choose a sugar thermometer that gives a digital reading, as precision is important when cooking sugar syrups. To accurately check the temperature of a syrup, ensure the thermometer is suspended in the syrup and not touching the pot.

Timer

A small digital timer can be used to precisely measure times required for proving, mixing or baking. (Oven timers can be unreliable.)

Whisk

A whisk is used for whisking together liquid ingredients. Choose a good-quality stainless-steel whisk; cheaper versions tend to fall apart before long.

Wire racks

Wire racks are used to elevate hot baked goods, allowing them to cool quickly. Choose a strong wire rack that will not buckle under the weight of a heavy cake.

Zester

This small metal grater is used to remove the outer skin of citrus fruits in fine strands, leaving behind the white pith. Zesters are available from cookware shops, but any fine grater will do the job.

Essential Baking Ingredients

Alcohol In some recipes wine, liqueur or a spirit may be used to enhance flavor. Choose good-quality products and purchase in small quantities if you'll only be using a small amount. Once opened, store liqueurs and spirits, tightly sealed, in a cool place; store white wine in the refrigerator for up to 3 days; and store red wine at room temperature for up to 3 days.

Baking powder This raising agent is used in cakes, brownies and biscuits. Baking powder begins to react as soon as moisture is added, therefore it is important to bake items as soon as they are mixed. Store baking powder in an airtight container in a cool dry place and check the use-by date before using, as it will lose its potency over time. Baking powder and bicarbonate of soda are not interchangeable.

Baking soda (bicarbonate of soda) This raising agent is used in cakes, brownies and biscuits. Like baking powder, it reacts when moisture is added and so needs to be baked immediately after mixing. Store in an airtight container in a cool dry place and check the use-by date before using, as it will lose its potency over time. Bicarbonate of soda and baking powder are not interchangeable.

Butter Unsalted butter is specified throughout this book because of its pure flavor. If you use salted butter it will change the flavor of the end product very slightly. Do not substitute margarine for butter, as it does not have the same taste or properties.

When a recipe calls for butter at room temperature, remove the butter from the refrigerator 1–2 hours before using, to allow it to come to room temperature. For softened butter, dice the butter into cubes and keep it in a warm place until soft but not melted. Butter can also be softened in the microwave: dice the butter and microwave for 5 seconds at a time until soft.

Butter can be melted in a saucepan over low heat, or in the microwave (be sure to check regularly). Keep butter well wrapped or in an airtight container in the refrigerator, as it will absorb the flavors and odors of other foods in the refrigerator.

Chocolate Choose chocolate with a high percentage of cocoa (between 50 and 75 per cent) remembering that the higher the percentage of cocoa, the darker and more bitter the chocolate. For most baking I prefer to use a dark

chocolate with 60 per cent cocoa. Store chocolate in a cool dry place out of direct sunlight.

Gianduja (gianduia) chocolate is a sweet chocolate made with about 30 per cent hazelnut paste.

'Couverture' chocolate must contain 32–39 per cent cocoa butter. It is now widely available in supermarkets and specialty baking stores. Couverture chocolate must be tempered if melted and used for decoration, otherwise it will set with a grainy texture and matte appearance. (See page 11 for how to temper chocolate.)

Cocoa A good-quality cocoa will give your baked goods a richer flavor and color. Choose cocoa that is unsweetened and has been alkalized (a process that reduces the acidity in the powder)—look for the words 'Dutch', 'Dutch process' or 'alkalized' on the packet.

Cornstarch Cornstarch is a fine white powder made from the inner grain of corn and commonly used as a thickening agent and in the rolling out of phyllo pastry. It is also often used in gluten-free cake recipes to replace a portion of the flour.

Cream All the recipes in this book use whipping cream with 35 per cent fat, also called pouring cream. Always ensure cream is well chilled before whipping. Note that reduced-fat or light cream is unable to be whipped, as the fat content is too low.

Eggs All the recipes in this book are designed to be made with 2 oz (60 g) eggs. Free-range and organic eggs are best. Keep eggs refrigerated, use them before the use-by date (or within 1 month of laying), and never use broken or cracked eggs. Bring eggs to room temperature before baking. Excess egg whites can be stored in the refrigerator in an airtight container for up to 4 days or frozen for up to 6 months (thaw thoroughly before using). Egg yolks cannot be frozen but can be stored in an airtight container in the refrigerator for 2 days.

Flour It is important to use the highest-quality flour available to get the best results. For cakes and pastries, an all-purpose (plain) flour is the best option. When baking bread, choose a specialty bread flour or baker's flour—all-purpose (plain) flour can be used, but will give inferior results.

Self-rising flour has a shorter shelf life than plain flour as it contains baking powder. Always check the use-by date of self-rising flour before baking; if you are unsure how old it is, it's safest to purchase a new packet. You can make your own self-rising flour by adding 2 teaspoons baking powder to 1 cup (150 g) plain flour, then sifting twice to combine thoroughly.

Milk Use full-cream milk for baking unless otherwise specified.

Nuts Store nuts in an airtight container in the refrigerator for up to 6 months.

Oil A vegetable-oil spray is convenient for greasing cake pans and baking sheets. Vegetable oil is best for deep-frying as it has a very mild flavor. When a recipe calls for olive oil, use a good-quality extra-virgin olive oil, which has a distinctive flavor that works well with many baked goods.

Salt Salt is used to enhance the flavor of baked goods. It also helps develop color in the crust of breads. For baking I generally use fine sea salt, as it has a good flavor and is easily dissolved (it has a much better flavor than table salt). Sea salt flakes are sometimes sprinkled on top of baked goods to add texture and flavor. Do not use rock salt, as it will not dissolve and is too hard to be edible.

Spices Buy spices in small quantities (they lose their potency over time) and store in airtight containers in a cool dark place. Grinding your own spices is a great way to get the freshest flavor, as whole spices keep much longer than ground. Invest in a small electric spice or coffee grinder for grinding whole spices such as cinnamon, cloves and peppercorns. Nutmeg can also be bought whole and then finely grated.

Sugar Superfine sugar or fine granulated sugar is most commonly used in this book. It is simply a finer version of white sugar and dissolves easily. Confectioner's (icing) sugar (white sugar that has been ground to a fine powder) is frequently used for making icing and for dusting baked goods. Soft brown sugar is also made from white sugar, but it contains a small amount of molasses, which adds a distinctive caramel flavor and color.

Vanilla Vanilla extract is used to flavor cakes, puddings and sweet breads. Ensure you purchase a good-quality liquid vanilla extract and avoid imitations such as vanilla essence, vanillin or imitation vanilla. Store in a cool dry place in a sealed jar or bottle.

The seeds from vanilla beans may be added to icings and fillings. (To remove the seeds, split the pod in half lengthwise then scrape out the seeds using a small knife.) Vanilla beans are also often used to impart flavor to custards, ice-creams and sauces: the pod and seeds are immersed in the liquid while it is being heated, then the pods are removed.

TIP Used vanilla-bean pods retain a lot of flavor. I often dry the used pods in a warm place until crisp (this can take 2–3 days), then transfer them to a jar of superfine sugar. The vanilla flavor eventually infuses the sugar. Another method is to process the dried pods in a food processor with superfine sugar, then sieve out any larger pieces of vanilla pod. The resultant vanilla sugar can be used in place of superfine sugar in your baking recipes for extra vanilla flavor.

Yeast I always use fresh yeast when baking, as it has a far better flavor and produces a better end result than dry yeast. Fresh yeast is available from supermarkets, specialty grocers, delis and health-food stores. Alternatively, your local bakery may sell you some. Fresh yeast only has a short life span (usually no longer than 1 month), so check the use-by date before baking. Store fresh yeast in the refrigerator in its original paper packaging. (Do not store it in an airtight container or wrapped in plastic wrap, as it needs to breathe.)

Dry yeast is easier to source and more convenient to use than fresh yeast, but its effectiveness also decreases over time. If using dry yeast for any of the recipes here, you will need to use half the amount specified in the ingredients list. You will also need to rehydrate the yeast before adding it to the mixture: mix the dry yeast with 10 per cent of the liquid required for your recipe and allow to stand for 20 minutes. The mixture will begin to foam, indicating that the yeast is now active. (If it does not begin to foam, discard and start again with new yeast.) Store dry yeast in an airtight container in the refrigerator.

Measures and Temperatures

US Imperial and metric measures

Although both (US) imperial and metric measures are included in this book, it is important to note that imperial measurements are not as accurate as metric. It is worth investing in a good set of metric scales, measuring spoons and jugs to ensure best results. Always follow one set of measures throughout a recipe.

Cup and spoon measures

Cup measures are given in this book although I find using a measuring jug for liquids and weighing out all dry ingredients is more precise and gives more consistent results. Spoon measures are based on United States standards. (Note that a US or UK tablespoon is 15 ml while an Australian tablespoon is equivalent to 20 ml.)

Temperatures

Oven temperatures can vary greatly from oven to oven, any large variation in temperature may affect the end result of the product and also the cooking time. For best results it may be worth purchasing an oven thermometer to ensure the oven temperature is correct.

Millilitres	US/UK Spoon/Cup
5 ml	*1 teaspoon
15 ml	1 tablespoon
60 ml	¼ cup
80 ml	⅓ cup
125 ml	½ cup
250 ml	1 cup

*the volume of a teaspoon is the same around the world

Volumes

US spoon/cup	Millilitres	US spoon/cup	Millilitres
4 teaspoons	20 ml	¾ cup	180 ml
2 tablespoons	30 ml	⅞ cup	200 ml
¼ cup	60 ml	1 cup	250 ml
6 tablespoons	90 ml	1¼ cups	300 ml
7 tablespoons	100 ml	1⅔ cups	400 ml
⅔ cup	150 ml	5¼ cups	1.25 liter

Weights

Ounces	Grams	Ounces	Grams
⅜ oz	20 g	7 oz	200 g
½ oz	15 g	11 oz	300 g
1 oz	30 g	14 oz	400 g
2 oz	60 g	16 oz (1 lb)	450 g
3 oz	90 g	1⅛ lb	500 g
4 oz	120 g	2¼ lb	1 kg
5 oz	150 g		

Oven Temperatures

Fahrenheit	Celcius	Fahrenheit	Celcius
210°F	100°C	360°F	180°C
230°F	110°C	375°F	190°C
250°F	120°C	390°F	200°C
265°F	130°C	410°F	210°C
285°F	140°C	430°F	220°C
300°F	150°C	450°F	230°C
325°F	160°C	460°F	240°C
340°F	170°C	480°F	250°C

Sizes

Inches	Centimeters	Inches	Centimeters
⅜ in	1 cm	6 in	15 cm
1 in	2.5 cm	8 in	20 cm
2 in	5 cm	12 in	30 cm
4 in	10 cm	16 in	40 cm

Basic Recipes

Frosting for Cakes and Cupcakes

MAKES ENOUGH TO ICE A 10-IN (25-CM) CAKE OR
  24 CUPCAKES
PREPARATION TIME: 15 MINS
STORE IN AN AIRTIGHT CONTAINER AT ROOM TEM-
  PERATURE FOR UP TO 2 DAYS

8 cups (1 kg) confectioner's (icing) sugar, sifted
1/3 cup (100 g) corn syrup (liquid glucose)
1/2 cup (1 stick/125 g) unsalted butter, softened
6 tablespoons water
1 teaspoon vanilla extract
Liquid food coloring and/or finely grated citrus zest (optional)

1 Combine the sifted icing sugar, corn syrup and butter in the bowl of an electric mixer fitted with the paddle attachment. Mix on low speed until well combined.
2 Add the water and vanilla, and beat on high speed for 5 minutes. If you wish to color or flavor the icing, do so now. If the frosting is too thick, add a little more water; if it is too runny, add some extra icing sugar. Beat well again on high speed.

Cream Cheese Frosting

MAKES 3 CUPS (ENOUGH TO ICE A 10-IN/25-CM CAKE)
PREPARATION TIME: 15 MINS
STORE IN AN AIRTIGHT CONTAINER IN THE REFRIG-
  ERATOR FOR UP TO 2 DAYS

1/2 cup (1 stick/125 g) unsalted butter, softened
9 oz (250 g) cream cheese, softened
2 teaspoons vanilla extract
4 3/4 cups (600 g) confectioner's (icing) sugar

1 Place the butter, cream cheese and vanilla in the bowl of an electric mixer fitted with the paddle attachment.
2 Sift in the icing sugar. Beat on low speed until combined, then beat on high speed for 2 minutes.

Almond Cream

MAKES 3/4 CUP
PREPARATION TIME: 15 MINS
STORE IN AN AIRTIGHT CONTAINER IN THE REFRIG-
  ERATOR FOR UP TO 3 DAYS

1/3 cup (2/3 stick/75 g) unsalted butter, softened
1/3 cup (90 g) superfine sugar
1 egg
1 tablespoon custard powder
3/4 cup (100 g) almond flour

1 Beat the butter and sugar, in the bowl of an electric mixer fitted with the paddle attachment, on high speed for 5 minutes until pale and creamy.
2 Add the egg and beat well. Add the custard powder and almond flour and mix on low speed until combined.

Lemon Curd

MAKES 2 CUPS
PREPARATION TIME: 20 MINS
STORE IN AN AIRTIGHT CONTAINER IN THE REFRIG-
  ERATOR FOR UP TO 1 WEEK

1 cup (225 g) sugar
4 eggs
3/4 cup (200 ml) freshly-squeezed lemon juice
Finely grated zest of 4 lemons
3/4 cup (1 1/2 sticks/175 g) unsalted butter, diced

1 Combine the sugar, eggs, lemon juice and zest in a saucepan and whisk together to combine well. Cook over medium heat, stirring continuously with a wooden spoon, until the mixture boils.
2 Remove from the heat, stir in the butter until combined, then strain the curd through a sieve into a clean bowl.
3 Press a plastic wrap onto the surface of the curd to prevent a skin forming, then chill.

Vanilla Custard

MAKES 1½ CUPS
PREPARATION TIME: 20 MINS
STORE IN AN AIRTIGHT CONTAINER IN THE REFRIG-
ERATOR FOR UP TO 2 DAYS

3 egg yolks
¼ cup (60 g) sugar
1 tablespoon custard powder
3 teaspoons all-purpose (plain) flour
1 cup (250 ml) milk
1 vanilla bean, split and seeds scraped
1 tablespoon unsalted butter

1 Whisk together the egg yolks, sugar, custard powder and
flour in a bowl.
2 Heat the milk, vanilla bean and seeds in a small saucepan
until hot. Remove the vanilla bean, then pour the hot milk into
the yolk mixture and whisk to combine. Return the mixture
to the saucepan and whisk constantly over low heat until the
custard thickens and boils, then cook for 1 minute more.
3 Remove the custard from the heat and add the butter. Stir
well to combine.
4 Pour the custard into a clean bowl and press a plastic wrap
onto the surface to prevent a skin forming.

VARIATION
Chocolate Custard: Add ¾ cup (100 g) chopped dark chocolate
with the butter.

Apricot Glaze

MAKES ¼ CUP
PREPARATION TIME: 5 MINS
STORE IN AN AIRTIGHT CONTAINER IN THE REFRIG-
ERATOR FOR UP TO 1 WEEK

5 tablespoons apricot jam
4 teaspoons water

Place the jam and water in a small saucepan and bring to a
boil. Pass through a fine sieve and leave to cool.

Sour Cream Pastry

*Sour cream pastry is very quick and simple to make. It
can be used in any recipe requiring savory pastry. The
texture is slightly less crumbly than the Shortcrust Pastry.*

MAKES 1½ LB (650 g)
PREPARATION TIME: 20 MINS + 2 HRS CHILLING TIME
STORE IN THE REFRIGERATOR FOR UP TO 3 DAYS OR
FREEZE FOR UP TO 1 MONTH

2 cups (300 g) all-purpose (plain) flour, sifted
1 cup (2 sticks/250 g) unsalted butter, diced
1 teaspoon fine sea salt
½ cup (100 g) sour cream

1 Combine the sifted flour, butter and salt in the bowl of an
electric mixer fitted with the paddle attachment. Mix on low
speed for 5 minutes, until pieces of butter are no longer visible. Add the sour cream and mix just until the dough comes
together. (Alternatively, make the dough by hand, using your
fingertips to rub the butter into the flour, then mixing in the
sour cream until a dough forms.)
2 Remove the dough from the bowl and wrap in a plastic
wrap. Refrigerate for at least 2 hours before using.

Pizza Sauce

MAKES ENOUGH FOR 2 PIZZAS
PREPARATION TIME: 10 MINS
COOKING TIME: 30 MINS
STORE IN AN AIRTIGHT CONTAINER IN THE REFRIG-
ERATOR FOR UP TO 3 DAYS

One × 14-oz (400-g) can crushed tomatoes
1 teaspoon dried oregano
4 teaspoons extra-virgin olive oil
Salt and freshly-ground black pepper

1 Combine the tomatoes, oregano and olive oil in a saucepan. Simmer over low heat for 20–30 minutes, until thickened.
2 Season the sauce to taste with salt and freshly-ground
black pepper. Leave to cool.

Breads

Classic White Bread

This is a good basic white bread that can be made in any shape or size—just adjust the cooking time if you make smaller loaves or rolls.

MAKES 1 LOAF
PREPARATION TIME: 30 MINS + 3
  HRS FOR THE DOUGH TO RISE
COOKING TIME: 30 MINS
BEST EATEN THE DAY YOU BAKE

8 teaspoons (40 g) fresh yeast
1¼ cups (310 ml) warm water
4 teaspoons superfine sugar
2 teaspoons fine sea salt
3⅓ cups (500 g) bread flour
2 tablespoons extra-virgin olive oil
3 teaspoons water, extra
1 teaspoon sesame seeds

1 Place the yeast and water in the bowl of an electric mixer, and stir to dissolve. Add the sugar, salt, flour and olive oil to the bowl. Using the dough hook attachment, mix on low speed for 10 minutes, until the dough is smooth and elastic.

2 Remove the dough hook, leaving the dough in the bowl. Cover the bowl with plastic wrap. Leave to rise in a warm place for 2 hours, or until the dough has doubled in size.

3 Turn the dough out onto a lightly floured work surface and knead into a log shape. Place the loaf on a greased baking sheet and use a sharp knife to cut shallow slashes, ¾ in (2 cm) apart, across the top. Leave to rise in a warm place for approximately 1 hour, until the dough has doubled in size.

4 Preheat the oven to 360°F (180°C).

5 Brush the loaf with the extra water and sprinkle with the sesame seeds. Bake for 30 minutes, until the bread is golden and sounds hollow when tapped. Cool on a wire rack.

Classic Rye Bread

This recipe uses light rye flour; if you prefer you can use dark rye flour.

MAKES 2 LOAVES
PREPARATION TIME: 30 MINS + 3
    HRS 30 MINS FOR THE DOUGH TO
    RISE
COOKING TIME: 30–40 MINS
BEST EATEN THE DAY YOU BAKE

2 tablespoons (30 g) fresh yeast
2$\frac{1}{2}$ cups (625 ml) warm water
3$\frac{1}{3}$ cups (500 g) light rye flour
3$\frac{1}{3}$ cups (500 g) bread flour
1 tablespoon fine sea salt
3 teaspoons caraway seeds

1 Place the yeast and water in the bowl of an electric mixer, and stir to dissolve. Add the flours, salt and caraway seeds to the bowl. Using the dough hook attachment, mix on low speed for 2 minutes, until a dough forms. Then mix on medium speed for 5 minutes, until the dough is smooth and elastic.

2 Remove the dough hook, leaving the dough in the bowl. Cover the bowl with plastic wrap. Leave to rise in a warm place for 2 hours, or until the dough has doubled in size.

3 Turn the dough out onto a lightly floured work surface and divide into two equal pieces. Shape each piece into a long oval shape and place on a greased baking sheet. Use a sharp knife to cut shallow slashes, $\frac{3}{8}$ in (1 cm) apart, across the top of each loaf. Leave to rise again for 1–1$\frac{1}{2}$ hours, until the loaves have doubled in size.

4 Preheat the oven to 390°F (200°C).

5 Bake the loaves for 30–40 minutes, until they sound hollow when tapped. Cool on a wire rack.

Whole Wheat Bread

This whole wheat bread has a great texture due to the addition of seeds and bulgur. You can find bulgur (also known as burghul or bulghur) in the health-food section of most supermarkets.

MAKE 1 LOAF
PREPARATION TIME: 30 MINS + 3 HRS
  FOR THE DOUGH TO RISE
COOKING TIME: 30 MINS
BEST EATEN THE DAY YOU BAKE

4 teaspoons (20 g) fresh yeast
1¼ cups (300 ml) warm water
1 teaspoon fine sea salt
¼ cup (30 g) sunflower seeds
2 teaspoons caraway seeds
¼ cup (60 g) fine bulgur, soaked in cold water
  for 15 minutes then drained
2 tablespoons extra-virgin olive oil
3⅓ cups (500 g) multigrain flour
3 teaspoons water, extra
1 teaspoon caraway seeds, extra

1 Place the yeast and warm water in the bowl of an electric mixer, and stir to dissolve. Add the salt, sunflower and caraway seeds, bulgur, olive oil and flour to the bowl. Using the dough hook attachment, mix on low speed for 10 minutes, or until the dough is smooth and elastic.
2 Remove the dough hook, leaving the dough in the bowl. Cover the bowl with plastic wrap. Leave to rise in a warm place for 2 hours, or until the dough has doubled in size.
3 Turn the dough out onto a lightly floured work surface and knead into a log shape. Place on a greased baking sheet and leave to rise in a warm place for approximately 1½ hours, until the dough has doubled in size.
4 Preheat the oven to 360°F (180°C).
5 Brush the loaf with the extra water and sprinkle the extra caraway seeds over the top.
6 Bake the loaf for 30 minutes, until it is golden and sounds hollow when tapped. Cool on a wire rack.

Ciabatta

This is one of my favorite bread recipes. The loaf has a crisp salty crust and a soft chewy center.

MAKES 1 LOAF
PREPARATION TIME: 30 MINS + 5 HRS
   FOR THE DOUGH TO RISE
COOKING TIME: 30 MINS
BEST EATEN THE DAY YOU BAKE

1 tablespoon (15 g) fresh yeast
1²/₃ cups (400 ml) warm water
3¹/₃ cups (500 g) bread flour
1½ teaspoons fine sea salt
2 tablespoons extra-virgin olive oil
2 teaspoons sea salt flakes

1 Place the yeast and water in the bowl of an electric mixer, and stir to dissolve. Add the flour and fine sea salt to the bowl. Using the dough hook attachment, mix on low speed until the ingredients are well combined. Mix the dough on medium speed for a further 5 minutes—the dough will be quite wet and will look elastic.

2 Remove the dough hook, leaving the dough in the bowl. Cover the bowl with plastic wrap. Leave to rise in a warm place for 2 hours, or until the dough has doubled in size.

3 Punch down the dough, then turn out onto a well-floured work surface and leave to rise (uncovered) for 2–3 hours more, until it has again doubled in size.

4 Preheat the oven to 450°F (230°C). Grease a baking sheet.

5 With well-floured hands, carefully shape the dough into a loaf, then lift it from the bench onto the prepared sheet, taking care not to punch any air out of the dough. Drizzle the olive oil over the dough and sprinkle with the sea salt flakes.

6 Place the loaf into the oven and immediately turn the temperature down to 360°F (180°C). Bake for 30 minutes, until golden brown. Cool on a wire rack.

Polenta Bread

This is a great bread to serve with a big bowl of soup in winter. The dough can also be used to make rolls.

MAKES 2 LOAVES
PREPARATION TIME: 45 MINS + 3
  HRS FOR THE DOUGH TO RISE
COOKING TIME: 40 MINS
BEST EATEN THE DAY YOU BAKE

1 cup (250 ml) milk
1/3 cup (60 g) instant polenta (cornmeal)
2 teaspoons (10 g) fresh yeast
3/4 cup (170 ml) warm water
3 1/3 cups (500 g) bread flour
2 teaspoons fine sea salt
3 teaspoons superfine sugar
1/3 cup (60 g) instant polenta (cornmeal),
  extra

1 Heat the milk in a small saucepan until simmering. Whisk in the polenta and stir over low heat for 2 minutes, until boiling and thick. Transfer the polenta to a bowl and press a plastic wrap onto the surface to prevent a skin forming. Leave to cool.

2 Place the yeast and water in the bowl of an electric mixer, and stir to dissolve. Add the flour, salt, sugar and polenta mixture to the bowl. Mix on low speed for 10 minutes, until the dough is smooth and elastic.

3 Remove the dough hook, leaving the dough in the bowl. Cover the bowl with plastic wrap. Leave to rise in a warm place for 1 1/2 hours, or until the dough has doubled in size.

4 Punch down the dough and transfer to a floured work surface. Divide into two equal pieces, and shape each into a round loaf. Dredge the loaves in the extra polenta. Use a sharp knife to cut a shallow criss-cross pattern in the top of each loaf. Place the loaves on a greased baking sheet. Leave to rise in a warm place for 1–1 1/2 hours, until the dough has doubled in size.

5 Preheat the oven to 360°F (180°C).

6 Bake the loaves for 40 minutes, until they are golden and sound hollow when tapped. Cool on a wire rack.

VARIATION

Polenta Rolls: Divide the prepared dough into 20 pieces. Bake for 20 minutes.

Sourdough Bread

Sourdough bread takes a few days to make but it is well worth the effort. This modern version is easier to make than some traditional recipes, but still has the desired sour flavor and a great chewy texture.

MAKES 2 LOAVES
PREPARATION TIME: 30 MINS + 2
  HRS FOR THE DOUGH TO RISE + 5
  DAYS FERMENTATION
COOKING TIME: 20 MINS
BEST EATEN THE DAY YOU BAKE

2 teaspoons (10 g) fresh yeast
1¼ cups (300 ml) warm water
1 portion prepared Sourdough
  Starter (see below)
2 cups (300 g) bread flour
⅔ cup (100 g) whole wheat flour
2 teaspoons fine sea salt
¼ cup (60 ml) extra-virgin olive oil
2 teaspoons sea salt flakes

SOURDOUGH STARTER
⅞ cup (125 g) bread flour
⅞ cup (125 g) whole wheat flour
½ cup (100 g) plain natural yogurt
1 cup (250 ml) apple juice
1 cup (150 g) bread flour, extra

1 To make the Sourdough Starter, combine the bread flour, whole wheat flour, yogurt and apple juice in a bowl and mix well. Cover the bowl loosely with plastic wrap and leave at room temperature for 24 hours. Every day (at the same time of day) for the next 5 days you need to mix the starter, then sprinkle the top with ¼ cup (30 g) extra bread flour. By the fifth day your starter should be fermented—it will smell sour and feel spongy. It is now ready to use. (Leftover starter can be frozen for later use.)

2 To make the bread, place the yeast and water in the bowl of an electric mixer, and stir to dissolve. Add the Sourdough Starter, flours and salt to the bowl. Using the dough hook attachment, mix on low speed for 5 minutes, until the dough is smooth and elastic.
3 Remove the dough hook, leaving the dough in the bowl. Cover the bowl with plastic wrap. Leave to rise in a warm place for 1 hour, or until the dough has doubled in size.
4 Turn the dough out onto a lightly floured work surface and divide into two equal pieces. Shape each piece into a loaf 16 in (40 cm) long and place on a greased baking sheet. Use a sharp knife to cut shallow slashes, ¾ in (2 cm) apart, across the top of each loaf. Drizzle the loaves with olive oil, then sprinkle with the sea salt flakes. Leave to rise in a warm place for approximately 1 hour, until the dough has slightly risen.
5 Preheat the oven to 480°F (250°C).
6 Place the loaves into the oven and immediately turn the temperature down to 360°F (180°C). Bake for 20 minutes, until golden. Cool on a wire rack.

Whole Wheat Honey Loaf

MAKE 1 LOAF
PREPARATION TIME: 30 MINS +
   2 HRS 30 MINS FOR THE DOUGH
   TO RISE
COOKING TIME: 30 MINS
BEST EATEN THE DAY YOU BAKE

2 teaspoons (10 g) fresh yeast
1¼ cups (300 ml) warm water
⅔ cup (100 g) bread flour
⅔ cup (100 g) rye flour
2 cups (300 g) multigrain flour
2 teaspoons fine sea salt
1 tablespoon honey
½ cup (60 g) sunflower seeds
Egg wash: 1 egg yolk whisked with 3
   teaspoons milk
¼ cup (30 g) rolled oats

1 Place the yeast and water in the bowl of an electric mixer, and stir to dissolve. Add the flours, salt, honey and sunflower seeds to the bowl. Using the dough hook attachment, mix on low speed for 10 minutes, until the dough is smooth and elastic.

2 Remove the dough hook, leaving the dough in the bowl. Cover the bowl with plastic wrap. Leave to rise in a warm place for 1½ hours, or until the dough has doubled in size.

3 Punch down the dough and transfer to a floured work surface. Knead the dough into an oval loaf shape and place on a greased baking sheet. Brush the loaf with the egg wash and sprinkle with the rolled oats. Use a sharp knife to cut a ¾ in (2 cm) deep slash lengthwise along the center of the loaf. Leave to rise in a warm place for approximately 1 hour, until the dough has risen slightly.

4 Preheat the oven to 360°F (180°C).

5 Bake the loaf for 30 minutes, until it is golden and sounds hollow when tapped. Cool on a wire rack.

Pita Bread

This versatile Middle Eastern flat-bread can be served as an accompaniment, or filled with ingredients to make a meal on its own. It can be cooked on a charcoal grill or barbecue—it's a real treat for guests to watch them inflate.

MAKES 12
PREPARATION TIME: 30 MINS +
  2 HRS FOR THE DOUGH TO RISE
COOKING TIME: 35 MINS

1 tablespoon (15 g) fresh yeast
1¹⁄₃ cups (325 ml) warm water
3 cups (450 g) bread flour
2 teaspoons fine sea salt
1 teaspoon superfine sugar

1 Place the yeast and water in the bowl of an electric mixer, and stir to dissolve. Add the flour, salt and sugar to the bowl. Using the dough hook attachment, mix on low speed for 2 minutes, until a dough forms. Then mix on medium speed for 5 minutes, until the dough is smooth and elastic.
2 Remove the dough hook, leaving the dough in the bowl. Cover the bowl with plastic wrap. Leave to rise in a warm place for 2 hours, or until the dough has doubled in size.
3 Preheat the oven to 480°F (250°C), placing a baking sheet on the bottom shelf to preheat. Alternatively, preheat a charcoal grill or barbecue grill to hot.
4 Turn the dough out onto a lightly floured work surface and roll into a log. Divide the log into 12 equal portions and roll each into a ball. Cover the balls with plastic wrap and stand for 10 minutes while the oven is heating.
5 Roll each ball out to a 6-in (15-cm) round. Place two rounds on the baking sheet in the oven (or on the grill). Bake or grill the pitas for 4 minutes, then turn over and cook for a further 2 minutes, until inflated and golden. Repeat with the remaining dough. Serve hot, or leave to cool on a wire rack.

Za'atar Spiced Flatbread

Za'atar is a Middle Eastern spice mix made with sesame seeds, thyme, marjoram, oregano, sumac and salt. You will find it at Middle Eastern grocers.

MAKES 12
PREPARATION TIME: 30
  MINS + 2 HRS FOR THE
  DOUGH TO RISE
COOKING TIME: 15 MINS
BEST EATEN THE DAY YOU
  BAKE

2 teaspoons (10 g) fresh yeast
1½ cups (350 ml) warm water
1 teaspoon fine sea salt
3⅓ cups (500 g) bread flour
¼ cup (60 ml) extra-virgin
  olive oil
1 clove garlic, crushed
¼ cup (50 g) za'atar
2 tablespoons extra-virgin
  olive oil, extra

1 Place the yeast and water in the bowl of an electric mixer, and stir to dissolve. Add the salt and flour to the bowl. Using the dough hook attachment, mix on low speed for 10 minutes, until the dough is smooth and elastic.
2 Remove the dough hook, leaving the dough in the bowl. Cover the bowl with plastic wrap. Leave to rise in a warm place for 1½ hours, or until the dough has doubled in size.
3 Punch down the dough and transfer to a floured work surface. Divide the dough into two equal portions and roll each out to an oval with a thickness of ⅜ in (1 cm). Place on greased baking sheets and use your fingertips to create indentations all over the dough.
4 Combine the olive oil and garlic, and brush over the dough. Sprinkle the dough liberally with the za'atar. Leave to rise in a warm place for approximately 30 minutes, until the dough has risen slightly.
5 Preheat the oven to 375°F (190°C).
6 Bake the bread for 15 minutes, until golden. Drizzle with the extra olive oil as soon as it comes out of the oven. Cool on a wire rack.

Garlic and Rosemary Focaccia

Focaccia makes great toasted sandwiches. It's also delicious cut into small pieces and served with dips.

MAKES 1 LOAF
PREPARATION TIME: 30 MINS
+ 2 HRS 30 MINS FOR THE
DOUGH TO RISE
COOKING TIME: 25 MINS
BEST EATEN THE DAY YOU
BAKE

1 tablespoon (15 g) fresh yeast
1²/₃ cups (400 ml) warm water
3¹/₃ cups (500 g) bread flour
1½ teaspoons fine sea salt
1 tablespoon finely chopped
fresh rosemary
4 cloves garlic, very finely
chopped
¼ cup (60 ml) extra-virgin
olive oil
1 teaspoon sea salt flakes
¼ cup (60 ml) extra-virgin olive
oil, extra

1 Place the yeast and water in the bowl of an electric mixer, and stir to dissolve. Add the flour and fine sea salt to the bowl. Using the dough hook attachment, mix on low speed until the ingredients are well combined. Mix the dough on medium speed for a further 5 minutes—the dough will be quite wet and will look elastic.

2 Remove the dough hook, leaving the dough in the bowl. Cover the bowl with plastic wrap. Leave to rise in a warm place for 2 hours, or until the dough has doubled in size.

3 Grease a 12-in × 16-in (30-cm × 40-cm) baking sheet with a little olive oil. On a lightly floured work surface, shape the dough into a rectangle slightly smaller than the baking sheet. Lift the dough onto the prepared sheet and, using floured hands, press the dough out to the edge of the sheet. Use your fingertips to create indents all over the dough.

4 Combine the rosemary, garlic and olive oil, then brush this mixture over the dough. Sprinkle with the sea salt flakes. Leave to rise in a warm place for approximately 30 minutes, until the dough has risen slightly.

5 Preheat the oven to 375°F (190°C).

6 Bake the focaccia for 20–25 minutes, until golden. Drizzle with the extra olive oil as soon as it comes out of the oven.

Olive Fougasse

This is a delicious French flatbread made in the shape of a leaf. It is best made with good-quality olives and extra-virgin olive oil.

MAKES 2
PREPARATION TIME: 20 MINS + 2
   HRS FOR THE DOUGH TO RISE
COOKING TIME: 20 MINS
BEST EATEN THE DAY YOU BAKE

1 tablespoon (15 g) fresh yeast
1¼ cups (300 ml) warm water
3⅓ cups (500 g) bread flour
2 teaspoons fine sea salt
3½ tablespoons extra-virgin olive oil
⅔ cup (100 g) green olives, pitted and
  chopped
¼ cup (60 ml) extra-virgin olive oil, extra
2 teaspoons sea salt flakes

1 Place the yeast and water in the bowl of an electric mixer, and stir to dissolve. Add the flour, fine sea salt and olive oil to the bowl. Using the dough hook attachment, mix on low speed for 2 minutes, until a dough forms. Then mix on medium speed for 5 minutes, until the dough is smooth and elastic. Add the chopped olives and mix until well combined.

2 Remove the dough hook, leaving the dough in the bowl. Cover the bowl with plastic wrap. Leave to rise in a warm place for 1–1½ hours, until the dough has doubled in size.

3 Turn the dough out onto a lightly floured work surface and divide into two equal pieces. Knead each piece into a ball, then roll out to a triangle 6 in (15 cm) wide at the base and 10 in (25 cm) long. Place each fougasse on a baking sheet that has been lightly greased with olive oil. Using a sharp knife, cut slits on an angle either side of the middle of the triangle. Brush the dough with half the extra olive oil and sprinkle with sea salt flakes. Leave to rise in a warm place for approximately 30 minutes, until the dough has risen slightly.

4 Preheat the oven to 390°F (200°C).

5 Bake the fougasses for 15–20 minutes, until golden. Brush liberally with olive oil as soon as they come out of the oven.

Raisins and Cinnamon Bagels

Serve these bagels toasted, spread with cream cheese and drizzled with honey for breakfast.

MAKES 12
PREPARATION TIME: 45 MINS +1 HR
   30 MINS FOR THE DOUGH TO RISE
COOKING TIME: 15 MINS
BEST EATEN THE DAY YOU BAKE

4 teaspoons (20 g) fresh yeast
¼ cup (60 g) sugar
7 tablespoons warm water
1⅛ cups (275 ml) warm milk
3 cups (450 g) bread flour
½ teaspoon fine sea salt
2 teaspoons ground cinnamon
1⅓ cups (200 g) golden raisins
   (sultanas)
Egg wash: 1 egg yolk whisked with 2
   teaspoons water

1 Place the yeast, sugar, water and milk in the bowl of an electric mixer, and stir to dissolve. Add the flour, salt, cinnamon and golden raisins to the bowl. Using the dough hook attachment, mix on low speed for 1 minute to combine the ingredients. Then mix on medium speed for 5 minutes, or until the dough is smooth and elastic.
2 Remove the hook, leaving the dough in the bowl. Cover the bowl with plastic wrap. Leave to rise in a warm place for 1 hour, or until the dough has doubled in size.
3 Turn the dough out onto a lightly floured work surface and knead into a ball. Divide into 12 equal portions and roll each into a ball. Press a finger through the center of each ball and gently stretch to form a hole that is a quarter the size of the bagel. Place the bagels, 2 in (5 cm) apart, on greased baking sheets. Leave to rise in a warm place for approximately 30 minutes, until the bagels have risen slightly.
4 Preheat the oven to 360°F (180°C). Grease a clean baking sheet.
5 Bring a large saucepan of water to a boil. Gently lift the bagels from the baking sheet and carefully drop into the boiling water. (It's important not to overcrowd, so cook only 2–3 bagels at a time, depending on the size of your saucepan.) Cook the bagels for 1 minute, then turn over using a slotted spoon and cook for a further minute. Remove from the water with the slotted spoon and place on the prepared baking sheet.
6 Brush the egg wash over the tops of the bagels, then bake for 15 minutes, until golden. Cool on a wire rack.

Grissini

Grissini (breadsticks) are a perfect accompaniment to an antipasto platter served at the beginning of a meal.

MAKES 50
PREPARATION TIME: 45 MINS + 1 HR 30
  MINS FOR THE DOUGH TO RISE
COOKING TIME: 10 MINS
BEST EATEN THE DAY YOU BAKE

½ tablespoon (7 g) fresh yeast
1¼ cups (300 ml) warm water
2 teaspoons fine sea salt
3⅓ cups (500 g) bread flour
1 egg white
3 teaspoons sea salt flakes
2 teaspoons sesame seeds

1 Place the yeast, water and fine sea salt in the bowl of an electric mixer, and stir to dissolve. Add the flour to the bowl. Using the dough hook attachment, mix on low speed for 10 minutes, until the dough is smooth and elastic.

2 Remove the dough hook, leaving the dough in the bowl. Cover the bowl with plastic wrap. Leave to rise in a warm place for 1½ hours, or until the dough has doubled in size.

3 Preheat the oven to 375°F (190°C). Grease a baking sheet.

4 Turn the dough out onto a lightly floured work surface and divide into five equal pieces. Divide each piece into ten equal portions. Roll each portion of dough into a snake that is thinner than a pencil. Place the grissini on the prepared baking sheet. Brush with the egg white and sprinkle with sea salt flakes and sesame seeds.

5 Bake the grissini for approximately 10 minutes, until golden. Cool on a wire rack.

Olive and Rosemary Rolls

MAKES 12
PREPARATION TIME: 20 MINS + 2 HRS
   FOR THE DOUGH TO RISE
COOKING TIME: 20 MINS
BEST EATEN THE DAY YOU BAKE

2 teaspoons (10 g) fresh yeast
1½ cups (350 ml) warm water
1 teaspoon fine sea salt
3⅓ cups (500 g) bread flour
1 cup (125 g) coarsely chopped pitted
   black olives
3 teaspoons finely chopped fresh
   rosemary

1 Place the yeast, water and salt in the
bowl of an electric mixer, and stir to dissolve. Add the remaining ingredients to the
bowl. Using the dough hook attachment,
mix on low speed for 1 minute to combine.
Then mix on medium speed for 5 minutes,
until the dough is smooth and elastic.
2 Turn the dough out onto a lightly
floured work surface and leave to rise
(uncovered) for 2 hours, or until the dough
has doubled in size.
3 Preheat the oven to 360°F (180°C).
Grease a baking tray.
4 Using a sharp knife, carefully cut the
dough into 12 equal portions, being careful not to punch any air out of the dough.
Gently place each roll, floured side up, on
the prepared tray.
5 Bake the rolls for 20 minutes, until
golden. Cool on a wire rack.

Parmesan Bread Rolls

MAKES 20
PREPARATION TIME: 30 MINS + 3 HRS
  FOR THE DOUGH TO RISE
COOKING TIME: 25 MINS
BEST EATEN THE DAY YOU BAKE

4 teaspoons (20 g) fresh yeast
1 cup (250 ml) warm water
2 eggs
3½ tablespoons extra-virgin olive oil
3⅓ cups (500 g) bread flour
2 teaspoons fine sea salt
1¼ cups (125 g) grated parmesan cheese
1 egg, extra
½ cup (50 g) grated parmesan cheese, extra

1 Place the yeast and water in the bowl of
an electric mixer, and stir to dissolve. Add the
eggs, olive oil, flour, salt and parmesan to
the bowl. Using the dough hook attachment,
mix on low speed for 2 minutes, until a dough
forms. Then mix on medium speed for 5 minutes, until the dough is smooth and elastic.
2 Remove the dough hook, leaving the dough
in the bowl. Cover the bowl with plastic wrap.
Leave to rise in a warm place for 2 hours, or
until the dough has doubled in size.
3 Turn the dough out onto a lightly floured
work surface and divide into 20 equal pieces.
Knead each piece into a ball and score the top
with a sharp knife. Place the rolls on a greased
baking sheet and leave to rise in a warm place
for approximately 1 hour, until doubled in size.
4 Preheat the oven to 390°F (200°C).
5 Beat the extra egg and brush it over the
rolls. Sprinkle with the extra parmesan.
6 Bake the rolls for 20–25 minutes, until
golden. Cool on a wire rack.

Fruit Bread

I am unable to resist slicing off a piece of this bread while it's still hot and spreading it liberally with butter.

MAKES 1 LOAF
PREPARATION TIME: 30 MINS + 2 HRS 30
   MINS FOR THE DOUGH TO RISE
COOKING TIME: 30 MINS
BEST EATEN THE DAY YOU BAKE

1 tablespoon (15 g) fresh yeast
1¹⁄₃ cups (330 ml) warm water
¼ cup (80 g) molasses
3¹⁄₃ cups (500 g) bread flour
1 teaspoon fine sea salt
1¹⁄₃ cups (200 g) dried figs, coarsely chopped
²⁄₃ cup (100 g) dried apricots, coarsely chopped
²⁄₃ cup (100 g) golden raisins (sultanas)

1 Place the yeast, water and molasses in the bowl of an electric mixer, and stir to dissolve. Add the flour and salt to the bowl. Using the dough hook attachment, mix on low speed for 10 minutes, until the dough is smooth and elastic. Add the dried figs, apricots and golden raisins, and mix for a further 2 minutes.

2 Remove the dough hook, leaving the dough in the bowl. Cover the bowl with plastic wrap. Leave to rise in a warm place for 1½ hours, or until the dough has doubled in size.

3 Turn the dough out onto a lightly floured work surface and shape into a loaf. Place on a greased baking sheet and leave to rise in a warm place for approximately 1 hour, until the dough has risen slightly.

4 Preheat the oven to 360°F (180°C).

5 Bake the loaf for 30 minutes, until it is golden brown and sounds hollow when tapped. Cool on a wire rack.

Three-seed Bagels

This bagel recipe was inspired by a famous bakery in Balaclava, Melbourne. I like to tear the bread apart and dip it into eggplant dip for a delicious snack.

MAKES 12
PREPARATION TIME: 45 MINS + 1 HR
   30 MINS FOR THE DOUGH TO RISE
COOKING TIME: 15 MINS
BEST EATEN THE DAY YOU BAKE

4 teaspoons (20 g) fresh yeast
4 teaspoons sugar
7 tablespoons warm water
1⅛ cups (275 ml) warm milk
3 cups (450 g) bread flour
1 teaspoon fine sea salt
Egg wash: 1 egg yolk whisked with 2
   teaspoons water
2 teaspoons poppy seeds
2 teaspoons sesame seeds
2 teaspoons caraway seeds
2 teaspoons sea salt flakes

1 Place the yeast, sugar, water and milk in the bowl of an electric mixer, and stir to dissolve. Add the flour and fine sea salt to the bowl. Using the dough hook attachment, mix on low speed for 1 minute to combine the ingredients. Then mix on medium speed for 5 minutes, or until the dough is smooth and elastic.

2 Remove the dough hook, leaving the dough in the bowl. Cover the bowl with plastic wrap. Leave to rise in a warm place for 1 hour, or until the dough has doubled in size.

3 Turn the dough out onto a lightly floured work surface and knead into a ball. Divide the dough into 12 equal portions and roll each into a ball. Press a finger through the center of each ball and gently stretch to form a hole that is a quarter the size of the bagel. Place the bagels, 2 in (5 cm) apart, on greased baking sheets. Leave to rise in a warm place for approximately 30 minutes, until the bagels have risen slightly.

4 Preheat the oven to 360°F (180°C). Grease a clean baking sheet.

5 Bring a large saucepan of water to a boil. Gently lift the bagels from the baking sheet and carefully drop into the boiling water. (It's important not to overcrowd the boiling water, so cook only 2–3 bagels at a time, depending on the size of your saucepan.) Cook for 1 minute, then turn over using a slotted spoon and cook for a further minute. Remove from the water with the slotted spoon and place on the prepared baking sheet.

6 Brush the egg wash over the tops of the bagels. Combine the poppy, sesame and caraway seeds, and the sea salt flakes, and sprinkle liberally over the bagels.

7 Bake the bagels for 15 minutes, until golden. Cool on a wire rack.

Stollen

In Germany this rich fruit bread is traditionally served at Christmas time.

MAKES 1 LOAF
PREPARATION TIME: 30 MINS +
    5 HRS FOR THE DOUGH TO RISE +
    1 HR FRUIT SOAKING TIME
COOKING TIME: 40 MINS
STORE IN AN AIRTIGHT CON-
    TAINER FOR UP TO 1 WEEK

²/₃ cup (90 g) currants

²/₃ cup (90 g) golden raisins (sultanas)

¹/₃ cup (90 g) candied cherries, cut in half

³/₄ cup (60 g) candied orange peel, chopped

4 tablespoons dark rum

4 teaspoons (20 g) fresh yeast

¹/₂ cup (125 ml) warm milk

1 egg

¹/₃ cup (90 g) superfine sugar

1 teaspoon fine sea salt

¹/₄ cup (¹/₂ stick/60 g) unsalted butter, softened

3 cups (450 g) all-purpose (plain) flour

1 teaspoon ground cinnamon

5 oz (150 g) marzipan

¹/₄ cup (30 g) confectioner's (icing) sugar, for dusting

1 Combine the currants, golden raisins, cherries, orange peel and rum in a bowl. Allow to stand for at least 1 hour (or overnight).

2 Place the yeast and milk in the bowl of an electric mixer, and stir to dissolve. Add the egg, sugar, salt, butter, flour and cinnamon to the bowl. Using the dough hook attachment, mix on low speed for 5 minutes, until the dough is smooth and elastic. Add the soaked dried fruit and mix until combined.

3 Remove the dough hook, leaving the dough in the bowl. Cover the bowl with plastic wrap. Leave to rise in a warm place for 3 hours, or until the dough has doubled in size.

4 Turn the dough out onto a lightly floured work surface and roll out to a rectangle 12 in × 8 in (30 cm × 20 cm). Roll the marzipan into a log 10 in (25 cm) long and place lengthwise in the center of the dough. Roll the dough into a log with the marzipan inside and press the edges together to seal. Place the loaf on a greased baking sheet and leave to rise in a warm place for approximately 2 hours, until risen slightly.

5 Preheat the oven to 360°F (180°C).

6 Bake the loaf for 10 minutes, then turn the oven down to 300°F (150°C) and bake for a further 30 minutes, until golden. Cool on a wire rack.

7 Dust the stollen with icing sugar and slice thinly to serve.

Apple and Cinnamon Buns

These buns are best served warm, spread with butter, for afternoon tea. They're also good toasted the next day.

MAKES 12
PREPARATION TIME: 45 MINS + 2
  HRS 30 MINS FOR THE DOUGH TO
  RISE
COOKING TIME: 30 MINS
BEST EATEN THE DAY YOU BAKE

2 tablespoons (30 g) fresh yeast
1½ cups (375 ml) warm milk
3¾ cups (550 g) all-purpose (plain) flour
3½ tablespoons superfine sugar
1 egg
2 tablespoons unsalted butter, softened
1 teaspoon ground cinnamon
2 tablespoons unsalted butter, melted
1 quantity Apricot Glaze (page 21)

FILLING
1½ cups (250 g) cooked or canned apple
  slices
¼ cup (60 g) soft brown sugar
2 teaspoons ground cinnamon

1 Make the Apricot Glaze by following the recipe on page 21.

2 Line a 10-in (25-cm) square cake pan with parchment baking paper.

3 Place the yeast and milk in the bowl of an electric mixer, and stir to dissolve. Add the flour, sugar, egg, softened butter and cinnamon to the bowl. Mix on low speed for 5 minutes, until the dough is smooth and elastic.

4 Remove the dough hook, leaving the dough in the bowl. Cover the bowl with plastic wrap. Leave to rise in a warm place for 1–1½ hours, until the dough has doubled in size.

5 Turn the dough out onto a lightly floured work surface and knead into a ball, then roll out to a rectangle 10 in × 16 in (25 cm × 40 cm). Brush the dough with the melted butter.

6 To make the Filling, scatter the apple slices over the dough. Combine the soft brown sugar and cinnamon and sprinkle over the apple.

7 Starting from a long side, roll up the dough into a log, then cut it into 12 even slices using a sharp knife. Place the slices cut side up in the prepared pan. Leave to rise in a warm place for approximately 1 hour, until the scrolls have doubled in size.

8 Preheat the oven to 360°F (180°C).

9 Bake the scrolls for 25–30 minutes, until golden and firm to the touch. Cool in the pan for 10 minutes, then turn out onto a wire rack to cool completely. Brush with the Apricot Glaze to serve.

Hot Cross Buns

This Easter-time bread is best served toasted and spread with butter.

MAKES 16
PREPARATION TIME: 45 MINS + 3 HRS
  FOR THE DOUGH TO RISE
COOKING TIME: 25 MINS
BEST EATEN THE DAY YOU BAKE

4 teaspoons (20 g) fresh yeast
1¼ cups (300 ml) warm water
3¾ cups (550 g) all-purpose (plain) flour
⅓ cup (90 g) superfine sugar
1 teaspoon fine sea salt
2 eggs
½ teaspoon ground cinnamon
Finely grated zest of 2 oranges
½ cup (1 stick/100 g) unsalted butter,
  softened
1 cup (125 g) golden raisins (sultanas)
⅓ cup (60 g) currants
⅓ cup (30 g) candied orange peel, finely
  chopped

FLOUR PASTE
⅔ cup (90 g) all-purpose (plain) flour
2 tablespoons sugar
6 tablespoons water

SYRUP
2 tablespoons sugar
2 tablespoons water

1 Place the yeast and water in the bowl of an electric mixer, and stir to dissolve. Add the flour, sugar, salt, eggs, cinnamon, orange zest and butter to the bowl. Using the dough hook attachment, mix on low speed for 2 minutes, until the ingredients are combined. Mix on medium speed for a further 5 minutes, until the dough is smooth and elastic. Add the golden raisins, currants and candied orange peel to the bowl, and mix on low speed until well combined.

2 Remove the dough hook, leaving the dough in the bowl. Cover the bowl with plastic wrap. Leave to rise in a warm place for 1½–2 hours, until the dough has doubled in size.

3 Punch down the dough and transfer to a floured work surface. Divide the dough into 16 equal portions and roll into balls. Place the buns, 2 in (5 cm) apart, on a baking sheet lined with parchment baking paper. Leave to rise in a warm place for approximately 1 hour, until risen slightly.

4 To make the Flour Paste, combine the flour and sugar in a bowl, and gradually stir in the water until smooth. Place the mixture into a piping bag fitted with a ¼ in (5 mm) plain nozzle.

5 Pipe crosses onto the top of the buns.

6 Preheat the oven to 340°F (170°C).

7 Bake the hot cross buns for 25 minutes, until golden. (Make the Syrup while the buns are in the oven.)

8 To make the Syrup, bring the sugar and water to a boil in a small saucepan.

9 Brush the hot cross buns with the Syrup as soon as they come out of the oven. Cool on a wire rack.

Coconut Icing Finger Buns

These buns are a childhood favorite of mine. Split and spread with a little butter to serve.

MAKES 12
PREPARATION TIME: 45 MINS + 30
   MINS FOR THE DOUGH TO RISE
COOKING TIME: 15 MINS
BEST EATEN THE DAY YOU BAKE

2 tablespoons (30 g) fresh yeast
1½ cups (375 ml) warm milk
¼ cup (60 g) superfine sugar
1 tablespoon honey
1 egg
1 teaspoon vanilla extract
⅓ cup (¾ stick/90 g) unsalted butter,
   diced, at room temperature
4 cups (600 g) all-purpose (plain) flour
1⅓ cups (200 g) golden raisins
   (sultanas)
¾ cup (60 g) candied orange peel, finely
   chopped
1¼ cups (120 g) desiccated coconut

ICING
3¼ cups (400 g) confectioner's (icing)
   sugar
¼ cup (½ stick/60 g) unsalted butter,
   melted
4–6 teaspoons water

1 Place the yeast and milk in the bowl of an electric mixer, and stir to dissolve. Add the sugar, honey, egg, vanilla, butter, flour, raisins and orange peel to the bowl. Mix on low speed for 10 minutes, until the dough is smooth and elastic.
2 Remove the dough hook, leaving the dough in the bowl. Cover the bowl with plastic wrap. Leave to rise in a warm place for 1 hour, or until the dough has doubled in size.
3 Preheat the oven to 360°F (180°C). Line two baking sheets with parchment baking paper.
4 Turn the dough out onto a lightly floured work surface, divide into 12 equal portions and roll each piece into a sausage 6 in (15 cm) long. Place the buns onto the prepared baking sheets and leave to rise in a warm place for approximately 30 minutes, until risen slightly.
5 Bake the buns for 12–15 minutes, or until golden and firm to the touch. Cool on a wire rack.
6 To make the Icing, sift the sugar into a bowl, add the butter and stir to combine. Continue stirring, adding a teaspoon of water at a time until a thick icing forms.
7 Spread the top of each bun with the Icing and sprinkle with desiccated coconut.

Vine Fruit and Rosemary Bread

This bread is an ideal accompaniment to a cheese platter. It can also be thickly sliced and toasted for breakfast.

MAKES 1 LOAF
PREPARATION TIME: 30 MINS + 3 HRS
  FOR THE DOUGH TO RISE
COOKING TIME: 45 MINS
BEST EATEN THE DAY YOU BAKE

2 teaspoons (10 g) fresh yeast
1¼ cups (300 ml) warm water
2⅔ cups (400 g) multigrain flour
⅔ cup (100 g) rye flour
2 teaspoons fine sea salt
1 tablespoon finely chopped fresh
  rosemary
1⅔ cups (250 g) golden raisins (sultanas)

1 Place the yeast and water in the bowl
of an electric mixer, and stir to dissolve.
Add the flours and salt to the bowl. Using
the dough hook attachment, mix on low
speed for 10 minutes, until the dough is
smooth and elastic. Add the rosemary
and golden raisins, and mix on low speed
until combined.
2 Remove the dough hook, leaving the
dough in the bowl. Cover the bowl with
plastic wrap. Leave to rise in a warm
place for 2 hours, or until the dough has
doubled in size.
3 Punch down the dough and transfer
to a floured work surface. Roll the dough
into an oval shape 8 in (20 cm) long and
place on a greased baking sheet. Use a
sharp knife to cut four or five ⅜ in (1 cm)
deep vertical slashes down each side of
the loaf. Leave to rise in a warm place for
approximately 1 hour, until risen slightly.
4 Preheat the oven to 375°F (190°C).
5 Bake the loaf for 45 minutes, until it is
golden and sounds hollow when tapped.

Panettone

This sweet bread originates from Milan in Italy. Serve slices with coffee or tea, or with a sweet wine.

SERVES 10
PREPARATION TIME: 45 MINS +
    5 HRS FOR THE DOUGH TO RISE
COOKING TIME: 55 MINS
BEST EATEN THE DAY YOU BAKE

8 teaspoons (40 g) fresh yeast

¼ cup (60 ml) warm water

¼ cup (60 g) honey

4 eggs

3 egg yolks

2 teaspoons vanilla extract

¾ cup (200 g) superfine sugar

4 cups (600 g) all-purpose (plain) flour

1 teaspoon fine sea salt

1¼ cups (2½ sticks/275 g) unsalted
    butter, diced, at room temperature

1⅔ cups (250 g) golden raisins (sultanas)

¼ cup (60 g) candied citron, finely
    chopped

¾ cup (60 g) candied orange peel, finely
    chopped

Finely grated zest of 2 oranges

Finely grated zest of 2 lemons

¼ cup (30 g) confectioner's (icing)
    sugar, for dusting

1 Place the yeast, water and honey in the bowl of an electric mixer, and stir to dissolve. Add the whole eggs, egg yolks, vanilla, sugar, sifted flour and salt to the bowl. Using the dough hook attachment, mix on low speed until the ingredients are well combined. Add the diced butter and continue to mix on low speed for 10 minutes, or until the butter is mixed in and the dough is smooth and elastic.

2 Remove the dough hook, leaving the dough in the bowl. Cover the bowl with plastic wrap. Leave to rise in a warm place for 2–3 hours, until the dough has doubled in size.

3 Line the base of a 8-in (20-cm) round cake pan with parchment baking paper, then line the sides of the pan, letting the paper come up 2 in (5 cm) higher than the height of the pan.

4 Turn the dough out onto a lightly floured work surface and add the golden raisins, candied citron and orange peel, orange zest and lemon zest. Knead until the ingredients are well mixed through the dough. Shape the dough into a ball and place in the cake pan. Use a sharp knife to cut a ⅜ in (1 cm) deep cross in the top of the dough. Leave to rise in a warm place for approximately 2 hours, until the dough has doubled in size.

5 Preheat the oven to 360°F (180°C).

6 Bake the panettone for 15 minutes, then reduce the oven temperature to 325°F (160°C) and bake for another 30–40 minutes or until a skewer inserted into the center comes out clean. Cool in the cake pan for 1 hour, then remove and transfer to a wire rack to cool completely.

7 Dust with icing sugar to serve.

Lavosh

The thinner you roll out the lavosh dough, the better—a pasta machine is ideal, but a rolling pin will also do the job.

SERVES 6
PREPARATION TIME: 45 MINS + 30
   MINS CHILLING TIME
COOKING TIME: 10 MINS
STORE IN AN AIRTIGHT CONTAINER
   FOR UP TO 3 DAYS

1²/₃ cups (250 g) all-purpose (plain) flour
1 teaspoon fine sea salt
2 tablespoons unsalted butter, diced
2 tablespoons milk
2 tablespoons water
1 egg yolk
Seeds (poppy, sesame or caraway) or
   coarsely ground black pepper, for
   sprinkling

1 Place the sifted flour, salt and butter in the bowl of an electric mixer fitted with the paddle attachment. Mix on low speed for 5 minutes or until the butter is completely mixed in. Add the milk, water and egg yolk, and mix on low speed until the dough forms a ball. Wrap the dough in plastic wrap and refrigerate for at least 30 minutes.

2 Preheat the oven to 360°F (180°C). Line two baking sheets with parchment baking paper.

3 Using a pasta machine, roll out the dough to a thickness of no more than ⅛ in (2 mm). (Alternatively, use a rolling pin to roll out the dough on a lightly floured work surface.) Cut the dough into desired shapes and place on baking sheets. Brush the dough with a little water and sprinkle with your choice of seeds or pepper.

4 Bake the lavosh for 10 minutes, until crisp and lightly golden. Cool, and serve alongside a cheese platter or with dips.

Chocolate and Walnut Babka

Babka is similar to brioche but is filled, rolled and twisted before being baked in a loaf pan. Serve warm for morning tea.

MAKES 1 LOAF
PREPARATION TIME: 45 MINS +
  2 HRS FOR THE DOUGH TO
  RISE
COOKING TIME: 45 MINS
BEST SERVED ON THE DAY OF
  BAKING

4 teaspoons (20 g) fresh yeast
¾ cup (180 ml) warm milk
½ cup (110 g) superfine sugar
3⅓ cups (500 g) all-purpose (plain)
  flour
2 eggs
1 egg yolk
1 teaspoon fine sea salt
⅔ cup (1⅓ sticks/150 g) unsalted
  butter, diced, softened
Egg wash: 1 egg yolk whisked with
  3 teaspoons milk

FILLING
½ cup (1 stick/100 g) unsalted but-
  ter, softened
1 cup (125 g) chopped dark choco-
  late
¾ cup (90 g) chopped walnuts
¼ cup (60 g) superfine sugar

1 Place the yeast and milk in the bowl of an electric mixer, and stir to dissolve. Add the sugar, flour, whole eggs, egg yolk and salt to the bowl. Using the dough hook attachment, mix on low speed for 2 minutes, until a dough forms. Then mix on medium speed for 5 minutes, until the dough is smooth and elastic. With the mixer running on medium speed, add the diced butter to the bowl a piece at a time, until incorporated.
2 Remove the dough hook, leaving the dough in the bowl. Cover the bowl with plastic wrap. Leave to rise in a warm place for 1½ hours, or until the dough has doubled in size.
3 Line a 8½-in × 4½-in (22-cm × 11-cm) loaf pan with parchment baking paper. Turn the dough out onto a lightly floured work surface and roll out to make a rectangle 14 in × 16 in (35 cm × 40 cm).
4 To make the Filling, spread the butter over the dough, then scatter the remaining Filling ingredients evenly on top, leaving a ¾ in (2 cm) border around the edge.
5 Brush the edges of the dough with the egg wash. (Reserve remaining egg wash.) Starting from a long side, roll the dough into a log, then pinch the long edge and the ends to seal. Fold the roll in half, then twist twice and place in the prepared pan. Leave the babka to rise in a warm place for 1 hour, until doubled in size.
6 Preheat the oven to 325°F (160°C).
7 Brush the top of the babka with the egg wash, then bake for 45 minutes, until golden. Remove from the cake pan and cool on a wire rack.

Basic Pizza Dough

This recipe makes a great pizza base. Keep uncooked bases in the freezer for a quick mid-week dinner.

MAKES 2 PIZZA BASES
PREPARATION TIME: 15 MINS + 1 HR
 FOR THE DOUGH TO RISE
COOKING TIME: 15 MINS
REFRIGERATE UNCOOKED BASES
 (WELL WRAPPED, ON THEIR BAK-
 ING SHEETS) FOR UP TO 1 DAY OR
 FREEZE FOR 1 WEEK. ALWAYS
 BRING BASES BACK TO ROOM TEM-
 PERATURE BEFORE BAKING.

2½ teaspoons (12 g) fresh yeast
²/₃ cup (160 ml) warm water
1⅞ cups (280 g) bread flour
2 teaspoons fine sea salt
2 tablespoons extra-virgin olive oil

1 Place the yeast and water in the bowl of an electric mixer, and stir to dissolve. Add the flour, salt and olive oil to the bowl. Using the dough hook attachment, mix on low speed for 2 minutes, until a dough forms. Then mix on medium speed for 5 minutes, until the dough is smooth and elastic.
2 Remove the dough hook, leaving the dough in the bowl. Cover the bowl with plastic wrap. Leave to rise in a warm place for 1 hour, or until the dough has doubled in size.
3 Grease two 12-in (30-cm) pizza trays or baking sheets. Turn the dough out onto a lightly floured work surface and divide into two equal pieces. Roll each piece into a ball, then roll out to a 12-in (30-cm) round. Carefully transfer each round to a tray and use your fingertips to press the dough out evenly.
4 Preheat the oven to 375°F (190°C).
5 Top the pizza bases with your favorite toppings and bake for 15 minutes, until the crusts are golden. Serve immediately.

Sausage Pizza

SERVES 4
PREPARATION TIME: 45 MINS + 1 HR
   FOR THE DOUGH TO RISE
COOKING TIME: 15 MINS

1 quantity Basic Pizza Dough (page 54)
1 quantity Pizza Sauce (page 21)
6 pork and fennel sausages
2 cups (200 g) grated mozzarella cheese
Fresh basil leaves, to serve
Extra-virgin olive oil, to serve

1 Make the Basic Pizza Dough and the Pizza Sauce by following their respective recipes on pages 54 and 21.

2 Preheat the oven to 375°F (190°C). Grease two 12-in (30-cm) pizza trays with a little olive oil.

3 Divide the Basic Pizza Dough into two equal pieces and roll out to fit the trays. Lift the dough rounds onto the trays and press out to the edges using your fingertips.

4 Spread the pizza bases with the Pizza Sauce. Remove the sausage meat from the skins and break the meat into small pieces. Scatter the sausage pieces over the pizza bases, then sprinkle with mozzarella.

5 Bake the pizzas for 15 minutes, until the crusts are golden. Garnish with fresh basil leaves and a drizzle of olive oil, and serve immediately.

Potato and Rosemary Pizza

This pizza is one of my favorite lunches when traveling in Italy—it's cheap, fresh and always tasty. Homemade it's even better.

SERVES 4
PREPARATION TIME: 1 HR + 1 HR
   FOR THE DOUGH TO RISE
COOKING TIME: 15 MINS

1¼ lb (600 g) potatoes
1 quantity Basic Pizza Dough (page 54)
1 tablespoon finely chopped fresh
   rosemary
4 teaspoons extra-virgin olive oil
Salt and freshly-ground black pepper
2 cups (200 g) grated mozzarella
   cheese

1 Make the Basic Pizza Dough by following the recipe on page 54.
2 Place the potatoes in a large saucepan and cover with cold water. Place the pan over medium heat and bring to a boil, then simmer until the potatoes are just tender. Drain and set aside to cool.
3 Preheat the oven to 375°F (190°C). Grease two 12-in (30-cm) pizza trays with a little olive oil.
4 Divide the Basic Pizza Dough into two equal pieces and roll out to fit the trays. Lift the dough rounds onto the trays and press out to the edges using your fingertips.
5 Peel and finely slice the cooled potatoes, then spread the slices over the pizza bases. Combine the rosemary and olive oil, and drizzle this mixture evenly over the sliced potatoes. Season lightly with salt and pepper, then scatter with the mozzarella.
6 Bake the pizzas for 15 minutes, until the crusts are golden. Serve immediately.

Prosciutto, Buffalo Mozzarella and Basil Pizza

SERVES 4
PREPARATION TIME: 45 MINS + 1 HR
   FOR THE DOUGH TO RISE
COOKING TIME: 15 MINS

1 quantity Basic Pizza Dough (page 54)
1 quantity Pizza Sauce (page 21)
½ lb (250 g) buffalo mozzarella
8 thin slices prosciutto
Fresh basil leaves, to serve
Extra-virgin olive oil, to serve

1 Make the Basic Pizza Dough and the Pizza Sauce by following their respective recipes on pages 54 and 21.
2 Preheat the oven to 375°F (190°C). Grease two 12-in (30-cm) pizza trays with a little olive oil.
3 Divide the Basic Pizza Dough into two equal pieces and roll out to fit the trays. Lift the dough rounds onto the trays and press out to the edges using your fingertips.
4 Spread the pizza bases with the Pizza Sauce, then break the mozzarella into small pieces and scatter over.
5 Bake the pizzas for 15 minutes, until the crusts are golden.
6 Arrange the sliced prosciutto and basil leaves on top of the pizzas. Drizzle with a little olive oil and serve immediately.

Pumpkin, Goat's Cheese and Caramelized Onion Pizza

SERVES 4
PREPARATION TIME: 1 HR 30 MINS +
    1 HR FOR THE DOUGH TO RISE
COOKING TIME: 15 MINS

2 tablespoons extra-virgin olive oil
2 tablespoons unsalted butter
1¹⁄₈ lb (500 g) red onions, finely sliced
Salt and freshly-ground black pepper
1¹⁄₈ lb (500 g) pumpkin, peeled and cut
    into ³⁄₈-in (1-cm) dice
2 tablespoons extra-virgin olive oil, extra
1 quantity Basic Pizza Dough (page 54)
2 cups (200 g) soft goat's cheese
Fresh rocket leaves, to serve

1 Make the Basic Pizza Dough by following the recipe on page 54.

2 Heat the olive oil and butter in a large saucepan. Add the onions and a good pinch of salt. Cover and cook over low heat for 20 minutes, stirring regularly, until the onions are very soft. Uncover and continue to cook for 20–30 minutes, until the onions are sweet and caramelized. Remove from the heat, season with salt and pepper to taste, and set aside to cool.

3 Preheat the oven to 375°F (190°C). Grease two 12-in (30-cm) pizza trays with a little olive oil.

4 In a baking dish, toss the diced pumpkin with the extra olive oil, and season with salt and pepper. Bake for 20 minutes, until the pumpkin is tender. Set aside to cool.

5 Divide the Basic Pizza Dough into two equal pieces and roll out to fit the trays. Lift the dough rounds onto the trays and press out to the edges using your fingertips.

6 Spread the caramelized onion over the pizza bases, then arrange the pumpkin over the top. Break the goat's cheese into small pieces and scatter it over.

7 Bake the pizzas for 15 minutes, until the crusts are golden. Scatter with fresh rocket leaves and serve immediately.

Olive and Anchovy Pissaladière

Only make this recipe with good-quality olives and anchovies—using poor-quality ingredients will disappoint.

SERVES 4
PREPARATION TIME: 1 HR 30 MINS + 1 HR
    FOR THE DOUGH TO RISE
COOKING TIME: 15 MINS

3½ tablespoons extra-virgin olive oil
2 tablespoons unsalted butter
1¼ lb (600 g) onions, finely sliced
2 cloves garlic, finely chopped
2 sprigs fresh thyme
1 bay leaf
Salt and freshly-ground black pepper
1 quantity Basic Pizza Dough (page 54)
15 pieces anchovy fillets (about 1¾ oz/50 g),
    neatly cut into long thin strips
⅓ cup (50 g) black olives, pitted and halved
2 teaspoons fresh thyme leaves, extra

1 Make the Basic Pizza Dough by following the recipe on page 54.

2 Heat the olive oil and butter in a large saucepan. Add the onions, garlic, thyme, bay leaf and a good pinch of salt. Cover and cook over low heat for 20 minutes, stirring regularly, until the onions are very soft. Uncover and continue to cook for 20–30 minutes, until the onions are sweet and caramelized. Remove the thyme sprigs and bay leaf. Season with salt and pepper to taste, and set aside to cool.

3 Preheat the oven to 360°F (180°C). Grease a 12-in × 16-in (30-cm × 40-cm) baking sheet with a little olive oil.

4 Roll out the Basic Pizza Dough to a rectangle to fit the prepared sheet. Lift the dough onto the sheet and press out to the edges using your fingertips.

5 Spread the caramelized onion evenly over the base, then arrange the anchovy slices in a lattice pattern over the onion. Place a piece of black olive in the center of each diamond.

6 Bake the pissaladière for 15 minutes, until the crust is golden. Sprinkle with fresh thyme leaves and serve immediately.

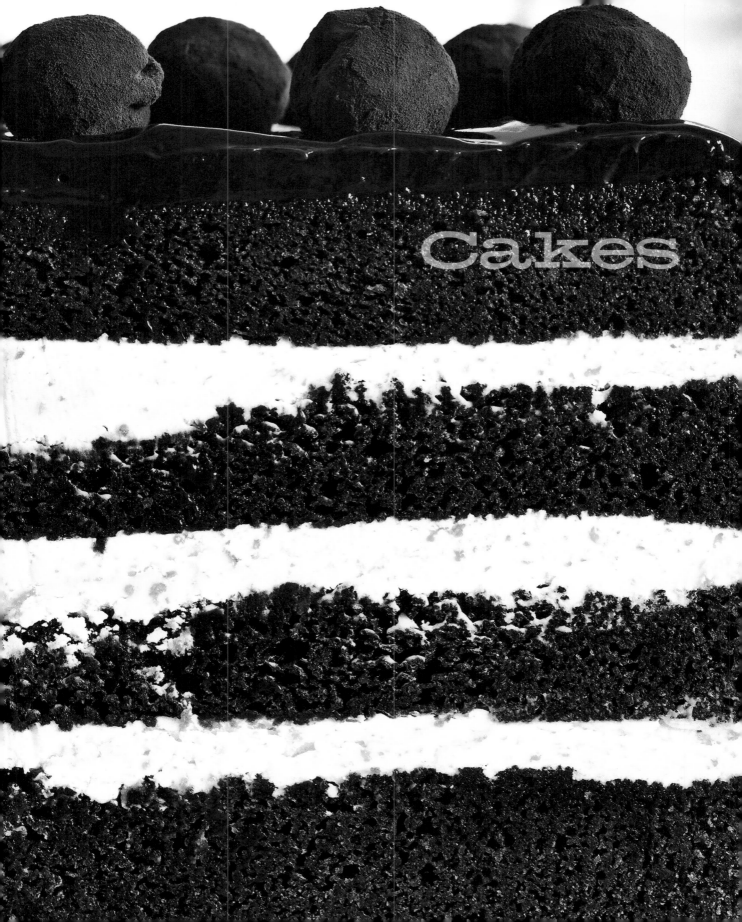

Cakes

Vanilla Butter Cake

This is a very versatile cake. Flavor it with your favorite ingredients, or bake it as cupcakes. It has a nice firm texture, so it's easy to cut into shapes that can be decorated for a children's birthday cake.

SERVES 12
PREPARATION TIME: 30 MINS
COOKING TIME: 40 MINS
STORE IN AN AIRTIGHT CONTAINER
   FOR UP TO 3 DAYS

1 cup (2 sticks/250 g) unsalted butter, softened
1⅛ cups (250 g) superfine sugar
2 teaspoons vanilla extract
5 eggs
1⅔ cups (250 g) self-rising flour
1 quantity Frosting for Cakes and Cupcakes (page 20)

VARIATIONS
Orange Butter Cake: Add the finely grated zest of 4 oranges with the vanilla.
Coconut Butter Cake: Add ½ cup (50 g) desiccated coconut with the flour.
Marbled Butter Cake: Divide the finished cake mixture into three equal portions: add pink food coloring to one portion, add ⅓ cup (30 g) cocoa to the second portion, and leave the last portion plain. Dollop large spoonfuls of the three different mixtures into the prepared pan, then drag a skewer or knife blade through the mixtures to create a marbled effect.
Cupcakes: Spoon the mixture into two 12-hole muffin trays that have been lined with paper cases. Bake for about 20 minutes.

1 Make the Frosting for Cakes and Cupcakes by following the recipe on page 20.
2 Preheat the oven to 325°F (160°C). Line a 8-in (20-cm) round cake pan with parchment baking paper.
3 Beat the butter, sugar and vanilla, in the bowl of an electric mixer fitted with the paddle attachment, on high speed for 5 minutes, until pale and creamy. Add the eggs one at a time, beating well after each addition. Sift in the flour and mix on low speed until well combined. Add any flavorings now, if using.
4 Pour the mixture into the prepared cake pan and spread out evenly. Bake for 40 minutes, or until a skewer inserted into the center of the cake comes out clean. Cool in the cake pan for 10 minutes, then turn out onto a wire rack to cool completely.
5 Color and flavor the frosting to your liking. Use a palette knife to spread the frosting over the entire cake.

Bread Cake

Bread Cake is a great way to turn stale bread into something delicious. It is best made the day before serving.

SERVES 10
PREPARATION TIME: 30 MINS
COOKING TIME: 1 HR
STORE IN AN AIRTIGHT CONTAINER
   FOR UP TO 2 DAYS

½ cup (60 g) golden raisins (sultanas)
2¾ tablespoons dark rum
10 slices (300 g) white bread, crusts
   removed
¾ cup (200 ml) milk
½ cup (1 stick/100 g) unsalted butter
1⅔ cups (400 ml) whipping cream
¾ cup (180 g) superfine sugar
Finely grated zest of 1 lemon
Finely grated zest of 1 orange
1 cup (150 g) dark chocolate chips
½ cup (50 g) pine nuts
4 eggs

VARIATIONS

- Instead of white bread, use panettone or brioche.
- Use your favorite nuts and dried fruits in place of the golden raisins (sultanas) and pine nuts.

1 Preheat the oven to 325°F (160°C). Line a 10-in (25-cm) round cake pan with parchment baking paper.

2 Soak the golden raisins in the rum while preparing the other ingredients. Cut the bread into large chunks and place in a large bowl.

3 Heat the milk, butter and cream in a saucepan until hot (but not boiling). Pour it over the bread and mix well with a spoon. Stand for 10 minutes.

4 Stir the bread mixture with a fork to break the bread into small pieces. Add the soaked golden raisins and rum, the sugar, lemon and orange zests, chocolate, pine nuts and eggs. Mix well.

5 Pour the cake mixture into the prepared pan. Bake for 1 hour, or until a skewer inserted into the center of the cake comes out clean. Cool the cake completely in the pan, preferably overnight to allow the flavors and texture to develop. Serve with cream if desired.

Apricot Streusel Cake

This cake can be made with other stone fruits, such as cherries, plums and peaches.

SERVES 8
PREPARATION TIME: 30 MINS
COOKING TIME: 1 HR 30 MINS
STORE IN AN AIRTIGHT CONTAINER
  FOR UP TO 2 DAYS

1 cup (2 sticks/250 g) unsalted butter,
  softened
2 cups (450 g) superfine sugar
6 eggs
2½ cups (375 g) all-purpose (plain) flour
½ cup (100 g) sour cream
8 ripe apricots, halved (or 16 canned
  apricot halves)
¼ cup (30 g) confectioner's (icing)
  sugar, for dusting

TOPPING
¾ cup (100 g) confectioner's (icing)
  sugar
1⅓ cups (200 g) all-purpose (plain) flour
⅓ cup (¾ stick/90 g) unsalted butter,
  melted

1 Preheat the oven to 325°F (160°C). Line a 10-in (25-cm) round springform cake pan with parchment baking paper.
2 Beat the butter and sugar, in the bowl of an electric mixer fitted with the paddle attachment, on high speed for 5 minutes until pale and creamy. Add the eggs one at a time, beating well after each addition. Sift in the flour, add the sour cream and mix on low speed until combined.
3 Spread the batter into the prepared pan. Arrange the apricot halves evenly over the batter, cut side down.
4 To make the Topping, place the icing sugar, flour and melted butter in a mixing bowl. Rub with your fingertips until the mixture is crumbly.
5 Sprinkle the streusel topping over the apricots. Bake the cake for 1 hour and 30 minutes, or until a skewer inserted into the center comes out clean. Cool in the pan for 10 minutes, then remove the sides of the pan and leave to cool completely. Dust with icing sugar to serve.

Apple and Walnut Cake

A lovely afternoon tea cake.

SERVES 10
PREPARATION TIME: 30 MINS
COOKING TIME: 1 HR
STORE IN AN AIRTIGHT CONTAINER
   FOR UP TO 2 DAYS

1⅓ cups (2⅔ sticks/300 g) unsalted
   butter, softened
½ cup (130 g) superfine sugar
1 egg
⅓ cup (60 g) self-rising flour, sifted
½ teaspoon baking powder
½ cup (80 g) almond flour
⅓ cup (80 ml) milk
1 teaspoon vanilla extract
2 teaspoons ground cinnamon
2½ tablespoons superfine sugar, extra
1½ tablespoons unsalted butter, softened, extra

TOPPING
¾ cup (80 g) finely chopped walnuts
2 tablespoons superfine sugar
2 green apples, peeled, cored and thinly
   sliced

1 Preheat the oven to 360°F (180°C). Line a 8-in (20-cm) round springform cake pan with parchment baking paper.
2 Beat the butter and sugar, in the bowl of an electric mixer fitted with the paddle attachment, on high speed for 5 minutes, until pale and creamy. Add the egg and beat for 2 minutes. Add the sifted flour and baking powder, and the almond flour, milk and vanilla. Mix on low speed until combined. Spread the batter into the prepared pan.
3 To make the Topping, combine the walnuts and sugar, and sprinkle the mixture over the batter. Arrange the apple slices decoratively over the top.
4 Bake the cake for 30 minutes. Remove from the oven and sprinkle with the combined cinnamon and extra sugar. Cut the extra butter into small pieces and scatter over the cake. Return to the oven and bake for a further 20–30 minutes, until a skewer inserted into the center comes out clean. Allow to cool completely in the pan. Serve warm or cold with cream.

Banana Cake with Cinnamon Buttercream

Use very ripe bananas for this recipe to achieve the best result. The addition of dried banana adds extra texture and flavor to the cake.

SERVES 12
PREPARATION TIME: 40 MINS
COOKING TIME: 1 HR 15 MINS
STORE IN AN AIRTIGHT CONTAINER
 FOR UP TO 3 DAYS

1 cup (2 sticks/250 g) unsalted butter, softened

2¼ cups (500 g) superfine sugar

4 eggs

2 teaspoons vanilla extract

Scant 1 cup (225 g) sour cream

3⅓ cups (500 g) all-purpose (plain) flour

2 teaspoons baking soda

6 very ripe bananas, mashed

¾ cup (125 g) chopped dried bananas

CINNAMON BUTTERCREAM

¾ cup (1¾ sticks/200 g) unsalted butter, softened

1¼ cups (150 g) confectioner's (icing) sugar

1 teaspoon ground cinnamon

1 Preheat the oven to 325°F (160°C). Line a 10-in (25-cm) round cake pan with parchment baking paper.

2 Beat the butter and sugar, in the bowl of an electric mixer fitted with the paddle attachment, on high speed for 5 minutes, until pale and creamy. Add the eggs one at a time, beating well after each addition. Add the vanilla and sour cream, then sift in the flour and baking soda, and mix on low speed. Add the mashed and dried banana, and mix on low speed until well combined.

3 Spread the batter into the prepared pan. Bake for 1 hour and 15 minutes, or until a skewer inserted into the center of the cake comes out clean. Cool in the pan for 10 minutes, then turn out onto a wire rack to cool completely.

4 To make the Cinnamon Buttercream, combine all the ingredients in the bowl of an electric mixer fitted with the paddle attachment. Beat on high speed for 5 minutes, until pale and creamy.

5 Use a palette knife to spread the Cinnamon Buttercream over the top of the cooled cake.

VARIATION

• I like to use dried whole bananas, which are quite soft and chewy. You could use crunchy dried banana slices instead; they will give the cake a slightly different texture.

Zucchini Bread

I first made this cake as a teenager and was surprised that zucchini could taste so good.

MAKES 2 LOAVES
(EACH SERVES 8)
PREPARATION TIME: 30 MINS
COOKING TIME: 1 HR
STORE IN AN AIRTIGHT CONTAINER
   FOR UP TO 3 DAYS

2½ cups (375 g) all-purpose (plain) flour
⅓ cup (40 g) powdered milk
2 teaspoons baking soda
½ teaspoon baking powder
½ cup (50 g) wheat germ
1 cup (225 g) superfine sugar
1 cup (225 g) raw sugar
3 teaspoons ground cinnamon
½ teaspoon ground nutmeg
1½ cups (200 g) finely crushed peanuts
1 cup (250 ml) vegetable oil
3 eggs
3 teaspoons vanilla extract
1¾ cups (400 g) grated zucchini

1 Preheat the oven to 340°F (170°C).
Lightly grease two 8½-in × 4½-in (22-cm
× 11-cm) loaf pans.
2 Place all the dry ingredients in a large
mixing bowl and make a well in the center. Add the oil, eggs, vanilla and grated
zucchini to the well, and stir to combine
thoroughly.
3 Press the mixture into the prepared
pans. Bake for 1 hour, or until a skewer
inserted into the center of a cake comes
out clean. Serve slices of the loaf warm
or cold, spread with butter.

Burnt Butter and Berry Friands

Burnt butter is made by simmering butter until a sweet, nutty smell develops—it is not actually taken to the point of burning.

MAKES 25 FRIANDS
PREPARATION TIME: 30 MINS
COOKING TIME: 12 MINS
BEST SERVED ON THE DAY OF BAKING.
  UNCOOKED FRIAND MIXTURE CAN
  BE STORED IN THE REFRIGERATOR
  FOR UP TO 3 DAYS.

¾ cup (1¾ sticks/200 g) unsalted
  butter, diced
¾ cup (200 g) superfine sugar
⅓ cup (60 g) all-purpose (plain) flour
⅓ cup (60 g) almond flour
6 egg whites
2 cups (250 g) fresh or frozen berries
  (blueberries, raspberries, blackberries)
2 quantities Apricot Glaze (page 21)

1 Make the Apricot Glaze by following the recipe on page 21.
2 Preheat the oven to 325°F (160°C). Grease 25 small friand molds or tart molds (or two 12-hole mini muffin trays).
3 Place the butter in a medium-sized saucepan and cook over medium heat, stirring regularly, until the butter begins to froth and a nutty smell develops. This process may take up to 10 minutes. Pour the butter immediately into a heatproof bowl and leave to cool to lukewarm.
4 Combine the sugar, sifted flour and almond flour in a mixing bowl. Add the egg whites and mix well with a spoon until combined. Pour in the cooled butter and mix thoroughly.
5 Spoon the mixture into the prepared molds, then press one or two berries into the center of each. Bake for 12 minutes, until golden. Cool the friands in the molds, then brush liberally with the Apricot Glaze.

Chocolate Orange Cake

The combination of chocolate and orange is very popular and this cake provides a double dose with its topping of Chocolate Orange Ganache.

SERVES 12
PREPARATION TIME: 40 MINS
COOKING TIME: 1 HR 15 MINS
STORE IN AN AIRTIGHT CONTAINER
  FOR UP TO 3 DAYS

²/₃ cup (1¹/₃ sticks/150 g) unsalted butter, softened
2³/₈ cups (600 g) soft brown sugar
Finely grated zest of 3 oranges
6 eggs
5 oz (150 g) dark chocolate, melted
2½ cups (375 g) all-purpose (plain) flour
2 teaspoons baking soda
1¼ cups (300 g) sour cream
½ cup (110 ml) boiling water

CHOCOLATE ORANGE GANACHE
1 cup (250 ml) whipping cream
2 cups (250 g) chopped dark chocolate
Finely grated zest of 1 orange

1 Preheat the oven to 325°F (160°C). Line a 10-in (25-cm) round cake pan with parchment baking paper.
2 Beat the butter, sugar and orange zest, in the bowl of an electric mixer fitted with the paddle attachment, on high speed for 3 minutes until pale and creamy. Add the eggs one at a time, beating well after each addition. Add the melted chocolate and mix well, then sift in the flour and baking soda and add the sour cream. Mix on low speed until well combined. Slowly add the boiling water and mix well.
3 Pour the batter into the prepared pan. Bake for 1 hour and 15 minutes, or until a skewer inserted into the center of the cake comes out clean. Cool in the pan for 10 minutes, then turn out onto a wire rack to cool completely.
4 To make the Chocolate Orange Ganache, bring the cream to a boil, then pour it over the chocolate and stir until smooth. Add the orange zest and mix well.
5 Use a palette knife to spread the Chocolate Orange Ganache over the top of the cooled cake.

White Chocolate Mud Cake

Similar to the Chocolate Mud Cake recipe (page 72), this is another cake that can't be beaten for simplicity and taste.

SERVES 12
PREPARATION TIME: 40 MINS
COOKING TIME: 1 HR 30 MINS
STORE IN AN AIRTIGHT CONTAINER
   FOR UP TO 5 DAYS

2¼ cups (4½ sticks/500 g) unsalted
   butter, diced
2 cups (500 ml) milk
2 cups (450 g) sugar
2½ cups (300 g) chopped white chocolate
4 eggs
2 teaspoons vanilla extract
4 cups (600 g) all-purpose (plain) flour,
   sifted
3 teaspoons baking powder

GANACHE
⅔ cup (150 ml) whipping cream
3¼ cups (400 g) chopped white chocolate

1 Preheat the oven to 325°F (160°C).
Line a 10-in (25-cm) round cake pan with
parchment baking paper.
2 Combine the butter, milk, sugar and
chocolate in a large saucepan. Stir over
low heat until smooth. Pour into a large
bowl and set aside to cool to lukewarm.
3 Add the eggs and vanilla to the chocolate mixture, and whisk together. Add the
sifted flour and baking powder, and mix
thoroughly with a whisk until smooth.

4 Pour the batter into the prepared pan.
Bake for 1½ hours, or until a skewer
inserted into the center of the cake
comes out clean. Cool in the pan for 10
minutes, then turn out onto a wire rack to
cool completely.
5 To make the Ganache, bring the cream
to a boil, then pour it over the chocolate
and stir until smooth. Pour the Ganache
over the top of the cooled cake.

Chocolate Mud Cake

This simple melt-and-mix cake is very moist. Use good-quality dark chocolate for that intense mud-cake flavor.

SERVES 12
PREPARATION TIME: 40 MINS
COOKING TIME: 1 HR 30 MINS
STORE IN AN AIRTIGHT CONTAINER FOR UP
   TO 5 DAYS

1⅔ cups (3¼ sticks/375 g) unsalted butter, diced
3 cups (675 g) sugar
11 oz (300 g) dark chocolate
3 cups (750 ml) boiling water
2 tablespoons instant coffee granules
3 eggs
2 teaspoons vanilla extract
2¼ cups (330 g) self-rising flour, sifted
⅔ cup (60 g) cocoa (unsweetened), sifted

GANACHE
¾ cup (200 ml) whipping cream
2 cups (250 g) chopped dark chocolate

1 Preheat the oven to 325°F (160°C). Line a 10-in (25-cm) round cake pan with parchment baking paper.

2 Combine the butter, sugar, chocolate, boiling water and coffee in a heavy-based saucepan. Stir over low heat until smooth. Pour the chocolate mixture into a large bowl and set aside to cool to lukewarm.

3 Add the eggs and vanilla to the chocolate mixture, and mix well using a whisk. Add the sifted flour and cocoa, and whisk again until smooth.

4 Pour the batter into the prepared pan. Bake for 1½ hours, or until a skewer inserted into the center of the cake comes out clean. Cool in the pan for 10 minutes, then turn out onto a wire rack to cool completely.

5 To make the Ganache, bring the cream to a boil, then pour it over the chocolate and stir until smooth.

6 Use a palette knife to spread the Ganache over the top of the cooled cake.

Boiled Pineapple Fruit Cake

This is my mother's recipe and it is the easiest way to make a fruit cake. The smell of the pineapple, dried fruits and spices cooking on the stove is unforgettable.

SERVES 12
PREPARATION TIME: 40 MINS
COOKING TIME: 1 HR
STORE IN AN AIRTIGHT CONTAINER
   FOR UP TO 2 WEEKS

2½ cups (375 g) mixed dried fruit (e.g. golden raisins (sultanas), currants, raisins, cherries)
One × 1-lb (450-g) can crushed pineapple
½ cup (1 stick/125 g) unsalted butter, diced
¾ cup (200 g) sugar
1 teaspoon mixed spice
1 teaspoon baking soda
2 eggs
1 cup (150 g) self-rising flour
1 cup (150 g) all-purpose (plain) flour

1 Place the mixed dried fruit, crushed pineapple (undrained), butter, sugar, mixed spice and baking soda in a saucepan. Bring to a boil over medium heat, stirring regularly. Boil for 10 minutes, then pour the mixture into a mixing bowl and allow to cool to room temperature.

2 Preheat the oven to 325°F (160°C). Line a 8-in (20-cm) round cake pan with parchment baking paper.

3 Stir the eggs into the cooled fruit mixture. Sift in the flours and stir until well combined. Pour the mixture into the prepared pan.

4 Bake for 1 hour, or until a skewer inserted into the center of the cake comes out clean. Allow to cool completely in the pan.

Chocolate Raisin Cake with Muscat Mascarpone

Serve this cake with a glass of tokaji for a simple dinner-party dessert.

SERVES 8
PREPARATION TIME: 40 MINS +
   1 HR FRUIT SOAKING TIME
COOKING TIME: 45 MINS
STORE IN AN AIRTIGHT CON-
   TAINER FOR UP TO 3 DAYS

⅔ cup (100 g) raisins
2 tablespoons tokaji or muscat
   liqueur
12-oz (350-g) dark chocolate
⅔ cup (1⅓ sticks/150 g) unsalted
   butter, diced
½ cup (110 g) superfine sugar
¼ cup (60 ml) strong brewed coffee
⅓ cup (50 g) self-rising flour
⅓ cup (30 g) cocoa (unsweetened)
4 eggs, separated
⅓ cup (80 g) superfine sugar, extra

MUSCAT MASCARPONE
12 oz (350 g) mascarpone cheese
¼ cup (60 ml) tokaji or muscat
   liqueur
¼ cup (30 g) confectioner's (icing)
   sugar

1 Preheat the oven to 325°F (160°C). Line a 10-in (25-cm) round springform cake pan with parchment baking paper.

2 Soak the raisins in the tokaji for 1 hour.

3 Heat the chocolate, butter, sugar and coffee over a double boiler or in the microwave until melted and smooth. Sift in the flour and cocoa, and whisk well to combine. Add the egg yolks and the raisins with the tokaji. Mix well.

4 Whip the egg whites, in the bowl of an electric mixer fitted with the whisk attachment, on medium speed until soft peaks form. Add the extra sugar and whisk on high speed until firm peaks form. Fold the egg whites into the chocolate mixture.

5 Pour the batter into the prepared pan. Bake for 45 minutes, or until a skewer inserted into the center of the cake comes out clean. Allow to cool completely in the pan.

6 To make the Muscat Mascarpone, whisk together the mascarpone, tokaji and icing sugar until smooth.

7 Serve slices of the cake with a dollop of Muscat Mascarpone.

Pumpkin, Orange and Poppy Seed Cake

The pumpkin in this recipe helps to keep the cake moist and also gives it a wonderful orange color.

SERVES 12
PREPARATION TIME: 40 MINS
COOKING TIME: 1 HR 30 MINS
STORE IN AN AIRTIGHT CON-
TAINER FOR UP TO 3 DAYS

1⅓ cups (2⅔ sticks/300 g) unsalted
  butter, diced, softened
1½ cups (330 g) superfine sugar
4 eggs
Grated zest of 3 oranges
Grated zest of 3 lemons
¼ cup (30 g) poppy seeds
2⅔ cups (400 g) self-rising flour,
  sifted
1¼ cups (300 g) pumpkin purée
  (boiled and mashed pumpkin)

SYRUP
1½ cups (330 g) sugar
6 tablespoons freshly-squeezed
  lemon juice
6 tablespoons freshly-squeezed
  orange juice

1 Preheat the oven to 325°F (160°C). Line a 10-in (25-cm) round cake pan with parchment baking paper.

2 Beat the butter and sugar, in the bowl of an electric mixer fitted with the paddle attachment, on high speed for 5 minutes until pale and creamy. Add the eggs one at a time, beating well after each addition. Add the orange and lemon zests, poppy seeds, sifted flour and pumpkin purée. Mix on low speed until combined.

3 Spread the mixture into the prepared pan. Bake for 1½ hours, or until a skewer inserted into the center of the cake comes out clean. (While the cake is baking, prepare the Syrup.)

4 To make the Syrup,combine the sugar, lemon juice and orange juice in a small saucepan. Bring to a boil, stirring, then remove from the heat.

5 Pour the hot Syrup over the cake as soon as it comes out of the oven. Allow the cake to cool completely in the pan.

Light Fruit Cake

This cake recipe, another from my great-grandmother, has a lot less fruit and a more buttery flavor than many traditional fruit cakes.

SERVES 20
PREPARATION TIME: 40 MINS
COOKING TIME: 1 HR 30 MINS
STORE IN AN AIRTIGHT CONTAINER
   FOR UP TO 2 WEEKS

1 cup (2 sticks/250 g) unsalted butter,
   softened
1⅛ cups (250 g) superfine sugar
5 eggs
⅔ cup (90 g) currants
¾ cups (120 g) raisins
1¾ cups (280 g) golden raisins
   (sultanas)
½ cup (60 g) whole blanched almonds
¾ cup (60 g) candied orange peel, finely
   chopped
½ cup (100 g) candied cherries
Finely grated zest and juice of 1 lemon
2 cups (300 g) all-purpose (plain) flour
Pinch of salt

1 Preheat the oven to 340°F (170°C).
Line a 8-in (20-cm) round cake pan with
parchment baking paper.
2 Beat the butter and sugar, in the bowl
of an electric mixer fitted with the paddle
attachment, on high speed for 5 minutes,
until pale and creamy. Add the eggs one
at a time, beating well after each addition.
Add the remaining ingredients and mix on
low speed until combined.
3 Spread the mixture into the prepared
pan, smoothing the top with the back of
a spoon.
4 Bake for 1½ hours, or until a skewer
inserted into the center of the cake
comes out clean. Allow to cool completely
in the pan.

Carrot Cake with Cream Cheese Frosting

This carrot cake recipe is great to try if you are new to baking as it is so simple to make, requiring only a quick mix with a spoon.

SERVES 12
PREPARATION TIME: 30 MINS
COOKING TIME: 1 HR 15 MINS
STORE THE UN-ICED CAKE IN AN
   AIRTIGHT CONTAINER FOR UP TO
   3 DAYS

3 cups (450 g) self-rising flour
2¼ cups (450 g) soft brown sugar
1½ teaspoons baking soda
1½ teaspoons ground cinnamon
5 eggs
2 cups (4 sticks/450 g) unsalted butter,
   melted
5 medium-sized carrots, peeled and grated
1⅓ cups (200 g) golden raisins (sultanas)
1 quantity Cream Cheese Frosting
   (page 20)
1 teaspoon ground cinnamon, for dusting

1 Make the Cream Cheese Frosting by following the recipe on page 20.
2 Preheat the oven to 325°F (160°C). Line a 10-in (25-cm) round cake pan with parchment baking paper.
3 Combine the sifted flour, sugar, baking soda and cinnamon in a large bowl. Make a well in the center of the dry ingredients and add the eggs and melted butter. Stir to combine, then add the grated carrot and golden raisins. Mix well.
4 Pour the mixture into the prepared pan. Bake for 1 hour and 15 minutes, or until a skewer inserted into the center of the cake comes out clean. Cool in the pan for 10 minutes, then turn out onto a wire rack to cool completely.
5 Use a palette knife to spread the Cream Cheese Frosting over the cooled cake, then dust with cinnamon.

Ginger Cake with Whipped Honey Buttercream

This is another quick-mix cake that is good for beginner bakers. The combination of ginger and the smooth honey buttercream is divine.

1 Preheat the oven to 325°F (160°C). Line a 10-in (25-cm) round cake pan with parchment baking paper.

2 Place the honey, milk, sugar, butter, and sifted flours, baking soda and ginger in the bowl of an electric mixer. Using the paddle attachment, mix on low speed until well combined, then mix on medium speed for 4 minutes.

3 Spread the mixture into the prepared pan. Bake for 45 minutes, or until a skewer inserted into the center of the cake comes out clean. Cool in the pan for 10 minutes, then turn out onto a wire rack to cool completely.

4 To make the Whipped Honey Buttercream, combine the water, sugar and honey in a small saucepan and bring to a boil. Remove from the heat, and refrigerate until completely cold. Beat the butter, in the bowl of an electric mixer fitted with the paddle attachment, on high speed for 5 minutes until pale and creamy. With the mixer on low speed, gradually add the syrup, mixing until well combined. Beat on high speed for a further 3 minutes.

5 Use a palette knife to spread the Whipped Honey Buttercream over the cooled cake.

SERVES 12
PREPARATION TIME: 40 MINS
COOKING TIME: 45 MINS
STORE IN AN AIRTIGHT CON-
TAINER FOR UP TO 3 DAYS

²/₃ cup (200 g) honey
²/₃ cup (160 ml) milk
1½ cups (140 g) soft brown sugar
1 cup (2 sticks/250 g) unsalted butter, melted
1½ cups (225 g) all-purpose (plain)
   flour
²/₃ cup (100 g) self-rising flour
½ teaspoon baking soda
1 tablespoon ground ginger

WHIPPED HONEY BUTTERCREAM
¹/₃ cup (80 ml) water
½ cup (100 g) sugar
3 tablespoons honey
²/₃ cup (1¹/₃ sticks/150 g) unsalted
   butter, at room temperature

Maple Syrup Tea Cake with Caramel Icing

If you are a lover of caramel, this cake is for you.

1 Preheat the oven to 340°F (170°C). Line a 8-in (20-cm) round cake pan with parchment baking paper.

2 Beat the butter, soft brown sugar and vanilla, in the bowl of an electric mixer fitted with the paddle attachment, on high speed for 5 minutes until pale and creamy. Add the eggs one at a time, beating well after each addition. Add the maple syrup to the bowl, then sift in the flours and cinnamon. Pour in the milk and mix on low speed until combined.

3 Spread the batter into the prepared pan. Bake for 1 hour, or until a skewer inserted into the center of the cake comes out clean. Cool in the pan for 10 minutes, then turn out onto a wire rack to cool completely.

4 To make the Caramel Icing, combine the soft brown sugar, butter and milk in a saucepan. Stir continuously over low heat until the sugar is dissolved,then simmer for 3 minutes. Remove from the heat and sift in the icing sugar. Mix well. Add the extra milk if required to make the icing of a spreadable consistency.

5 Use a palette knife to spread the Caramel Icing over the top of the cooled cake.

SERVES 8
PREPARATION TIME: 40 MINS
COOKING TIME: 1 HR
STORE IN AN AIRTIGHT CONTAINER FOR UP TO 3 DAYS

¾ cup (1⅔ sticks/180 g) unsalted butter, softened
1¼ cups (300 g) soft brown sugar
2 teaspoons vanilla extract
3 eggs
¼ cup (75 g) maple syrup (or golden syrup)
1½ cups (225 g) all-purpose (plain) flour
¾ cup (120 g) self-rising flour
1 teaspoon ground cinnamon
¾ cup (180 ml) milk

CARAMEL ICING
¾ cup (200 g) soft brown sugar
¼ cup (½ stick/60 g) unsalted butter, diced
3½ tablespoons milk
1 cup (120 g) confectioner's (icing) sugar
3½ tablespoons milk, extra (if needed)

Lemon and Raspberry Pavlova Roulade

Use fresh strawberries if raspberries are not available.

SERVES 8
PREPARATION TIME: 30 MINS
COOKING TIME: 30 MINS
BEST SERVED ON THE DAY OF BAKING

4 egg whites
1 cup (225 g) superfine sugar
2 teaspoons cornstarch
1 teaspoon white vinegar
2 teaspoons vanilla extract
½ cup (60 g) confectioner's (icing) sugar

LEMON CURD FILLING
1¼ cups (300 ml) whipping cream
¼ cup (60 g) superfine sugar
½ quantity Lemon Curd (page 20)
1¼ cups (150 g) fresh raspberries

1 Make the Lemon Curd by following the recipe on page 20.
2 Preheat the oven to 285°F (140°C). Line a 8-in × 12-in (20-cm × 30-cm) baking sheet with parchment baking paper.
3 Whip the egg whites, in the bowl of an electric mixer fitted with the whisk attachment, on high speed until soft peaks form. With the mixer running on low speed, gradually add the sugar. Beat on high speed for a further 5 minutes, until the mixture is thick and shiny. Add the cornstarch, vinegar and vanilla, and mix well.
4 Using a palette knife, spread the meringue mixture evenly over the prepared sheet. Bake for 25–30 minutes, until set and slightly firm to the touch. Remove from the oven and stand for 5 minutes.

5 Dust the icing sugar evenly over a large sheet of parchment baking paper. Carefully turn the meringue out onto the parchment baking paper. Allow to cool completely.
6 To make the Lemon Curd Filling, whip the cream and sugar in the bowl of an electric mixer fitted with the whisk attachment until firm peaks form. Fold in the Lemon Curd and raspberries.
7 Spread the Lemon Curd Filling evenly over the meringue. Starting from a long side, roll up the meringue, using the parchment baking paper to help you. Place join side down on a serving plate.

Fruit Cake

My great-grandmother Lucy Cleland was a wonderful cook. Her cakes were outstanding, especially this fruit cake.

SERVES 40

PREPARATION TIME: 40 MINS +
 OVERNIGHT FRUIT SOAKING TIME
COOKING TIME: 4 HRS

BRUSHED WITH A LITTLE BRANDY
 ONCE A MONTH, THIS CAKE WILL
 KEEP (WELL WRAPPED IN PLASTIC
 WRAP AND ALUMINUM FOIL) IN AN
 AIRTIGHT CONTAINER FOR UP TO
 12 MONTHS.

4 cups (600 g) golden raisins (sultanas)
$2^3/4$ cups (400 g) raisins
$1^1/4$ cups (200 g) currants
$3/4$ cup (150 g) candied cherries
$3/4$ cup (60 g) candied orange peel, finely
 chopped
1 cup (150 g) whole blanched almonds
7 tablespoons brandy
$1^3/4$ cups ($3^1/2$ sticks/400 g) unsalted
 butter, softened
$1^3/4$ cups (400 g) superfine sugar
6 eggs
$2^2/3$ cups (400 g) all-purpose (plain) flour
$2/3$ cup (100 g) self-rising flour
$1/2$ teaspoon fine sea salt
1 teaspoon mixed spice
$1/8$ cup (40 g) orange marmalade
Finely grated zest and juice of 1 lemon
Finely grated zest of 1 orange

1 Combine the golden raisins, raisins, currants, cherries, orange peel, almonds and brandy in a large mixing bowl. Cover with plastic wrap and leave to soak overnight at room temperature.

2 Preheat the oven to 300°F (150°C). Line a 10-in (25-cm) round cake pan with parchment baking paper.

3 Beat the butter and sugar, in the bowl of an electric mixer fitted with the paddle attachment, on high speed for 5 minutes until pale and creamy. Add the eggs one at a time, beating well after each addition. Sift the flours, salt and mixed spice into the bowl. Add the marmalade, brandy-soaked fruit mix, lemon juice and zest, and orange zest. Mix on low speed until combined.

4 Spread the cake mixture into the prepared pan, smoothing the top with the back of a spoon. To help prevent burning, wrap the outside of the cake pan in a thick layer of newspaper, securing it with butcher's twine, and also sit the pan on a thick layer of newspaper.

5 Bake for $3^1/2$–4 hours, until a skewer inserted into the center of the cake comes out clean. Allow to cool completely in the pan.

Hummingbird Cake

Hummingbird cake is a lovely afternoon tea cake. It's easy to make, and so moist and packed full of flavor.

SERVES 12
PREPARATION TIME: 30 MINS
COOKING TIME: 1 HR 15 MINS
STORE THE UN-ICED CAKE IN AN
    AIRTIGHT CONTAINER FOR UP
    TO 3 DAYS

1½ cups (225 g) all-purpose (plain)
    flour
1 teaspoon fine sea salt
1 teaspoon ground cinnamon
1 teaspoon baking soda
2 cups (450 g) superfine sugar
¾ cup (100 g) chopped walnuts
3 eggs
1 teaspoon vanilla extract
3 very ripe bananas, mashed
1 cup (250 ml) vegetable oil
1 cup (250 g) drained crushed pine-
    apple
1 quantity Cream Cheese Frosting
    (page 20)

1 Make the Cream Cheese Frosting by following the recipe on page 20.

2 Preheat the oven to 300°F (150°C). Line a 10-in (25-cm) square cake pan with parchment baking paper.

3 Sift the flour, salt, cinnamon and baking soda into a large mixing bowl. Add the sugar and walnuts, and stir until combined. Make a well in the center of the dry ingredients. Add the eggs, vanilla, banana, oil and pineapple to the well, and mix thoroughly.

4 Pour the mixture into the prepared pan. Bake for 1 hour and 15 minutes, or until a skewer inserted into the center of the cake comes out clean. Cool in the pan for 10 minutes, then turn out onto a wire rack to cool completely.

5 Use a palette knife to spread the Cream Cheese Frosting over the top of the cooled cake.

Rhubarb and Apple Cake

I love this cake. The soft brown sugar crumbled over the top before baking creates a lovely sweet crust that pairs well with the acidity of the rhubarb.

SERVES 10
PREPARATION TIME: 40 MINS
COOKING TIME: 1 HR
STORE IN AN AIRTIGHT CON-
TAINER FOR UP TO 3 DAYS

¾ cup (1½ sticks/175 g) unsalted
butter, softened

1½ cups (375 g) soft brown sugar

2 eggs

1 teaspoon vanilla extract

2 cups (300 g) all-purpose (plain)
flour

1 teaspoon ground cinnamon

1 teaspoon baking soda

7 oz (200 g) rhubarb, chopped into
⅜-in (1-cm) pieces

11 oz (300 g) green apples, peeled,
cored and cut into ⅜-in (1-cm)
dice

Finely grated zest of 1 lemon

1 cup (250 g) sour cream

⅜ cup (80 g) soft brown sugar,
extra

1 teaspoon ground cinnamon, extra

1 Preheat the oven to 340°F (170°C). Line a 10-in (25-cm) round springform cake pan with parchment baking paper.

2 Beat the butter and sugar, in the bowl of an electric mixer fitted with the paddle attachment, on high speed for 5 minutes until pale and creamy. Add the eggs one at a time, beating well after each addition. Add the vanilla, then sift in the flour, cinnamon and baking soda. Add the rhubarb, apple, lemon zest and sour cream, and mix on low speed until combined.

3 Spread the batter into the prepared pan. Combine the extra soft brown sugar and cinnamon, and sprinkle it over the top of the cake. Bake for 1 hour, or until a skewer inserted into the center of the cake comes out clean. Cool in the pan for 10 minutes, then remove the sides of the pan and leave to cool completely. Serve with whipped cream if desired.

Lamingtons

While living in London, I developed this recipe for work colleagues who had never before tried this Australian favorite.

MAKES 12
PREPARATION TIME: 1 HR
COOKING TIME: 30 MINS
BEST SERVED ON THE DAY OF
  BAKING

8 eggs
1⅛ cups (250 g) superfine sugar
1⅔ cups (250 g) all-purpose
  (plain) flour, sifted
⅓ cup (⅔ stick/80 g) unsalted but-
  ter, melted
5 tablespoons raspberry jam
2½ cups (250 g) desiccated coco-
  nut

CHOCOLATE ICING
4 cups (500 g) confectioner's (icing)
  sugar
¾ cup (80 g) cocoa (unsweetened)
2 tablespoons unsalted butter,
  melted
⅔ cup (150 ml) water

1 Preheat the oven to 325°F (160°C). Line a 10-in (25-cm) square cake pan with parchment baking paper.
2 Beat the eggs and sugar, in the bowl of an electric mixer fitted with the whisk attachment, on high speed for 10 minutes until pale and creamy. Gently fold in the sifted flour, then stir in the melted butter until combined.
3 Pour the mixture into the prepared pan. Bake for 30 minutes, until the cake springs back when pressed gently in the center. Cool in the pan for 10 minutes, then turn out onto a wire rack to cool completely.
4 Split the sponge in half using a serrated knife. Spread the base with the raspberry jam, then place the other half of the sponge back on top. Trim off the edges, then cut the cake into 12 equal pieces.
5 To make the Chocolate Icing, sift the icing sugar and cocoa into a bowl. Add the melted butter and water, and whisk until smooth.
6 Spread the coconut on a large tray. Using a fork, dip each lamington into the Chocolate Icing, then dredge it in the coconut. Place the lamingtons on a clean plate or tray. Allow the icing to set for at least 30 minutes before serving.

Date Cake with Sweet Marsala Icing

Marsala icing pairs impeccably with this spicy, moist date cake. It's great served with coffee.

SERVES 12
PREPARATION TIME: 40 MINS
COOKING TIME: 1 HR
STORE IN AN AIRTIGHT CON-
TAINER FOR UP TO 3 DAYS

**2 cups (200 g) dried dates, pitted
and chopped**
¾ cup (180 ml) boiling water
**¾ cup (1¾ sticks/200 g) unsalted
butter, softened**
1¼ cups (300 g) soft brown sugar
3 eggs
3 cups (450 g) self-rising flour
1 teaspoon ground nutmeg
1 teaspoon ground cloves
Pinch of salt
1¼ cups (300 ml) milk

MARSALA ICING
**¼ cup (½ stick/60 g) unsalted but-
ter, melted**
**3¼ cups (400 g) confectioner's
(icing) sugar**
¼ cup (60 ml) sweet marsala wine

1 Preheat the oven to 325°F (160°C). Line a 8-in (20-cm) square cake pan with parchment baking paper.

2 Place the dates in a bowl and cover with the boiling water. Stand for 10 minutes, then mash with a fork until the dates are puréed.

3 Beat the butter and sugar, in the bowl of an electric mixer fitted with the paddle attachment, on high speed for 5 minutes, until pale and creamy. Add the eggs one at a time, beating well after each addition. Add the date mixture, then sift in the flour, nutmeg, cloves and salt. Pour in the milk and mix well on low speed until combined.

4 Spread the batter into the prepared pan. Bake for 1 hour, or until a skewer inserted into the center of the cake comes out clean. Cool in the pan for 10 minutes, then turn out onto a wire rack to cool completely.

5 To make the Marsala Icing, combine the butter and icing sugar in a large bowl. Gradually add the marsala while stirring, until the icing is of a spreadable consistency.

6 Use a palette knife to spread the Marsala Icing over the cooled cake.

Ricotta Cake

Good-quality fresh ricotta cheese is available from most delis. Do not use smooth ricotta as you will not get the same result.

SERVES 10
PREPARATION TIME: 45 MINS + 2
   HRS FREEZING TIME
COOKING TIME: 1 HR
STORE IN AN AIRTIGHT CONTAINER
   FOR UP TO 3 DAYS

2²/₃ cups (400 g) all-purpose (plain)
   flour, sifted

3 teaspoons baking powder

½ cup (125 g) soft brown sugar

¾ cup (100 g) almond flour

1 teaspoon vanilla extract

1 cup (2 sticks/250 g) unsalted butter,
   diced, at room temperature

1 egg

¼ cup (30 g) confectioner's (icing)
   sugar, for dusting

FILLING

2¼ lb (1 kg) ricotta cheese

¾ cup (170 g) superfine sugar

½ cup (100 g) coarsely chopped candied
   cherries

1 cup (100 g) coarsely chopped pistachios

2 tablespoons kirsch (cherry brandy)

2 teaspoons vanilla extract

1 Combine the sifted flour, baking powder, sugar, almond flour, vanilla and butter in the bowl of an electric mixer fitted with the paddle attachment. Mix on low speed until there are no lumps of butter visible. Add the egg and mix on low speed until a dough forms. Wrap the dough in cling wrap and place in the freezer for 2 hours, or until firm.

2 Preheat the oven to 360°F (180°C). Line a 10-in (25-cm) round springform cake pan with parchment baking paper.

3 To make the Filling, place all the ingredients in a mixing bowl and mix with a spoon until well combined.

4 Grate half the dough into the bottom of the prepared pan, ensuring the entire base is covered (do not press down). Spread the Filling evenly on top. Grate the remaining dough over the Filling, ensuring even coverage.

5 Bake the cake for 1 hour, until golden. Allow to cool completely in the pan. Dust with the icing sugar to serve.

VARIATION

• Replace the cherries and pistachios in the Filling with other dried fruits, nuts or chocolate—try dried apricot and almond, chocolate and hazelnut, or pine nut and orange.

Sponge Cake

To check if a sponge cake is cooked, press it very gently in the center. When ready, the cake should spring back; if your finger mark remains in the cake, it requires more cooking. Avoid opening the oven door too often during baking, as this will lower the temperature and the cake may sink.

SERVES 12
PREPARATION TIME: 40 MINS
COOKING TIME: 30 MINS
BEST SERVED ON THE DAY OF BAKING

8 eggs
1⅛ cups (250 g) superfine sugar
1⅔ cups (250 g) all-purpose (plain) flour, sifted
⅓ cup (⅔ stick/80 g) unsalted butter, melted
5 tablespoons strawberry jam
¼ cup (30 g) confectioner's (icing) sugar, for dusting

VANILLA CREAM
1 cup (250 ml) whipping cream
¼ cup (60 g) superfine sugar
1 teaspoon vanilla extract

1 Preheat the oven to 325°F (160°C). Line a 10-in (25-cm) round cake pan with parchment baking paper.
2 Beat the eggs and sugar, in the bowl of an electric mixer fitted with the whisk attachment, on high speed for 10 minutes until pale and creamy. Gently fold in the sifted flour, then stir in the melted butter.
3 Pour the mixture into the prepared pan.

Bake for 30 minutes, until the cake springs back when pressed gently in the center. Cool in the pan for 10 minutes, then turn out onto a wire rack to cool completely.
4 Split the cooled cake in half using a serrated knife. Spread the base with the strawberry jam.
5 To make the Vanilla Cream, whip the cream, sugar and vanilla in the bowl of an electric mixer fitted with the whisk attachment on high speed until thick.
6 Spread the Vanilla Cream over the jam, then place the other half of the cake back on top. Dust with the icing sugar to serve.

Spiced Roulade with Vanilla Buttercream

From start to finish this cake takes only 1 hour to make, so it's great if you need a cake for an impromptu get-together.

SERVES 8
PREPARATION TIME: 40 MINS
COOKING TIME: 15 MINS
STORE IN AN AIRTIGHT CONTAINER
 FOR UP TO 2 DAYS

¼ cup (½ stick/60 g) unsalted butter,
  softened
¾ cup (250 g) honey (or golden syrup)
¾ cup (110 g) all-purpose (plain) flour
½ cup (75 g) self-rising flour
1 teaspoon baking soda
1 teaspoon ground cinnamon
2½ teaspoons ground ginger
½ teaspoon ground nutmeg
¼ teaspoon ground cloves
2 eggs
¼ cup (60 ml) milk
3½ tablespoons superfine sugar

VANILLA BUTTERCREAM
⅔ cup (1⅓ sticks/150 g) unsalted
  butter, softened
1 cup (120 g) confectioner's (icing)
  sugar
1 vanilla bean, split and seeds scraped

1 Preheat the oven to 360°F (180°C). Line a 8-in × 12-in (20-cm × 30-cm) baking sheet with parchment baking paper.
2 Beat the butter, in the bowl of an electric mixer fitted with the paddle attachment, on low speed until smooth. Add the honey, then sift in the flours, baking soda and spices. Add the eggs and mix well on low speed, then add the milk and mix until combined.

3 Spread the batter evenly over the baking sheet. Bake for 12–15 minutes, or until the cake springs back when pressed gently in the center. Remove the cake from the oven and stand for 5 minutes.
4 Sprinkle a large sheet of parchment baking paper with the superfine sugar, then turn the cake out onto the paper. Starting from a long side, roll up the cake into a log, using the paper to help you. Set aside for 10 minutes. Unroll the cake, then leave to cool completely.
5 To make the Vanilla Buttercream, beat the butter, icing sugar and vanilla seeds in the bowl of an electric mixer fitted with the paddle attachment, on high speed for 5 minutes, until pale and creamy.
6 Spread the Vanilla Buttercream over the cake, then roll up. Place the roulade join side down on a serving plate.

White Wine and Olive Oil Cake with White Chocolate Ganache

I trained as a chef in a winery restaurant. We used a lot of wine in our cooking, but I was always particularly interested in adding it to cakes and desserts. Be sure to use good-quality white wine and olive oil in this cake to achieve best results.

SERVES 12
PREPARATION TIME: 30 MINS
COOKING TIME: 1 HR
STORE IN AN AIRTIGHT CONTAINER
    FOR UP TO 3 DAYS

2 cups (450 g) superfine sugar
2½ cups (375 g) self-rising flour
½ teaspoon fine sea salt
4 eggs
1 cup (250 ml) extra-virgin olive oil
1 cup (250 ml) white dessert wine

GANACHE
⅔ cup (150 ml) whipping cream
3¼ cups (400 g) chopped white chocolate

1 Preheat the oven to 300°F (150°C). Line a 10-in (25-cm) round cake pan with parchment baking paper.

2 Combine the sugar, sifted flour and salt in a large mixing bowl. Add the eggs, oil and white wine, and whisk until smooth.

3 Pour the batter into the prepared pan. Bake for 1 hour, or until a skewer inserted into the center of the cake comes out clean. Cool in the pan for 10 minutes, then turn out onto a wire rack to cool completely.

4 To make the Ganache, bring the cream to a boil, then pour it over the chocolate and stir until smooth.

5 Pour the white chocolate Ganache over the top of the cooled cake.

Passionfruit and Lemon Sponge Cake with Raspberries

This is a great party cake for summer. Use any fresh berries you like to decorate it.

SERVES 16
PREPARATION TIME: 1 HR 25 MINS
COOKING TIME: 1 HR
BEST SERVED ON THE DAY OF BAKING

1 quantity Lemon Curd (page 20), chilled
3 cups (750 ml) whipping cream
$^2/_3$ cup (150 g) superfine sugar
$^3/_4$ cup (150 g) passionfruit pulp (from about 5 fresh passionfruits)
2 Sponge Cakes (page 88), cooled
$^2/_3$ cup (200 g) raspberry jam
3$^1/_4$ cups (400 g) fresh raspberries
2$^3/_4$ tablespoons passionfruit pulp, extra

1 Make the Lemon Curd and the Sponge Cakes by following their respective recipes on pages 20 and 88.
2 Whip the Lemon Curd, cream, sugar and passionfruit pulp, in the bowl of an electric mixer fitted with the whisk attachment, on high speed until thick.
3 Split each cooled cake into two layers using a serrated knife. Place one cake layer on a serving plate and spread with a third of the raspberry jam, followed by a quarter of the passionfruit cream. Place another cake layer on top and spread with another third of the raspberry jam, then with a quarter of the passionfruit cream. Repeat with the remaining cake layers, raspberry jam and cream, finishing with a layer of passionfruit cream on top.
4 Decorate the cake with fresh raspberries and the extra passionfruit pulp to serve.

Banana and Walnut Layer Cake with Caramel Buttercream and Caramelized Walnuts

Cook the caramel for the buttercream until it's as dark as you would like the buttercream to be—I like it very dark, for a rich caramel taste.

SERVES 16
PREPARATION TIME: 2 HRS + 25 MINS
COOKING TIME: 1 HR + 30 MINS
BEST SERVED ON THE DAY OF BAKING

2 Banana Cakes (page 67) with 1¼ cups (150 g) chopped walnuts added to the batter of each cake before baking, cooled

CARAMEL BUTTERCREAM
1¼ cups (300 ml) whipping cream
1⅓ cups (300 g) sugar
14 egg yolks
1¾ cups (400 g) sugar, extra
¾ cup (180 ml) water
2½ cups (5 sticks/550 g) unsalted butter, softened

CARAMELIZED WALNUTS
½ cup (125 g) sugar
3 tablespoons water
3 cups (300 g) walnut halves
1 teaspoon unsalted butter

1 Make the Banana Cakes by following the recipe on page 67. Allow the cakes to cool completely before turning them out and frosting them.

2 To make the Caramel Buttercream, place the cream in a small saucepan and heat until hot, then set aside. Place the sugar in a medium-sized saucepan and cook over medium heat, stirring occasionally, until the sugar is liquid and caramel-colored. Keep cooking until it turns into a dark caramel. Remove from the heat and immediately add the cream, stirring to combine, being careful not to burn yourself on the steam that rises. Pour the caramel into a heatproof bowl and set aside to cool.

3 Beat the egg yolks, in the bowl of an electric mixer fitted with the whisk attachment, on high speed for 10 minutes until pale and creamy. Place the extra sugar and the water in a small saucepan and bring to a boil, then simmer until the syrup reaches 250°F (120°C)—check temperature using a sugar thermometer. With the mixer running on medium speed, slowly pour the sugar syrup into the egg yolks. Beat on high speed for 10 minutes until cool. With the mixer running on medium speed, add the softened butter a piece at a time, allowing each piece to mix in before adding the next one. Beat on high speed for 2 minutes. Add the cooled caramel to the bowl and beat again for 2 minutes.

4 To make the Caramelized Walnuts, combine the sugar and water in a large saucepan and bring to a boil, then simmer until the syrup reaches 250°F (120°C). Add the walnuts and stir continuously over medium heat until the sugar coats the walnuts and caramelizes. When the walnuts are golden, remove the pan from the heat and add the butter. Mix well, then pour onto a baking sheet lined with parchment baking paper. Separate the walnuts while still warm, then set aside to cool.

5 Split each cooled cake into two layers using a serrated knife. Place the base of one cake on a serving plate and use a palette knife to spread it with a sixth of the Caramel Buttercream. Place another cake layer on top and spread with another sixth of the Caramel Buttercream. Repeat the process with one more cake layer. Put the top cake layer on top and press gently to ensure it is level. Spread a very thin layer of Caramel Buttercream all over the cake, then use the remainder to evenly cover the entire cake. Decorate the cake with the Caramelized Walnuts.

Chocolate Orange Layer Cake with Orange Buttercream and Chocolate Orange Truffles

SERVES 16
PREPARATION TIME: 2 HRS 25 MINS +
   1 HR CHILLING TIME
COOKING TIME: 1 HR 15 MINS
BEST SERVED ON THE DAY OF BAKING

2 Chocolate Orange Cakes (page 70),
   cooled
2 quantities Chocolate Orange Ganache
   (page 70)

CHOCOLATE ORANGE TRUFFLES
1 cup (250 ml) whipping cream
2½ cups (300 g) chopped dark chocolate
4 teaspoons orange liqueur
1½ cups (150 g) cocoa (unsweetened),
   for coating

ORANGE SYRUP
Juice of 3 oranges
¼ cup (60 g) sugar

ORANGE BUTTERCREAM
1⅔ cups (3¼ sticks/375 g) unsalted
   butter, softened
2½ cups (300 g) confectioner's (icing)
   sugar
Finely grated zest of 3 oranges

1 Make the Chocolate Orange Cakes by following the recipe on page 70.

2 To make the Chocolate Orange Truffles, place the cream in a small saucepan and bring to a boil. Pour it over the chopped chocolate and orange liqueur, and stir until smooth. Refrigerate the chocolate mixture for 2 hours, until firm. Using a small metal scoop or melon baller that has been heated in hot water, scoop out balls from the set chocolate. Dredge the chocolate balls in the cocoa. Store in a cool place until required.

3 To make the Orange Syrup, bring the orange juice and sugar to a boil in a small saucepan. Set aside to cool.

4 To make the Orange Buttercream, beat the butter, icing sugar and orange zest in the bowl of an electric mixer fitted with the paddle attachment on high speed for 5 minutes, until pale and creamy.

5 Split each cooled cake into two layers using a serrated knife. Place the base of one cake on a serving plate and brush with a third of the Orange Syrup, then use a palette knife to spread with a third of the Orange Buttercream. Place another cake layer on top and brush with another third of the Orange Syrup, then spread with a third of the Orange Buttercream. Repeat the process with one more cake layer and the remaining syrup and buttercream. Put the top cake layer on top and press gently to ensure it is level. Use a palette knife to spread any buttercream that oozes out evenly around the sides of the cake. Chill the cake for 1 hour.

6 Prepare the Chocolate Orange Ganache by following the recipe on page 70, then pour it over the cake and use a palette knife to spread it over the top and sides of the cake.

7 Decorate the top of the cake with the Chocolate Orange Truffles to serve.

VARIATION
Chocolate Orange Cupcakes with Orange Buttercream and Chocolate Orange Truffles
Spoon the Chocolate Orange Cake batter into two 12-hole muffin trays that have been lined with paper cases. Bake for about 20 minutes. Once cooled, brush the cupcakes with the Orange Syrup, spread with Orange Buttercream, and top each with a Chocolate Orange Truffle.

Chocolate Mud Layer Cake with Coffee Buttercream and Swiss Meringues

SERVES 16
PREPARATION TIME: 2 HRS 25 MINS
COOKING TIME: 1 HR 40 MINS
BEST SERVED ON THE DAY OF BAKING

2 Chocolate Mud Cakes (page 72), cooled

1 quantity Swiss Chocolate Meringues (page 144) piped into 4-in (10-cm) sticks

COFFEE SYRUP
¼ cup (60 ml) water
¼ cup (60 g) sugar
1 tablespoon instant coffee granules

COFFEE BUTTERCREAM
1⅔ cups (3¼ sticks/375 g) unsalted butter, softened
2½ cups (300 g) confectioner's (icing) sugar
2 tablespoons instant coffee granules dissolved in 2 teaspoons boiling water
1 teaspoon vanilla extract

GANACHE
1¼ cups (300 ml) whipping cream
3½ cups (450 g) chopped dark chocolate

1 Make the Chocolate Mud Cakes by following the recipe on page 72. Allow them to cool completely before turning them out for frosting.

2 Make the Swiss Chocolate Meringues by following the recipe on page 144.

3 To make the Coffee Syrup, combine the water, sugar and coffee granules in a small saucepan. Bring to a boil and simmer for 1 minute, then set aside to cool.

4 To make the Coffee Buttercream, beat the butter and icing sugar in the bowl of an electric mixer fitted with the paddle attachment, on high speed for 5 minutes until pale and creamy. Add the dissolved coffee and the vanilla extract to the buttercream, and beat again on high speed for 2 minutes.

5 Split each cooled cake into two layers using a serrated knife. Place the base of one cake on a serving plate and brush with a third of the cooled Coffee Syrup, then use a palette knife to spread with a third of the Coffee Buttercream. Place another cake layer on top, brush with a third of the cooled Coffee Syrup and spread with a third of the Coffee Buttercream. Repeat the process with one more cake layer and the remaining syrup and buttercream. Put the top cake layer on top and press gently to ensure it is level. Use a palette knife to spread any buttercream that oozes out evenly around the sides of the cake. Chill in the refrigerator for 1 hour.

6 To make the Ganache, bring the cream to a boil, then pour it over the chocolate and stir until smooth.

7 Pour the Ganache over the cake and use a palette knife to spread it over the top and sides of the cake.

8 While the Ganache is still wet, position the sticks of Swiss Chocolate Meringues vertically around the sides of the cake.

VARIATION
Chocolate Mud Cupcakes with Coffee Buttercream and Swiss Meringues
Spoon the Chocolate Mud Cake batter into two 12-hole muffin trays that have been lined with paper cases. Bake for about 20 minutes. Once cooled, brush the cupcakes with the Coffee Syrup, spread with the Coffee Buttercream, then decorate with sticks of Swiss Chocolate Meringues.

White Chocolate Mud Layer Cake with Limoncello Syrup, Lemon Buttercream and Strawberries

SERVES 16
PREPARATION TIME: 1 HR 55 MINS
COOKING TIME: 1 HR 30 MINS
BEST SERVED ON THE DAY OF BAKING

**2 White Chocolate Mud Cakes (page 71),
cooled**
**2½ cups (500 g) strawberries, hulled and
cut into thin slices**
1 quantity Apricot Glaze (page 21)

LIMONCELLO SYRUP
7 tablespoons water
½ cup (100 g) sugar
Juice of 1 lemon
2 tablespoons limoncello (lemon liqueur)

LEMON BUTTERCREAM
**2¼ cups (4½ sticks/500 g) unsalted
butter, softened**
**3¼ cups (400 g) confectioner's (icing)
sugar**
1 quantity Lemon Curd (page 20)

1 Make the White Chocolate Mud Cakes by following the recipe on page 71. Allow the cakes to cool completely before turning them out for frosting.
2 Make the Apricot Glaze and the Lemon Curd by following their respective recipes on pages 21 and 20.
3 To make the Limoncello Syrup, combine the water, sugar and lemon juice in a saucepan, and bring to a boil. Allow to cool, then stir in the limoncello.
4 To make the Lemon Buttercream, beat the butter and icing sugar in the bowl of an electric mixer fitted with the paddle attachment, on high speed for 5 minutes, until pale and creamy. Add the Lemon Curd and beat again for 2 minutes.
5 Split each of the cooled cakes into two layers using a serrated knife. Place the base of one cake on a serving plate and brush liberally with the Limoncello Syrup, then use a palette knife to spread with a sixth of the Lemon Buttercream. Place another cake layer on top, brush with the Limoncello Syrup and spread with another sixth of the Lemon Buttercream. Repeat the process with one more cake layer. Put the top cake layer on top and press gently to ensure it is level. Brush the top with some more syrup, then spread a thin layer of buttercream over the entire cake. Spread the remaining buttercream around the sides of the cake, leaving just a thin layer of buttercream on the top.
6 Arrange the strawberry slices decoratively over the top of the cake. Brush the strawberries with the Apricot Glaze.

VARIATION
White Chocolate Cupcakes with Limoncello Syrup, Lemon Buttercream and Strawberries
Spoon the White Chocolate Cake batter into two 12-hole muffin trays that have been lined with paper cases. Bake for 20 minutes. Once cooled, brush the cupcakes with the Limoncello Syrup, spread the tops with the Lemon Buttercream, and garnish with a strawberry slice.

Hazelnut and Chocolate Meringue Layer Cake

SERVES 16
PREPARATION TIME: 1 HR 30 MINS
COOKING TIME: 1 HR
BEST SERVED ON THE DAY OF BAKING

One × 9-oz (250-g) block gianduja chocolate

MERINGUE

16 egg whites

1²/₃ cups (375 g) superfine sugar

1²/₃ cups (250 g) hazelnut flour

2 cups (250 g) confectioner's (icing) sugar

CHOCOLATE BUTTERCREAM

16 egg yolks

2 cups (450 g) sugar

²/₃ cup (150 ml) water

7 oz (200 g) dark chocolate, melted

2²/₃ cups (5¼ sticks/600 g) unsalted butter, diced, softened

1 Preheat the oven to 265°F (130°C). Line two baking sheets with parchment baking paper draw two 8-in (20-cm) circles on each piece of paper (trace around a dinner plate or cake pan).

2 To make the Meringue, whip the egg whites in the bowl of an electric mixer fitted with the whisk attachment, on high speed until soft peaks form. With the mixer on medium speed, gradually add the sugar. Beat on high speed for 10 minutes, until the mixture is thick and glossy. Combine the hazelnut flour and icing sugar, then fold this into the beaten egg whites.

3 Divide the Meringue mixture between the four circles on the baking sheets and spread out using a palette knife. Bake for 1 hour, until firm to the touch. Cool completely on the sheets.

4 To make the Chocolate Buttercream, beat the egg yolks in the bowl of an electric mixer fitted with the whisk attachment, on high speed for 10 minutes. Meanwhile, combine the sugar and water in a small saucepan, bring to a boil, and simmer until the syrup reaches 250°F (120°C)—check the temperature using a sugar thermometer. With the mixer running on medium speed, slowly drizzle the sugar syrup into the egg yolks. Beat on high speed for 10 minutes, until cool. Meanwhile, melt the chocolate. Add the melted chocolate to the bowl with the eggs and quickly mix in. With the mixer on medium speed, gradually add the softened butter a little at a time, then beat on high speed for 3 minutes until smooth.

5 Scrape the sharp edge of a round biscuit cutter across the surface of the block of gianduja chocolate, to make decorative curls.

6 Place one Meringue layer on a serving plate and use a palette knife to spread with a quarter of the Chocolate Buttercream. Place another Meringue layer on top and spread with another quarter of the Chocolate Buttercream. Repeat with the remaining Meringue layers and buttercream, finishing with a layer of buttercream on top.

7 Decorate the top of the cake with the chocolate curls. Refrigerate for at least 2 hours before serving.

Coconut Layer Cake with Coconut Rum Syrup and Coconut Frosting

1 Make the Vanilla Butter Cakes and the Frosting for Cakes and Cupcakes by following their respective recipes on pages 62 and 20.

2 To make the Coconut Rum Syrup, bring the sugar and water to a boil in a small saucepan. Allow to cool completely, then add the coconut rum. Set aside.

3 Split each cooled cake into two layers using a serrated knife. Place the base of one cake on a serving plate and brush with a quarter of the syrup, then use a palette knife to spread with a sixth of the frosting. Place another cake layer on top and brush with another quarter of the syrup, then spread with a sixth of the frosting. Repeat the process with one more cake layer. Put the top cake layer on top and brush with the remaining syrup. Spread a very thin layer of frosting all over the cake, then use the remaining frosting to evenly cover the entire cake.

4 While the frosting is still wet, sprinkle the cake liberally with the desiccated coconut to decorate.

SERVES 16
PREPARATION TIME: 1 HR 30 MINS
COOKING TIME: 40 MINS
BEST SERVED ON THE DAY OF
  BAKING

2 Vanilla Butter Cakes (page 62)—
  ½ cup (50 g) desiccated coco-
  nut added to each batter before
  baking—cooled
2 quantities Frosting for Cakes and
  Cupcakes (page 20)
2 cups (200 g) desiccated coconut

COCONUT RUM SYRUP
½ cup (100 g) sugar
7 tablespoons water
3½ tablespoons coconut rum

VARIATION

Coconut Cupcakes with Coconut Rum Syrup and Coconut Frosting
Spoon the Vanilla Butter Cake batter (with extra coconut added) into two 12-hole muffin trays that have been lined with paper cases. Bake for about 20 minutes. Once cooled, brush the cupcakes with the Coconut Rum Syrup, spread with the coconut icing, and decorate with the desiccated coconut.

Lemon Butter Cake with Lime and Orange Buttercreams and White Chocolate Ganache

1 Make the Vanilla Cakes by following the recipe on page 62.

2 To make the Ganache, bring the cream to a boil, then pour it over the chocolate and stir until smooth. Refrigerate for 2 hours or until of a spreadable consistency.

3 Make each Buttercream as follows. Beat the butter, icing sugar and zest in the bowl of an electric mixer fitted with the paddle attachment, on high speed for 5 minutes, until pale and creamy.

4 Split each cooled cake into two layers using a serrated knife. Place the base of one cake on a serving plate and use a palette knife to spread with half of the Lime Buttercream. Place another cake layer on top and spread with the Orange Buttercream. Place the third cake layer on top and spread with the remaining Lime Buttercream. Put the top cake layer on top and press gently to ensure it is level. Spread a very thin layer of white chocolate Ganache all over the cake, then use the remaining Ganache to evenly cover the entire cake.

5 Use a vegetable peeler to make chocolate curls from the block of white chocolate.

6 Sprinkle the chocolate curls over the cake to decorate.

SERVES 16
PREPARATION TIME: 1 HR 30 MINS
COOKING TIME: 40 MINS
BEST SERVED ON THE DAY OF
  BAKING

2 Vanilla Butter Cakes (page 62)—finely grated zest of 4 lemons added to each batter before baking—cooled

One × 7-oz (200-g) block white chocolate

GANACHE
³/₄ cup (200 ml) whipping cream
4³/₄ cups (600 g) chopped white chocolate

LIME BUTTERCREAM
1¹/₃ cups (2²/₃ sticks/300 g) unsalted butter, softened
2 cups (250 g) confectioner's (icing) sugar
Finely grated zest of 4 limes

ORANGE BUTTERCREAM
²/₃ cup (1¹/₃ sticks/150 g) unsalted butter, softened
1 cup (125 g) confectioner's (icing) sugar
Finely grated zest of 2 oranges

Red Velvet Cake with Cream Cheese Frosting

SERVES 16
PREPARATION TIME: 1 HR + 2 HRS
   COOLING TIME
COOKING TIME: 45 MINS
BEST SERVED ON THE DAY OF BAKING

1 cup (2 sticks/250 g) unsalted butter,
  softened
2⅔ cups (600 g) superfine sugar
4 eggs
1 cup (100 g) cocoa (unsweetened)
2 teaspoons vanilla extract
⅓ cup (80 ml) red liquid food coloring
1⅔ cups (400 ml) buttermilk
4 cups (600 g) all-purpose (plain) flour
2 teaspoons baking soda
4 teaspoons white vinegar
3 quantities Cream Cheese Frosting
  (page 20)

1 Make the Cream Cheese Frosting by following the recipe on page 20.

2 Preheat the oven to 325°F (160°C). Line two 8-in (20-cm) round cake pans with parchment baking paper.

3 Beat the butter and sugar in the bowl of an electric mixer fitted with the paddle attachment, on high speed for 5 minutes until pale and creamy. Add the eggs one at a time, beating well after each addition. Combine the cocoa, vanilla and red food coloring in a small bowl, then add this to the butter mixture and mix on low speed to combine well. Add half the buttermilk and half the flour, and mix on low speed. Add the remaining buttermilk and flour, mix well, then add the baking soda and vinegar, scrape down the sides of the bowl, and beat on medium speed for 2 minutes.

4 Divide the mixture between the two cake pans and spread out evenly. Bake for 45 minutes, or until a skewer inserted into the center of a cake comes out clean. Cool in the pans for 30 minutes, then turn out onto wire racks to cool completely.

5 Split each cake into two layers using a serrated knife (reserving any crumbs for decoration). Place one cake layer on a serving plate and use a palette knife to spread with a sixth of the Cream Cheese Frosting. Place another cake layer on top and spread with another sixth of the frosting. Repeat the process with one more cake layer. Put the top cake layer on top and press gently to ensure it is level. Spread a very thin layer of Cream Cheese Frosting all over the cake, then use the remaining frosting to evenly cover the entire cake.

6 Sprinkle the top of the cake with the reserved cake crumbs. Keep refrigerated until ready to serve.

VARIATION

Red Velvet Cupcakes with Cream Cheese Frosting: Spoon the prepared batter into two 12-hole muffin trays that have been lined with paper cases. Bake for about 20 minutes. Once cooled, spread the cupcakes with Cream Cheese Frosting (you will need only 2 quantities of frosting).

Baked
Desserts

Baked Cheesecake with Spiced Blueberries

This is the recipe that turned me into a cheesecake fan. It is a little lighter than most cheesecakes and has an amazing smooth texture. It pairs well with fruit that is a little tart, like these spiced blueberries.

SERVES 12
PREPARATION TIME: 45 MINS
COOKING TIME: 35 MINS
BEST SERVED ON THE DAY OF BAKING

BASE

1¾ cups (160 g) crushed graham
 crackers
½ cup (1 stick/100 g) unsalted butter,
 melted
1 tablespoon unsalted butter, melted,
 extra

FILLING

2¼ lb (1 kg) cream cheese, softened
1⅛ cups (250 g) superfine sugar
¼ cup (40 g) all-purpose (plain) flour,
 sifted
Zest and juice of 1 lemon
4 eggs
1 cup (250 g) sour cream

SPICED BLUEBERRIES

4 cups (500 g) fresh or frozen (defrosted)
 blueberries
1 vanilla bean, split and seeds scraped
1 star anise
¾ cup (200 g) sugar
Zest of ½ orange
¾ cup (200 ml) red wine

1 Preheat the oven to 375°F (190°C). Line the base of a 8-in (20-cm) round springform cake pan with parchment baking paper.

2 To make the Base, combine the crushed biscuits and melted butter in a bowl. Press the mixture evenly over the base of the pan. Brush the sides of the cake pan with the extra melted butter.

3 To make the Filling, beat the cream cheese in the bowl of an electric mixer fitted with the paddle attachment, on medium speed until smooth. Mix together the sugar and sifted flour, then add this to the cream cheese and mix on low speed until combined. Add the lemon zest and juice, eggs and sour cream, and mix until smooth.

4 Pour the Filling into the prepared pan. Bake for 15 minutes, then reduce the oven temperature to 210°F (100°C) and bake for a further 20 minutes. Allow the cheesecake to cool for 2 hours before removing the sides of the pan.

5 To make the Spiced Blueberries, combine all the ingredients in a small saucepan and simmer gently for 2 minutes. Refrigerate until cold, then remove the vanilla bean and star anise.

6 Serve the cheesecake with the Spiced Blueberries at the side or drizzled on top.

Cherry and Coconut Clafoutis

A traditional French bistro dessert, the clafouti is about as simple as it gets.

SERVES 8
PREPARATION TIME: 20 MINS
COOKING TIME: 30 MINS

2¼ lb (1 kg) fresh ripe cherries, pitted
1½ cups (140 g) desiccated coconut
¾ cup (200 g) superfine sugar
3 tablespoons all-purpose (plain) flour, sifted
2 cups (500 ml) whipping cream
5 eggs
5 egg yolks

1 Preheat the oven to 360°F (180°C).
2 Place the cherries in a 3 pt 3 fl oz (1.5 l) pudding dish.
3 Toast the coconut in a skillet over low heat for about 3 minutes, stirring constantly, until golden. Remove from the skillet and set aside to cool.
4 Combine the sugar, sifted flour and coconut in a mixing bowl. Add the cream, whole eggs and egg yolks, and mix well with a whisk until smooth.
5 Pour the batter over the cherries.
6 Bake the clafoutis for 30 minutes, until golden and set. Serve hot with vanilla ice-cream.

Impossible Pies

These pies are more magical than impossible. They separate into three layers while baking: a sweet base, smooth custard filling and coconut topping.

SERVES 8
PREPARATION TIME: 20 MINS
COOKING TIME: 30 MINS

4 eggs
³⁄₄ cup (200 g) superfine sugar
½ cup (1 stick/125 g) unsalted butter, diced, at room temperature
³⁄₄ cup (90 g) desiccated coconut
½ cup (70 g) all-purpose (plain) flour
2 teaspoons vanilla extract
2 cups (500 ml) milk

1 Preheat the oven to 340°F (170°C). Grease eight 8-fl oz (250-ml) individual pudding dishes with melted butter.
2 Place all the ingredients in a food processor or blender. Mix on high for 1 minute, until the ingredients are well combined.
3 Pour the mixture into the prepared pudding dishes and bake for 20 minutes, until set. Remove from the oven and allow to cool at room temperature for at least 30 minutes before serving.

VARIATION
Large Impossible Pie: To make one large pie instead of eight small ones, simply use a 10-in (25-cm) pie dish and bake for 1 hour.

Apple and Cinnamon Charlottes

The bread in this recipe creates a golden-brown crust around the sweet apple filling. Take your time to butter and layer the slices of bread neatly for a perfect finish.

MAKES 4
PREPARATION TIME: 45 MINS
COOKING TIME: 30 MINS
BEST EATEN THE DAY YOU
   BAKE

2 tablespoons superfine sugar, for coating
20 slices white bread, crusts removed
½ cup (1 stick/100 g) unsalted butter, melted

FILLING
¼ cup (½ stick/60 g) unsalted butter, diced
2½ tablespoons sugar
1 teaspoon ground cinnamon
1¼ lb (600 g) green apples, peeled, cored and sliced

1 To make the Filling, melt the butter in a skillet, then add the sugar, cinnamon and apple, and cook over high heat until the apple slices are caramelized. Remove from the skillet and allow to cool.

2 Preheat the oven to 360°F (180°C).

3 Grease four 8-fl oz (250-ml) round individual pudding dishes with butter. Sprinkle the superfine sugar into the molds to coat, then shake out the excess.

4 Cut out four rounds of bread the same size as the pudding dishes, brush them with melted butter and place one in the base of each mold. Cut each of the remaining slices of bread into three strips. Brush the strips of bread with the melted butter and use to line the sides of the pudding dishes, slightly overlapping each strip so there are no gaps, and leaving the ends of the strips sticking up above the top of the dish.

5 Fill each dish with the Filling. Fold over the strips of bread to meet at the top, completely covering the Filling.

6 Cover each dish with aluminum foil and bake for 30 minutes, until golden. Allow to cool for 10 minutes in the dishes before carefully unmolding onto serving plates. Serve immediately, with cream or ice-cream.

Individual Pavlovas

Pavlova is my favorite dessert. This recipe is to die for; it creates baked pavlovas with a crisp outer shell and soft meringue center.

SERVES 6
PREPARATION TIME: 30 MINS
COOKING TIME: 1 HR
STORE UNDECORATED PAVLOVAS IN
AN AIRTIGHT CONTAINER FOR UP
TO 3 DAYS

Fresh fruit of your choice (berries, chopped mango, passionfruit pulp), to decorate

MERINGUE
9 egg whites
3 teaspoons boiling water
1⅓ cups (300 g) superfine sugar
1 teaspoon white vinegar
2 teaspoons vanilla extract

SWEETENED CREAM
1¼ cups (300 ml) whipping cream
¼ cup (60 g) superfine sugar

VARIATION
Large Pavlova: To make one large pavlova instead of six mini ones, simply spread the meringue in a single round on the baking sheet and bake for 1½ hours.

1 Preheat the oven to 265°F (130°C). Line a baking sheet with parchment baking paper.
2 To make the Meringue, whip all the ingredients in the bowl of an electric mixer fitted with the whisk attachment, on high speed for 10–15 minutes, until thick and glossy.
3 Spoon six mounds of Meringue onto the prepared baking sheet. Bake for 1 hour. Cool completely on the baking sheet.
4 To make the Sweetened Cream, whip the cream and sugar in the bowl of an electric mixer fitted with the whisk attachment, on high speed until thick.
5 Just before serving, spread the pavlovas with the Sweetened Cream and decorate with fresh fruit.

Apple Crumble

Living very close to a number of apple orchards, I always have a plentiful supply of apples when they are in season. This dessert is a family favorite that I have been making for over 20 years.

SERVES 6
PREPARATION TIME: 30 MINS
COOKING TIME: 50 MINS

8 green apples, peeled, cored and sliced
6 tablespoons water
1 teaspoon ground cinnamon
¾ cup (200 g) soft brown sugar
½ cup (75 g) all-purpose (plain) flour
1¾ cups (170 g) desiccated coconut
½ cup (1 stick/125 g) unsalted butter, softened

1 Preheat the oven to 360°F (180°C).
2 Combine the sliced apple, water and cinnamon in a bowl, then transfer to a 3 pt 3 fl oz (1.5 l) pudding dish. Cover with aluminum foil and bake for 20 minutes to soften the apples.
3 Combine the soft brown sugar, sifted flour and coconut in another bowl. Add the butter and use your fingertips to rub it in until the mixture resembles bread-crumbs. Sprinkle this mixture over the apples.
4 Return the dish to the oven and bake, uncovered, for 30 minutes, until golden. Serve hot with custard and ice-cream.

Lemon Delicious Puddings

I learnt to make this recipe as an apprentice. It's an excellent last-minute dessert, as it is quick to prepare and the ingredients are nearly always in the pantry and fridge.

MAKES 4
PREPARATION TIME: 30 MINS
COOKING TIME: 25 MINS

$^1/_3$ cup ($^3/_4$ stick/90 g) unsalted butter, softened
$^2/_3$ cup (150 g) superfine sugar
3 eggs, separated
Finely grated zest and juice of 3 lemons
$^2/_3$ cup (90 g) self-rising flour, sifted
$1^1/_4$ cups (300 ml) milk

1 Preheat the oven to 325°F (160°C).
2 Beat the butter and sugar, in the bowl of an electric mixer fitted with the paddle attachment, on high speed for 5 minutes, until pale and creamy. Add the egg yolks one at a time, beating well after each addition. Add the lemon juice and zest, sifted flour and milk. Mix on low speed until combined. Transfer the mixture to another bowl. Thoroughly wash and dry the bowl of the mixer.
3 Place the egg whites in the bowl of the electric mixer. Using the whisk attachment, whip the whites on high speed until firm peaks form. Fold the whipped egg whites into the lemon mixture.
4 Divide the batter evenly between four 8-fl oz (250-ml) individual pudding dishes. Bake for 25 minutes, until set. Serve hot, in the pudding dishes, with cream or ice-cream.

VARIATION
Large Lemon Delicious Pudding: Use a 34-fl oz (1-l) dish instead of individual dishes and bake for 45 minutes, until set.

Pear and Raspberry Sponge Pudding

This versatile recipe can be made with almost any fruit you like, which means you can bake it all year round, using whatever is in season.

SERVES 6
PREPARATION TIME: 30 MINS
COOKING TIME: 40 MINS

10 ripe pears, peeled, cored and sliced
1²⁄₃ cups (200 g) fresh raspberries
1 cup (225 g) sugar
Zest of 1 lemon
2 tablespoons water

SPONGE
½ cup (1 stick/100 g) unsalted butter,
  softened
⅓ cup (80 g) superfine sugar
2 eggs
1 cup (150 g) all-purpose (plain) flour
½ teaspoon baking powder

1 Preheat the oven to 340°F (170°C). Grease a 3-pt 3 fl oz (1.5-l) pudding dish with melted butter.

2 Place the pear slices in the prepared dish, then stir in the raspberries, sugar, lemon zest and water.

3 To make the Sponge, beat the butter and sugar in the bowl of an electric mixer fitted with the paddle attachment, on high speed for 5 minutes, until pale and creamy. Add the eggs one at a time, beating well after each addition. Sift the flour and baking powder into the bowl and mix well.

4 Spread the Sponge mixture over the pears. Bake the pudding for 40 minutes, until golden. Serve hot with cream or ice-cream.

Soft-centered Chocolate Puddings

The trick with these puddings—also called chocolate fondants—is not to overcook them. Too long in the oven and the center will cook solid, rather than be oozy and melted.

MAKES 4

PREPARATION TIME: 30 MINS

COOKING TIME: 12 MINS

THE UNCOOKED PUDDINGS CAN BE KEPT IN THE REFRIGERATOR FOR UP TO 2 DAYS. ADD 2 MINUTES TO THE COOKING TIME IF COOKING THEM STRAIGHT FROM THE FRIDGE.

1¼ cups (150 g) chopped dark chocolate

⅔ cup (1⅓ sticks/150 g) unsalted butter, diced

3 eggs

1 egg yolk

¼ cup (60 g) superfine sugar

½ cup (85 g) all-purpose (plain) flour

1½ tablespoons cocoa (unsweetened)

1 teaspoon baking powder

1 quantity Vanilla Custard (page 21) (optional)

1 Make the Vanilla Custard by following the recipe on page 21.

2 Preheat the oven to 360°F (180°C). Grease four 8-fl oz (250-ml) individual pudding dishes with melted butter.

3 Melt the chocolate and butter together in a double boiler or in the microwave until smooth.

4 Beat the whole eggs, egg yolk and sugar in the bowl of an electric mixer fitted with the whisk attachment, on high speed for 10 minutes, until pale and creamy.

5 Gently fold the melted chocolate and butter into the egg mixture, then sift in the flour, cocoa and baking powder. Fold together carefully until just combined. Spoon the mixture into the prepared pudding molds.

6 Bake the puddings for 12 minutes (they should feel soft in the center when pressed lightly). Serve hot with Vanilla Custard and/ or cream or ice-cream.

Banana and Walnut Puddings with Honey Custard

The honey custard complements this pudding perfectly. To avoid curdling the custard, strain the mixture through a sieve as soon as it reaches the correct temperature (check using a cooking thermometer).

MAKES 6
PREPARATION TIME: 45 MINS
COOKING TIME: 20 MINS

3 large very ripe bananas, chopped
2 tablespoons water
1 cup (2 sticks/250 g) unsalted butter, softened
1 cup (225 g) superfine sugar
4 eggs
⁷/₈ cup (125 g) self-rising flour
1 teaspoon baking powder
1 teaspoon vanilla extract
½ cup (60 g) finely chopped walnuts

HONEY CUSTARD
2 cups (500 ml) whipping cream
1 vanilla bean, split and seeds scraped
6 egg yolks
⅓ cup (100 g) honey

1 Place the chopped banana in a saucepan with the water. Cook over low heat, stirring constantly, until softened. Transfer to a bowl and set aside to cool.

2 Preheat the oven to 300°F (150°C). Grease six 8-fl oz (250-ml) individual pudding dishes with melted butter.

3 Beat the butter and sugar, in the bowl of an electric mixer fitted with the paddle attachment, on high speed for 5 minutes, until pale and creamy. Add the eggs one at a time, beating well after each addition. Sift the flour and baking powder into the bowl, and fold in. Add the banana, vanilla and walnuts, and stir to combine.

4 Divide the mixture between the six pudding dishes. Bake for 25 minutes, or until a skewer inserted into the center of a pudding comes out clean. You can make the Honey Custard while the puddings are in the oven. (Alternatively, make the custard in advance and refrigerate until ready to serve.)

5 To make the Honey Custard, heat the cream and vanilla bean and seeds in a saucepan until hot (but not boiling). Remove from the heat. Combine the egg yolks and honey in a bowl and whisk well, then pour in the hot cream and stir well. Return the mixture to the saucepan and cook over low heat, stirring constantly, until the custard thickens enough to coat the back of the spoon—the temperature of the custard should be 175°F (80°C). Immediately strain the custard into a clean bowl to stop the cooking process.

6 Serve the puddings hot, with hot or cold Honey Custard.

Sticky Date Pudding with Butterscotch Sauce

Everyone needs a good sticky date pudding recipe, and you'll never try another after baking this one.

SERVES 6
PREPARATION TIME: 45 MINS
COOKING TIME: 30 MINS

2¼ cups (225 g) dried dates, pitted
   and coarsely chopped
1 teaspoon vanilla extract
⅞ cup (220 ml) water
¾ cup (200 g) sour cream
¼ cup (½ stick/60 g) unsalted
   butter, diced
¾ cup (180 g) sugar
1¼ cups (180 g) self-rising flour,
   sifted
3 eggs

BUTTERSCOTCH SAUCE
⅜ cup (90 g) soft brown sugar
⅝ cup (150 g) sour cream
¼ cup (½ stick/60 g) unsalted
   butter, diced
1 teaspoon vanilla extract

1 Preheat the oven to 360°F
(180°C). Line a 8-in (20-cm) square
cake pan with parchment baking
paper.
2 Place the dates, vanilla, water
and sour cream in a saucepan over
medium heat. Simmer until the dates
are tender and the mixture is the
consistency of jam. Stir in the diced
butter. Pour the mixture into a bowl
and set aside to cool for 10 minutes.

3 Add the sugar, sifted flour and the eggs to the date mixture. Stir until combined, then pour
the batter into the prepared pan.
4 Bake the pudding for 30 minutes, or until a skewer inserted into the center comes out clean.
5 To make the Butterscotch Sauce, combine the soft brown sugar, sour cream, butter and
vanilla in a small saucepan. Simmer for 5 minutes, until the sugar is dissolved and the sauce
is slightly thickened.
6 Cut the pudding into squares and serve hot with the Butterscotch Sauce and vanilla ice-cream.

Mandarin and Chocolate Cheesecake

I make this recipe with oranges when mandarins are out of season—either fruit is a winning combination with chocolate.

SERVES 12
PREPARATION TIME: 45 MINS
COOKING TIME: 1 HR
BEST SERVED ON THE DAY OF
    BAKING

BASE

**3 cups (300 g) crushed plain choco-
    late biscuits**
**²⁄₃ cup (1¹⁄₃ sticks/150 g) unsalted
    butter, melted**

FILLING

**1⁵⁄₈ lb (750 g) cream cheese,
    softened**
1³⁄₄ cups (450 g) sour cream
3 eggs
1 cup (225 g) superfine sugar
2 teaspoons vanilla extract
Finely grated zest of 4 mandarins

GANACHE

7 tablespoons whipping cream
3¹⁄₂ oz (100 g) dark chocolate

1 Preheat the oven to 300°F
(150°C). Line the base of a 8-in (20-
cm) round springform cake pan with
parchment baking paper.
2 To make the Base, combine the
crushed biscuits and melted butter
in a bowl. Press the mixture evenly
over the base and up the sides of
the prepared pan.

3 To make the Filling, beat the cream cheese in the bowl of an electric mixer fitted with the
paddle attachment, on medium speed until smooth. Add the sour cream, eggs, sugar, vanilla
and mandarin zest, and beat until well combined.
4 Pour the Filling into the prepared pan and bake for 1 hour, until set. Allow the cheesecake
to cool for 2 hours before removing the sides of the pan.
5 To make the Ganache, bring the cream to a boil, then pour it over the chocolate and stir
until smooth.
6 Drizzle the chocolate Ganache over the cheesecake.

Bread and Butter Pudding

It's good to prepare this recipe a day before baking—this allows the custard to soak into the bread, giving the pudding a better texture.

SERVES 6
PREPARATION TIME: 30 MINS
COOKING TIME: 1 HR

14 slices (400 g) white bread, fruit bread
  or brioche, crusts removed
¾ cup (100 g) grated dark chocolate
½ cup (60 g) golden raisins (sultanas)
3 eggs
3 egg yolks
½ cup (100 g) superfine sugar
1⅔ cups (400 ml) whipping cream
1⅔ cups (400 ml) milk
2 teaspoons vanilla extract
Finely grated zest of 1 orange

1 Preheat the oven to 325°F (160°C). Grease a 3-pt 3 fl oz (1.5-l) pudding dish with melted butter.
2 Cut the bread into slices ⅜ in (1 cm) thick. Arrange the slices in the baking dish, sprinkling the grated chocolate and golden raisins between the layers.
3 Whisk together the whole eggs, egg yolks, sugar, cream, milk, vanilla and orange zest in a bowl until well combined. Pour the mixture over the bread. For best results, refrigerate the pudding for at least 1 hour (and up to 24 hours) before baking, to allow the custard to soak into the bread.
4 Bake the pudding for 45 minutes to 1 hour, until golden. Serve hot with vanilla ice-cream.

Self-saucing Chocolate and Orange Pudding

As a teenager I was always impressed by recipes that changed in some surprising way during baking. In this recipe, the sauce starts off on top of the pudding but ends up underneath. Clever and delicious!

SERVES 8
PREPARATION TIME: 30 MINS
COOKING TIME: 35 MINS

1⅓ cups (200 g) self-rising flour
½ cup (50 g) cocoa (unsweetened)
½ cup (100 g) superfine sugar
¾ cup (180 ml) milk
¼ cup (½ stick/60 g) unsalted butter, melted
1 teaspoon vanilla extract
1 egg
1 egg yolk
Finely grated zest of 4 oranges

SAUCE
1 cup (250 g) soft brown sugar
½ cup (50 g) cocoa (unsweetened)
1¼ cups (300 ml) boiling water
6 tablespoons orange juice

1 Preheat the oven to 360°F (180°C). Grease a 3-pt 3 fl oz (1.5-l) pudding dish with melted butter.
2 Sift the flour and cocoa into a bowl. Add the sugar, milk, melted butter, vanilla, whole egg, egg yolk and orange zest. Mix well with a spoon, then spread into the pudding dish.
3 To make the Sauce, combine the soft brown sugar and cocoa, and sprinkle evenly over the batter. Combine the boiling water and orange juice, and carefully pour over the top of the pudding.
4 Bake the pudding for 35 minutes, until firm to the touch. Serve hot with whipped cream or ice-cream.

Sweet Muffins

Muffins are a great way to introduce children to cooking, and this recipe is super simple, requiring only a quick stir with a wooden spoon. An important selling point for children is that the muffins can be made and eaten within 30 minutes.

MAKES 12
PREPARATION TIME: 20 MINS
COOKING TIME: 15 MINS
BEST SERVED ON THE DAY OF BAKING

2 cups (300 g) self-rising flour
¾ cup (170 g) superfine sugar
3 eggs
½ cup (1 stick/125 g) unsalted butter, melted
½ cup (125 ml) milk
Flavorings of your choice (see Variations)

1 Preheat the oven to 360°F (180°C). Grease a 12-hole muffin tray, or line with paper cases.

2 Sift the flour into a large bowl, then add the sugar, eggs, butter and milk. Add your flavorings of choice and mix until only just combined. (Do not overmix, or the muffins will be tough.)

3 Divide the mixture between the muffin-tray holes. Bake for 20 minutes, or until a skewer inserted into the center of a muffin comes out clean. Cool for 10 minutes in the pan, then transfer to a wire rack.

VARIATIONS

Raspberry and White Chocolate Muffins (pictured): Add 1¼ cups (150 g) raspberries and ¾ cup (100 g) chopped white chocolate.

Blueberry Muffins (pictured): Add 1⅔ cups (200 g) blueberries and 2 teaspoons vanilla extract.

Banana and Cinnamon Muffins: Add 2 teaspoons ground cinnamon and 2 mashed bananas.

Date and Orange Muffins: Add 2 cups (200 g) chopped pitted dates and the finely grated zest of 2 oranges.

Spiced Apple Muffins: Add 1¼ cups (200 g) canned apple slices, 1 teaspoon ground ginger, 1 teaspoon ground cinnamon and ¼ teaspoon ground nutmeg.

Chocolate and Hazelnut Muffins: Add ⅔ cup (100 g) roasted chopped hazelnuts and 1¼ cups (150 g) chopped dark chocolate.

Savory Muffins

Savory muffins make a tasty snack for lunchboxes. Try the flavor variations provided or create some of your own.

MAKES 12
PREPARATION TIME: 20 MINS
COOKING TIME: 15 MINS
BEST SERVED ON THE DAY OF BAKING

2 cups (300 g) self-rising flour
1 teaspoon fine sea salt
1 egg
1/3 cup (2/3 stick/80 g) unsalted butter, melted
1 cup (250 ml) milk
Flavorings of your choice (see Variations below)

VARIATIONS

Three Cheese Muffins: Add ½ cup (60 g) grated tasty cheddar, ¼ cup (30 g) grated parmesan, ¼ cup (30 g) crumbled blue cheese and 2 tablespoons chopped fresh chives.

Spinach and Feta Muffins: Add ½ cup (100 g) chopped cooked spinach (excess moisture squeezed out), 1 cup (100 g) crumbled feta and ¼ cup (30 g) grated parmesan.

Sun-dried Tomato, Prosciutto and Basil Muffins (pictured): Add ¾ cup (90 g) chopped prosciutto, ¼ cup (60 g) chopped sun-dried tomatoes and 2 tablespoons chopped fresh basil.

Bacon and Onion Muffins: Add ½ cup (125 g) chopped bacon that has been cooked in a skillet until crispy, 1 finely grated onion, 2 chopped green onions (scallions) and 2 tablespoons chopped fresh chives.

1 Preheat the oven to 360°F (180°C). Grease a 12-hole muffin tray, or line with paper cases.
2 Sift the flour into a large bowl, then add the salt, egg, butter and milk. Add the flavorings of your choice and mix until only just combined. (Be careful not to overmix, or the muffins will be tough.)
3 Divide the mixture between the muffin-tray holes. Bake for 15 minutes, or until a skewer inserted into the center of a muffin comes out clean. Allow to cool for 10 minutes in the pan, then transfer to a wire rack.

Savory Scones

To avoid ending up with tough, chewy scones, do not overmix the dough; stop mixing as soon as the dough has formed.

MAKES 12
PREPARATION TIME: 30 MINS
COOKING TIME: 20 MINS
BEST SERVED ON THE DAY OF BAKING

2²/₃ cups (400 g) self-rising flour, sifted
½ teaspoon fine sea salt
3½ tablespoons unsalted butter, diced
1 cup (250 ml) milk
Flavorings of your choice (see Variations)
2 tablespoons milk, extra

1 Preheat the oven to 340°F (170°C). Grease a baking sheet.
2 Combine the sifted flour with the salt and diced butter in the bowl of an electric mixer fitted with the paddle attachment. Mix on low speed until there are no lumps of butter visible. (Alternatively, this step can be done in a food processor.) Add the milk and flavorings of your choice, and mix on low speed (or by hand) until a dough forms. (Be careful not to overmix, as this will result in dry, tough scones.)
3 Turn the dough out onto a lightly floured work surface and roll out to a thickness of 1¼ in (3 cm). Cut the dough into 2-in (5-cm) squares, or cut out rounds using a 2-in (5-cm) cutter. Place the scones on the prepared baking sheet and brush the tops with the extra milk.
4 Bake the scones for 15–20 minutes, until golden.

VARIATIONS

Smoked Salmon and Dill Scones (pictured): Add ½ cup (125 g) chopped smoked salmon and 2 tablespoons chopped fresh dill with the milk.
Cheese and Mustard Scones: Add 1¼ cups (125 g) grated tasty cheese and 1 tablespoon Dijon mustard with the milk. After brushing the finished scones with milk, scatter them with 1 cup (90 g) extra grated cheese.
Bacon and Chive Scones: Add ½ cup (125 g) chopped bacon that has been cooked in a skillet until crispy, and 2 tablespoons chopped chives with the milk.

Sweet Scones

To test if the scones are cooked, break one in half—if it is still doughy in the middle, return scones to the oven for a few more minutes.

MAKES 16
PREPARATION TIME: 30 MINS
COOKING TIME: 20 MINS
BEST SERVED ON THE DAY OF BAKING

$4^2/_3$ cups (700 g) self-rising flour
$^3/_4$ cup (180 g) superfine sugar
Pinch of salt
$^1/_4$ cup ($^1/_2$ stick/60 g) unsalted butter, diced
1 teaspoon vanilla extract
$1^1/_2$ cups (375 ml) milk
2 tablespoons milk, extra

1 Preheat the oven to 340°F (170°C). Grease a baking sheet.
2 Combine the sifted flour, sugar, salt and diced butter in the bowl of an electric mixer fitted with the paddle attachment. Mix on low speed until there are no lumps of butter visible. (Alternatively, this step can be done in a food processor.) Add the vanilla and milk, and mix on low speed (or by hand) until a dough forms. (Be careful not to overmix, as this will result in dry, tough scones.)
3 Turn the dough out onto a lightly floured work surface and roll out to a thickness of $1^1/_4$ in (3 cm). Cut out rounds using a 2-in (5-cm) cutter. Place the scones on the prepared baking sheet and brush the tops with the extra milk.
4 Bake the scones for 15–20 minutes, until golden. Serve with jam and whipped cream.

VARIATION
Sultana Scones: Add 1 cup (150 g) golden raisins (sultanas) to the dry ingredients.

Pumpkin Scones

If you have a glut of pumpkins (as I usually do in autumn) these scones are a fantastic way to use up some of the excess. Also try the Pumpkin, Orange and Poppy Seed Cake (page 75) or the Pumpkin Pie (page 194).

MAKES 16
PREPARATION TIME: 30 MINS
COOKING TIME: 20 MINS
BEST SERVED ON THE DAY OF BAKING

4^2/$_3$ cups (700 g) self-rising flour
^{3}/$_4$ cup (180 g) superfine sugar
Pinch of salt
^{1}/$_4$ cup (^{1}/$_2$ stick/60 g) unsalted butter, diced
^{3}/$_4$ cup (200 ml) milk
1 cup (250 g) pumpkin purée (boiled and mashed pumpkin)
2 tablespoons milk, extra

1 Preheat the oven to 340°F (170°C). Grease a baking sheet.
2 Combine the sifted flour, sugar, salt and diced butter in the bowl of an electric mixer fitted with the paddle attachment. Mix on low speed until there are no lumps of butter visible. (Alternatively, this step can be done in a food processor.) Add the milk and pumpkin to the bowl, and mix on low speed (or by hand) until a dough forms. (Be careful not to overmix, as this will result in dry, tough scones.)
3 Turn the dough out onto a lightly floured work surface and roll out to a thickness of 1^1/$_4$ in (3 cm). Cut out rounds using a 2-in (5-cm) cutter. Place the scones on the prepared baking sheet and brush with the extra milk.
4 Bake the scones for 15–20 minutes, until golden. Serve warm or cold with jam and whipped cream.

Cookies and Brownies

Ginger Snaps

One of my favorite desserts as a teenager was made from ginger snaps: ginger nuts, crushed pineapple and whipped cream layered in a pudding dish, then chilled for at least 6 hours before serving.

MAKES 24
PREPARATION TIME: 30 MINS
COOKING TIME: 12 MINS
STORE IN AN AIRTIGHT CONTAINER
   FOR UP TO 1 WEEK

1½ cups (225 g) all-purpose (plain) flour
2 teaspoons baking soda
2 teaspoons mixed spice
2 teaspoons ground cinnamon
3 teaspoons ground ginger
¼ cup (60 g) superfine sugar
½ cup (1 stick/125 g) unsalted butter, diced
½ cup (125 g) honey (or golden syrup)
½ cup (110 g) superfine sugar, extra

1 Preheat the oven to 360°F (180°C). Line two baking sheets with parchment baking paper.

2 Sift the flour, baking soda, mixed spice, cinnamon, ginger and sugar into a large bowl. Melt the butter and honey in a small saucepan, over medium heat, then pour it over the dry ingredients. Mix with a spatula until a dough forms.

3 Roll the dough into walnut-sized balls, then dredge the balls in the extra superfine sugar. Place the balls 2 in (5 cm) apart on the baking sheets.

4 Bake the ginger snaps for 10–12 minutes, until firm to the touch. Cool on the baking sheets for 5 minutes before transferring to a wire rack to cool completely.

Oatmeal Coconut Cookies (Anzacs)

Parcels of these traditional Australian biscuits were sent to the serving soldiers during World War I.

MAKES 16
PREPARATION TIME: 30 MINS
COOKING TIME: 15 MINS
STORE IN AN AIRTIGHT CONTAINER
FOR UP TO 1 WEEK

**2 cups (300 g) all-purpose (plain) flour,
sifted**
2½ cups (250 g) rolled oats
1¼ cups (130 g) desiccated coconut
1¼ cups (300 g) soft brown sugar
1 teaspoon baking powder
**1 cup (2 sticks/250 g) unsalted butter,
diced**
½ cup (130 g) honey

1 Preheat the oven to 300°F (150°C).
Line two baking sheets with parchment
baking paper.
2 Combine the sifted flour with the oats,
coconut, soft brown sugar and baking
powder in a mixing bowl.
3 Place the butter and honey in a small
saucepan and stir over low heat until the
butter is melted. Pour into the bowl with
the dry ingredients and stir until thoroughly combined.
4 Roll the mixture into 16 balls and place
them, 2 in (5 cm) apart, on prepared baking sheets. Press the balls gently to flatten.
5 Bake the cookies for 15 minutes, until
golden. Allow to cool slightly on the baking sheets before transferring to a wire
rack to cool completely.

Coconut Chocolate Macaroons

The only word I can use to describe these biscuits is 'irresistible'. Try them for yourself.

MAKES 32
PREPARATION TIME: 30 MINS
COOKING TIME: 10 MINS
STORE IN AN AIRTIGHT CONTAINER
  FOR UP TO 1 WEEK

4 egg whites
1⅓ cups (300 g) superfine sugar
3 cups (300 g) desiccated coconut
2 teaspoons vanilla extract
1½ tablespoons apricot jam
7 oz (200 g) dark chocolate, tempered
  (see page 11)

1 Preheat the oven to 390°F (200°C). Line two baking sheets with parchment baking paper.

2 Combine the egg whites, sugar, coconut and vanilla in a bowl. Heat the apricot jam in the microwave for about 15 seconds, until warm, then add to the mixture. Using a spatula, mix the ingredients until well combined.

3 Press tablespoonfuls of the mixture into firm mounds on the baking sheets. Bake for 7–10 minutes, until golden around the edges. Cool on the sheet.

4 Dip the base of each macaroon into the melted chocolate, then place chocolate side down on the baking sheets to set.

Double Chocolate Cookies

This is a great dough to store in the freezer—the cookies can be baked from frozen and are ready to eat within 20 minutes.

MAKES 16
PREPARATION TIME: 30 MINS
COOKING TIME: 15 MINS
STORE COOKED COOKIES IN AN AIR-
   TIGHT CONTAINER FOR UP TO 1
   WEEK. UNCOOKED COOKIES CAN
   BE FROZEN (ON THE SHEETS) FOR
   UP TO 1 MONTH. TO COOK FROM
   FROZEN, ADD 5 MINUTES TO THE
   COOKING TIME.

½ cup (1 stick/125g) unsalted butter,
   softened
¾ cups (180 g) soft brown sugar
2 eggs
1 teaspoon vanilla extract
1 cup (150 g) all-purpose (plain) flour
½ cup (40 g) cocoa (unsweetened)
½ teaspoon baking soda
Pinch of salt
¾ cup (125 g) white chocolate chips
¾ cup (125 g) dark chocolate chips

1 Preheat the oven to 300°F (150°C).
Line two baking sheets with parchment
baking paper.
2 Beat the butter and sugar in the bowl
of an electric mixer fitted with the paddle
attachment, on high speed for 5 minutes,
until pale and creamy. Add the eggs one
at a time, beating well after each addition. Add the vanilla, then sift in the flour,
cocoa, baking soda and salt. Mix on
low speed until combined, then add the
chocolate chips and stir well.

3 Roll the mixture into 1¾ oz (50 g) balls
(about the size of a golf ball) and place
on the prepared baking sheets. Press the
balls gently to flatten.

4 Bake the cookies for 15 minutes, until
lightly golden and firm to the touch. Cool
on a wire rack.

Macadamia Nut Chocolate Chip Cookies

This is a good basic cookie recipe. It can easily be adjusted with different nuts or chocolate to suit your taste.

MAKES 25
PREPARATION TIME: 30 MINS
COOKING TIME: 12 MINS
STORE COOKED COOKIES IN AN AIR-
TIGHT CONTAINER FOR UP TO 1
WEEK. UNCOOKED DOUGH CAN
BE STORED, WRAPPED IN PLASTIC
WRAP, IN THE REFRIGERATOR FOR
UP TO 3 DAYS.

¾ cup (170 g) superfine sugar

¾ cup (200 g) soft brown sugar

1 cup (2 sticks/250 g) unsalted butter, softened

2 teaspoons vanilla extract

2 eggs

3 cups (450 g) all-purpose (plain) flour

¾ teaspoon baking powder

¾ teaspoon fine sea salt

2¾ cups (500 g) dark chocolate chips

1¼ cups (200 g) chopped macadamia nuts

1 Preheat the oven to 325°F (160°C). Line two baking sheets with parchment baking paper.

2 Beat the superfine sugar, soft brown sugar, butter and vanilla in the bowl of an electric mixer fitted with the paddle attachment, on high speed for 5 minutes, until pale and creamy. Add the eggs one at a time, beating well after each addition. Sift in the flour, baking powder and salt, and mix on low speed until combined. Add the chocolate chips and macadamia nuts, and mix until combined.

3 Roll the cookie dough into 2½ oz (70 g) balls (about the size of a golf ball), place on the baking sheets and press gently with your hand to flatten. Bake for 12 minutes, until lightly golden and firm to the touch. Cool on a wire rack.

VARIATIONS

White Chocolate and Pistachio Cookies: Use white chocolate buttons instead of the dark chocolate and replace the macadamias with pistachios.

Hazelnut and Milk Chocolate Cookies: Use milk chocolate buttons instead of the dark chocolate and replace the macadamias with chopped roasted hazelnuts.

Almond, Vanilla and White Chocolate Cookies: Use white chocolate buttons instead of the dark chocolate, replace the macadamias with chopped blanched almonds, and add the seeds of 1 vanilla bean.

Jammy Dodgers

While working as a pastry chef in London, I was asked to make jammy dodgers—I had no idea what they were! In fact they are known by various names around the world, including Happy Faces, Monkey Faces and Raspberry Shortcakes. I have made these jam biscuits dozens of times since then, as I find they are always popular.

MAKES 12
PREPARATION TIME: 30 MINS + 30
  MINS CHILLING TIME
COOKING TIME: 10 MINS
STORE IN AN AIRTIGHT CONTAINER
  FOR UP TO 1 WEEK

¾ cup (1¾ sticks/200 g) unsalted butter, softened
¾ cup (200 g) superfine sugar
2 teaspoons vanilla extract
1 egg
2⅔ cups (400 g) all-purpose (plain) flour
5 tablespoons raspberry jam
½ cup (60 g) confectioner's (icing) sugar

1 Beat the butter, sugar and vanilla in the bowl of an electric mixer fitted with the paddle attachment, on medium speed until smooth. Add the egg and beat well. Sift in the flour and mix on low speed until combined. Remove the dough from the bowl, wrap in plastic wrap and refrigerate for 30 minutes.
2 Preheat the oven to 325°F (160°C). Line two baking sheets with parchment baking paper.
3 On a lightly floured work surface, roll out the dough to a thickness of ¼ in (5 mm). Cut out rounds using a 2¼ in (6 cm) round biscuit cutter. Using a ⅜ in (1 cm) round cutter, cut holes in the center of half the dough rounds. Roll out the leftover dough and cut out more cookies.
4 Place all the dough rounds on the prepared baking sheets and bake for 10 minutes, until lightly golden. Cool on a wire rack.
5 Spread the raspberry jam onto the whole cookies. Dust the remaining cookies (those with a hole in the center) with icing sugar, then place on top of the raspberry jam.

Shortbread

The melt-in-the-mouth texture of shortbread is incredible, and it's so easy to make. The orange and poppy seed version is well worth a try.

MAKES 2
PREPARATION TIME: 30 MINS
COOKING TIME: 10 MINS
STORE IN AN AIRTIGHT CONTAINER
  FOR UP TO 1 WEEK

1¼ cups (150 g) confectioner's (icing) sugar
2 cups (300 g) all-purpose (plain) flour
1 cup (150 g) rice flour
1⅓ cups (2⅔ sticks/300 g) unsalted butter, softened
⅓ cup (30 g) superfine sugar

1 Preheat the oven to 300°F (150°C). Line a baking sheet with parchment baking paper.
2 Sift the icing sugar and flours into the bowl of an electric mixer fitted with the paddle attachment. Add the butter and mix on low speed until the mixture comes together to form a dough.
3 Turn the dough out onto a lightly floured work surface and roll out to a thickness of ⅜ in (1 cm). Cut the dough into rectangles 1½ in × 2¼ in (4 cm x 6 cm) and transfer to the prepared baking sheet. Decorate the shortbread by pricking with a fork and sprinkling with the superfine sugar.
4 Bake the shortbread for 10 minutes, until firm to the touch and a pale golden color. Cool on a wire rack.

VARIATION
Orange and Poppy Seed Shortbread (pictured): Add ¼ cup (30 g) poppy seeds and the finely grated zest of 2 oranges to the dry ingredients before mixing.

Lemon Vanilla Cookies

The icing for these cookies sets to a crisp, smooth glaze.

MAKES 30
PREPARATION TIME: 30 MINS + 30
   MINS CHILLING TIME + 2–4 HRS
   ICING DRYING TIME
COOKING TIME: 8 MINS
STORE IN AN AIRTIGHT CONTAINER
   FOR UP TO 1 WEEK

³/₄ cup (1³/₄ sticks/200 g) unsalted butter, softened
³/₄ cup (200 g) superfine sugar
2 teaspoons vanilla extract
Finely grated zest of 2 lemons
1 egg
2²/₃ cups (400 g) all-purpose (plain) flour

LEMON ICING
1 egg white
2 cups (250 g) confectioner's (icing)
   sugar
Juice of 1–2 lemons
Yellow liquid food coloring

1 Beat the butter and sugar in the bowl of an electric mixer fitted with the paddle attachment, on medium speed until smooth. Add the vanilla, lemon zest and egg, and mix until combined. Do not overbeat. Add the sifted flour and mix on low speed until the dough comes together. Remove the dough from the bowl and roll into a log, wrap in plastic wrap and chill for at least 30 minutes.

2 Preheat the oven to 300°F (150°C). Line two baking sheets with parchment baking paper.

3 On a lightly floured work surface, roll out the cookie dough to a thickness of ¼ in (5 mm). Using a 1½ in (4 cm) round bis-

cuit cutter (or cutter of your choice), cut out cookies. Roll out the leftover dough and cut out more cookies. Place the cookies on baking sheets and bake for 8 minutes, until a light golden color. Cool on a wire rack.

4 To make the Lemon Icing, whip the egg white in the bowl of an electric mixer fitted with the whisk attachment, until soft peaks form. Add the icing sugar and beat on high speed for 3 minutes. Add enough

lemon juice to achieve a runny icing. (Ensure it is the right consistency by drizzling a figure of eight in the icing; the figure of eight should disappear within 10 seconds.) Add enough yellow food coloring to create a pale lemon color.

5 Dip the top of each cookie into the icing, letting any excess drip off. Place the cookies on a baking sheet and leave to set for 2–4 hours.

Yo-Yos

MAKES 14
PREPARATION TIME: 30 MINS
COOKING TIME: 15 MINS
STORE IN AN AIRTIGHT CONTAINER
  FOR UP TO 1 WEEK

1 cup (2 sticks/250 g) unsalted butter, softened
³⁄₄ cup (100 g) confectioner's (icing) sugar
2 cups (300 g) all-purpose (plain) flour, sifted
5 tablespoons custard powder
2 teaspoons vanilla extract

FILLING
1¼ cups (160 g) confectioner's (icing) sugar
¹⁄₃ cup (²⁄₃ stick/80 g) unsalted butter, softened
1 tablespoon custard powder
1 teaspoon vanilla extract

1 Preheat the oven to 325°F (160°C). Line two baking sheets with parchment baking paper.
2 In the bowl of an electric mixer fitted with the paddle attachment, combine the butter, icing sugar, sifted flour, custard powder and vanilla extract. Mix on low speed until a dough forms.
3 Roll tablespoonfuls of the dough into balls. Place the balls on the prepared baking sheets and flatten slightly with a fork.
4 Bake the cookies for 15 minutes, until firm to the touch. Cool on a wire rack.
5 To make the Filling, combine all the ingredients in the bowl of an electric mixer. Using the paddle attachment, beat on low speed until combined, then beat on high speed for 3 minutes.
6 Sandwich the cooled biscuits together with the Filling.

Swiss Chocolate Meringues

I first used this recipe to decorate a birthday cake similar to the Chocolate Mud Layer Cake (page 97). Pipe the meringues in any shape you like. Serve with coffee.

MAKES 40
PREPARATION TIME: 30 MINS
COOKING TIME: 10 MINS
STORE IN AN AIRTIGHT CONTAINER
  FOR UP TO 1 WEEK

4 egg whites
¾ cup (180 g) superfine sugar
3 oz (80 g) dark chocolate, melted

1 Preheat the oven to 300°F (150°C). Line a baking sheet with parchment baking paper.

2 Heat the egg whites and sugar in a double boiler until the sugar is dissolved and the mixture is blood temperature (about 105°F/40°C)—check with a sugar thermometer if possible. Whip the meringue mixture in the bowl of an electric mixer fitted with the whisk attachment, on high speed for 10 minutes, until thick. Fold in the melted chocolate.

3 Place the mixture into a piping bag fitted with a ⅜ in (1 cm) plain nozzle. Pipe desired shapes onto the prepared baking sheet.

4 Bake the meringues for 10 minutes, until firm. Cool completely on the sheet.

Orange and Almond Snowballs

These Italian biscuits are said to resemble snow on the mountains.

MAKES 36
PREPARATION TIME: 30 MINS
COOKING TIME: 15 MINS
STORE IN AN AIRTIGHT CONTAINER
FOR UP TO 1 WEEK

1 cup (125 g) almond flour
½ cup (125 g) superfine sugar
1¼ cups (150 g) confectioner's (icing) sugar
1 cup (80 g) candied orange peel, very finely chopped
1 egg white
1¼ cups (150 g) confectioner's (icing) sugar, for coating

1 Preheat the oven to 325°F (160°C). Line two baking sheets with parchment baking paper.
2 Place the almond flour, superfine sugar, icing sugar and orange peel in the bowl of an electric mixer fitted with the paddle attachment. Mix on low speed to combine, then continue mixing as you add the egg white a teaspoon at a time, until the ingredients form a dough.
3 Remove the dough from the bowl and roll tablespoonfuls of the dough into balls. Spread the extra icing sugar on a baking sheet or large flat plate. Dredge the balls of dough in the sugar to coat evenly. Transfer to the prepared baking sheets.
4 Bake the snowballs for 15 minutes, until golden but still soft in the center. Cool on a wire rack.

Pine Nut Cookies

MAKES 40
PREPARATION TIME: 45 MINS + 2 HRS
  CHILLING TIME
COOKING TIME: 12 MINS
BEST SERVED ON THE DAY OF BAKING

3/4 cup (100 g) hazelnuts
2 1/2 cups (350 g) almond flour
2 cups (250 g) confectioner's (icing) sugar
3 1/2 tablespoons unsalted butter, melted
1 tablespoon honey
5 egg whites
5 cups (500 g) pine nuts
3/4 cup (100 g) confectioner's (icing) sugar,
  for dusting

1 Preheat the oven to 325°F (160°C).
2 Place the hazelnuts on a baking sheet
and bake for 10 minutes until the skins
begin to loosen. Cool the hazelnuts slightly,
then rub them between the palms of your
hands to remove the skins. Grind the hazelnuts to a fine powder in a food processor or
chop very finely.
3 Place the ground hazelnuts, almond flour,
icing sugar, butter, honey and egg whites in
the bowl of an electric mixer fitted with the
paddle attachment. Mix on low speed until
the ingredients form a paste. Refrigerate the
mixture for at least 2 hours. (The mixture will
keep in the refrigerator for up to 1 week.)
4 Preheat the oven to 325°F (160°C). Line
two baking sheets with parchment baking
paper.
5 Spread the pine nuts on a baking sheet
or on a clean work surface. Drop tablespoonfuls of the cookie mixture onto the
pine nuts. Using the palm of your hand,
roll each piece into a ball until the dough is
completely coated with pine nuts. Place on
the prepared baking sheets.
6 Bake the cookies for 12 minutes, until
golden. Cool on the baking sheets, then
dust liberally with the icing sugar.

Almond Biscotti

Biscotti are excellent served with tea and coffee—I always keep some in the pantry for unexpected guests.

MAKES 60
PREPARATION TIME: 30 MINS + 2 HRS
  COOLING TIME
COOKING TIME: 50 MINS
STORE IN AN AIRTIGHT CONTAINER
  FOR UP TO 1 MONTH

1⅓ cups (200 g) self-rising flour
1⅓ cups (200 g) all-purpose (plain) flour
1½ cups (250 g) blanched whole almonds
1 cup (250 g) superfine sugar
3 eggs
1 teaspoon vanilla extract
1 teaspoon bitter almond extract

1 Preheat the oven to 325°F (160°C). Grease a baking sheet.

2 Place all the ingredients in the bowl of an electric mixer fitted with the paddle attachment. Mix on low speed for 3 minutes, until the dough comes together. (Alternatively, combine the ingredients in a large mixing bowl using your hands.)

3 Turn the dough out onto a lightly floured work surface and divide into two equal pieces. Roll each piece into a log about 12 in (30 cm) long. Place the logs on the baking sheet and bake for 25 minutes, until golden and firm to the touch. Cool on the baking sheets at room temperature for at least 2 hours (or overnight).

4 Preheat the oven to 210°F (100°C).

5 Using a serrated knife, cut the logs at an angle into slices ⅜ in (1 cm) thick. Place the biscotti flat on ungreased baking sheets and bake for 25 minutes. Cool on the baking sheets.

Pistachio, Chocolate and Orange Biscotti

MAKES 60
PREPARATION TIME: 30 MINS + 2
   HRS COOLING TIME
COOKING TIME: 50 MINS
STORE IN AN AIRTIGHT CONTAINER
   FOR UP TO 1 MONTH

1$\frac{1}{3}$ cups (200 g) all-purpose (plain) flour
1$\frac{1}{3}$ cups (200 g) self-rising flour
1$\frac{1}{2}$ cups (250 g) dark chocolate buttons
1$\frac{1}{2}$ cups (250 g) pistachios
1 cup (250 g) superfine sugar
$\frac{3}{4}$ cup (60 g) candied orange peel, finely
   chopped
Finely grated zest of 2 oranges
1 teaspoon vanilla extract
3 eggs

1 Preheat the oven to 325°F (160°C).
Grease a baking sheet.
2 Place all the ingredients in the bowl
of an electric mixer. Using the paddle
attachment, mix on low speed until the
dough comes together. (Alternatively,
combine the ingredients in a large mixing
bowl using your hands.)
3 Turn the dough out onto a lightly
floured work surface and divide into two
equal pieces. Roll each piece into a log
12 in (30 cm) long. Place the logs on the
baking sheet and bake for 25 minutes,
until golden and firm to the touch. Cool
on the baking sheet at room temperature
for at least 2 hours (or overnight).
4 Preheat the oven to 210°F (100°C).
5 Using a serrated knife, cut the logs at
an angle into slices $\frac{3}{8}$ in (1 cm) thick.
Place the biscotti on ungreased baking
sheets and bake for 25 minutes. Cool on
the baking sheets.

Macadamia Wafers

I usually serve these crisp wafers alongside a dessert such as crème brûlée or chocolate mousse.

SERVES 12
PREPARATION TIME: 30 MINS +
  OVERNIGHT COOLING TIME
COOKING TIME: 1 HR 15 MINS
STORE IN AN AIRTIGHT CONTAINER
  FOR UP TO 1 WEEK

9 egg whites
$1^2/_3$ cups (375 g) superfine sugar
3 teaspoons vanilla extract
$2^1/_2$ cups (375 g) all-purpose (plain) flour
$2^1/_2$ cups (375 g) macadamia nuts

1 Preheat the oven to 325°F (160°C). Line a $8^1/_2$-in × $4^1/_2$-in (22-cm x 11-cm) loaf pan with parchment baking paper.
2 Whip the egg whites in the bowl of an electric mixer fitted with the whisk attachment, on high speed until firm peaks form. With the mixer on low speed, gradually add the sugar. Whip on high speed for 5 minutes until glossy. Add the vanilla to the whites, then sift in the flour and add the nuts. Fold together gently.
3 Pour the mixture into the prepared pan and bake for 45 minutes, until firm to the touch. Cool in the pan at room temperature overnight.
4 Preheat the oven to 210°F (100°C).
5 Cut the macadamia bread into wafer-thin slices. Arrange the slices on a baking sheet and bake for 30 minutes—when ready the bread should be crisp but its color should not have altered. Cool on a wire rack.

Mocha Hazelnut Meringues

These crisp little meringues are a good way to use up excess egg whites. They can be made without the coffee if you prefer.

MAKES 50
PREPARATION TIME: 30 MINS
COOKING TIME: 1 HR 30 MINS
STORE IN AN AIRTIGHT CONTAINER FOR
  UP TO 1 WEEK

$3\frac{1}{2}$ cups (500 g) raw shelled hazelnuts
4 cups (500 g) confectioner's (icing) sugar
$\frac{2}{3}$ cup (60 g) cocoa (unsweetened)
2 teaspoons cornstarch
4 egg whites
$1\frac{1}{2}$ tablespoons very fine coffee powder

1 Preheat the oven to 325°F (160°C).
2 Place the hazelnuts on a baking sheet and bake for 10 minutes until the skins begin to loosen. Cool the hazelnuts slightly, then rub them between the palms of your hands to remove the skins. (Reduce oven temperature to 230°F/110°C.)
3 Sift together the icing sugar, cocoa and cornstarch. Whip the egg whites in the bowl of an electric mixer fitted with the whisk attachment, on high speed until firm peaks form. With the mixer running on low speed, gradually add the icing sugar mixture. Add the coffee powder, then beat the mixture on high speed for 1 minute. Fold in the hazelnuts.
4 Place tablespoonfuls of the mixture onto baking sheets that have been lined with parchment baking paper.
5 Bake the meringues for $1\frac{1}{2}$ hours. Cool on the baking sheets.

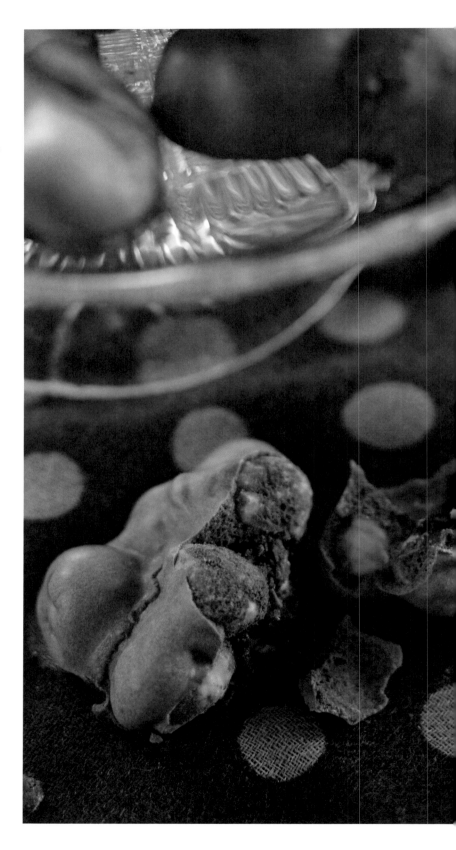

Brandy Snaps

Be sure to bake the brandy snaps in batches, as you need to roll them while still warm.

MAKES 24
PREPARATION TIME: 30 MINS
COOKING TIME: 10 MINS
STORE, UNFILLED, IN AN AIRTIGHT
  CONTAINER FOR UP TO 3 DAYS

½ cup (1 stick/125 g) unsalted butter
½ cup (125 g) superfine sugar
½ cup (125 g) honey (or golden syrup)
2 teaspoons ground ginger
1 cup (125 g) self-rising flour

VANILLA CREAM
1²/₃ cups (400 ml) whipping cream
⅓ cup (90 g) superfine sugar
1 teaspoon vanilla extract

1 Preheat the oven to 325°F (160°C). Line two baking sheets with parchment baking paper.
2 Combine the butter, sugar and honey in a saucepan, and stir over low heat until the butter has melted. Sift together the ginger and flour, and add to the saucepan, stirring well to combine.
3 Place half-tablespoonfuls of the mixture on the baking sheets, 4 in (10 cm) apart (to allow plenty of room for spreading). Bake for 8–10 minutes, until golden brown. Remove from the oven and allow to cool for 2 minutes. Carefully lift the brandy snaps from the sheets and mold into desired shapes (e.g. basket) or wrap around a wooden spoon handle to make a tube, holding for a few seconds until set. Cool on a wire rack.
4 To make the Vanilla Cream, whip the cream, sugar and vanilla in the bowl of an electric mixer fitted with the whisk attachment, on high speed until thick.
5 Pipe or spoon the Vanilla Cream into the brandy snaps just before serving.

Gingerbread People

Children will be impressed by gingerbread people, but for real wow factor try building a gingerbread house and decorating it with your favorite confectionery.

MAKES 24
PREPARATION TIME: 45 MINS + 2
   HRS CHILLING TIME
COOKING TIME: 12 MINS
STORE IN AN AIRTIGHT CONTAINER
   FOR UP TO 1 WEEK

7 tablespoons water
¾ cup (200 g) soft brown sugar
½ cup (180 g) honey (or golden syrup)
3 tablespoons ground ginger
3 tablespoons ground cinnamon
1 teaspoon ground cloves
1 cup (2 sticks/250 g) unsalted butter, diced
1 teaspoon baking soda
3¾ cups (550 g) all-purpose (plain) flour

LEMON ICING
2 egg whites
4 cups (500 g) confectioner's (icing) sugar
Juice of ½ lemon

1 Place the water, soft brown sugar, honey, ginger, cinnamon and cloves in a saucepan, and bring to a boil over medium heat, stirring constantly. Add the butter and stir until melted, then add the baking soda. Pour the mixture into a bowl and allow to cool to luke-warm. Sift in the flour and stir until a dough forms. Wrap the dough in plastic wrap and chill for 2 hours before using.

2 Preheat the oven to 325°F (160°C). Line two baking sheets with parchment baking paper.

3 On a lightly floured work surface, roll out the dough to a thickness of ¼ in (5mm). Using a gingerbread man cookie cutter, cut out shapes and place on prepared baking sheets.

4 Bake the gingerbread people cookies for 10–12 minutes, until firm to the touch. Cool on a wire rack.

5 To make the Lemon Icing, whip the egg whites in the bowl of an electric mixer fitted with the whisk attachment, on high speed until soft peaks form. Gradually add the icing sugar, beating until the icing is thick, then beat on high speed for a further 3 minutes. Add the lemon juice and mix well.

6 Place the Lemon Icing into a piping bag fitted with a small nozzle. Pipe decorations onto the gingerbread people. (If the icing is too thick, add a little more water.) Leave the icing to set for 2 hours.

VARIATION

Gingerbread House: Multiply the recipe above by three. Roll out the dough to a thickness of ¼ in (5 mm), then use the plan on page 265 to cut out the panels for the house. Make a double recipe of lemon icing. Assemble the house, using the icing to join the pieces (use cans of food to hold up the walls while the icing dries). Decorate the house with extra icing and confectionery of your choice.

Chocolate Panforte

Panforte is thought to originate from Siena, Italy. There are many versions, each with a different combination of nuts, fruits and spices. This recipe has to be my favorite; the chocolate and cinnamon work perfectly together.

SERVES 20
PREPARATION TIME: 30 MINS
COOKING TIME: 20 MINS
STORE IN AN AIRTIGHT CONTAINER
  FOR UP TO 1 MONTH

1½ cups (500 g) blanched whole
  almonds
1 cup (300 g) honey
½ cup (70 g) confectioner's (icing) sugar
¾ cup (100 g) chopped dark chocolate
1⅓ cups (200 g) dried figs, chopped
1¼ cups (180 g) all-purpose (plain) flour,
  sifted

½ cup (40 g) cocoa (unsweetened)
2 tablespoons ground cinnamon
1 tablespoon cocoa (unsweetened), extra

1 Preheat the oven to 325°F (160°C). Line a 8-in (20-cm) round pan with parchment baking paper.
2 Place the almonds on a baking sheet and roast for 5 minutes, until light golden. Remove from the oven and set aside. (Reduce oven temperature to 250°F/120°C.)

3 Combine the honey and icing sugar in a large saucepan, and bring to a boil. Add the chocolate and stir until melted, then add the figs and almonds, and sifted flour, cocoa and cinnamon. Stir over low heat for 3 minutes. Press the mixture into the prepared pan.
4 Bake the panforte for 20 minutes. Allow to cool completely in the pan, then dust with the extra cocoa. Serve very thin slices with coffee or tea.

Garibaldi Pastry

Two layers of sweet, crisp pastry filled with raisins (or currants if you prefer).

MAKES 16 PIECES
PREPARATION TIME: 20 MINS + 2
  HRS 30 MINS CHILLING TIME
COOKING TIME: 30 MINS
STORE IN AN AIRTIGHT CONTAINER
  FOR UP TO 1 WEEK

**2 quantities Sweet Shortcrust Pastry
(page 175)**
1 egg, beaten
3¹/₃ cups (500 g) raisins

CARAMEL
¹/₂ cup (125 g) sugar
1 tablespoon corn syrup (liquid glucose)
¹/₃ cup (80 ml) water
¹/₄ cup (60 ml) water, extra

1 Make the Sweet Shortcrust Pastry by following the recipe on page 175.
2 Line a 8-in × 12-in (20-cm x 30-cm) brownie pan with parchment baking paper.
3 Break off one-third of the pastry. On a lightly floured work surface, roll out the larger piece of pastry to a rectangle 8 in × 12 in (20 cm x 30 cm). Place in the base of the prepared pan. Brush the base with beaten egg, then press the raisins evenly over the pastry. Brush the raisins with some more beaten egg.
4 Roll out the remaining piece of pastry to the same size, then lay it on top of the raisins in the pan. Brush the top piece of pastry with beaten egg. Chill in the refrigerator while you make the caramel.
5 To make the Caramel, combine the sugar, corn syrup and water in a small saucepan, and stir over medium heat until the sugar is dissolved. Bring the syrup to a boil and cook until it is a dark golden color—do not stir during this process or the sugar will crystallize. Remove the saucepan from the heat and gradually stir in the extra water, a spoonful at a time, until the Caramel has cooled and thickened to a spreadable consistency.
6 Pour the Caramel over the pastry and spread out evenly. Use a fork to create a wave pattern in the caramel. Chill the pastry again for at least 30 minutes before baking.
7 Preheat the oven to 340°F (170°C).
8 Bake the pastry for 25–30 minutes, until golden. Allow to cool completely in the pan, then cut into slices.

Date and Coconut Brownies

This is the perfect brownie for a lunchbox. Substitute dried apricots, raisins or cranberries for the dates.

MAKES 16 SQUARES
PREPARATION TIME: 20 MINS
COOKING TIME: 25 MINS
STORE IN AN AIRTIGHT CONTAINER
   FOR UP TO 1 WEEK

2¼ cups (330 g) self-rising flour, sifted
1¾ cups (180 g) desiccated coconut
3¾ cups (375 g) dried dates, pitted and chopped
2 cups (425 g) superfine sugar
3 eggs
1¼ cups (2½ sticks/275 g) unsalted butter, melted

1 Preheat the oven to 360°F (180°C). Line an 8-in × 12-in (20-cm x 30-cm) brownie pan with parchment baking paper.

2 Place the sifted flour, coconut, dates, sugar and eggs in a mixing bowl. Add the melted butter and mix well. Press the mixture into the prepared pan.

3 Bake the brownies for 20–25 minutes, until golden. Allow to cool completely in the baking pan, then cut into squares.

Apple and Golden Raisins Brownies

MAKES 12 SQUARES
PREPARATION TIME: 30 MINS
COOKING TIME: 35 MINS
STORE IN AN AIRTIGHT CONTAINER
  FOR UP TO 3 DAYS

¾ cup (1⅔ sticks/180 g) unsalted butter, softened
1 cup (280 g) soft brown sugar
1 egg
1½ cups (225 g) self-rising flour, sifted
¾ cup (110 g) all-purpose (plain) flour, sifted
13 oz (375 g) stewed apple (or canned apple)
2 cups (300 g) golden raisins (sultanas)
3 teaspoons mixed spice
1½ teaspoons baking soda
1½ teaspoons vanilla extract

1 Preheat the oven to 360°F (180°C). Line a 8-in × 12-in (20-cm x 30-cm) brownie pan with parchment baking paper.
2 Beat the butter and sugar in the bowl of an electric mixer fitted with the paddle attachment, on high speed for 5 minutes until pale and creamy. Add the egg and beat well, then add the sifted flours and remaining ingredients and mix on low speed until combined. Spread the mixture into the prepared pan.
3 Bake the brownies for 30–35 minutes, until a skewer inserted into the center comes out clean. Cool completely in the pan, then cut into squares.

Chocolate Brownies

Brownies should be rich and moist, so be careful not to overcook them. The walnuts can be replaced with pecans, hazelnuts or almonds.

MAKES 12 SQUARES
PREPARATION TIME: 30 MINS
COOKING TIME: 30 MINS
STORE IN AN AIRTIGHT CONTAINER FOR
  UP TO 3 DAYS

2½ cups (300 g) chopped dark chocolate
1 cup (2 sticks/250 g) unsalted butter, diced
4 eggs
1¾ cups (400 g) superfine sugar
1⅓ cups (200 g) all-purpose (plain) flour
1¼ cups (150 g) chopped dark chocolate,
  extra
1¼ cups (150 g) finely chopped walnuts

1 Preheat the oven to 325°F (160°C). Line a 8-in × 12-in (20-cm x 30-cm) brownie pan with parchment baking paper.
2 Melt the chocolate and butter together in a double boiler or in the microwave until smooth.
3 Whip the eggs and sugar in the bowl of an electric mixer fitted with the whisk attachment, on high speed for 10 minutes until pale and creamy. Fold in the melted chocolate. Sift the flour into the bowl and add the extra chocolate and walnuts. Fold gently until combined. Pour the mixture into the prepared pan.
4 Bake the brownies for 30 minutes, until risen and firm to the touch. Allow to cool completely in the pan, then cut into squares.

Chocolate Fudge Brownies

MAKES 12 SQUARES
PREPARATION TIME: 20 MINS
COOKING TIME: 30 MINS
STORE IN AN AIRTIGHT CONTAINER
  FOR UP TO 3 DAYS

1½ cups (225 g) self-rising flour, sifted
¾ cup (75 g) desiccated coconut
⅔ cup (150 g) soft brown sugar
½ cup (50 g) cocoa (unsweetened)
¾ cup (1⅔ sticks/180 g) unsalted but-
  ter, melted
2 cups (600 g) sweetened condensed
  milk
1½ cups (180 g) chopped dark chocolate

1 Preheat the oven to 340°F (170°C). Line a 8-in × 12-in (20-cm x 30-cm) brownie pan with parchment baking paper.
2 Combine the sifted flour, coconut, sugar and cocoa in a mixing bowl. Add the melted butter and condensed milk, and stir to combine.
3 Spread half the mixture into the prepared pan and scatter the chopped chocolate over. Spread the remaining mixture over the top.
4 Bake the brownies for 30 minutes, or until a skewer inserted into the center comes out clean. Allow to cool completely in the pan, then cut into squares or rectangles.

Florentines

Originating in Florence, Italy, this recipe is so simple to make. To get the best results, ensure you cook them until golden—if undercooked it will not set.

MAKES 40 SQUARES
PREPARATION TIME: 30 MINS + 2
   HRS CHILLING TIME
COOKING TIME: 45 MINS
STORE IN AN AIRTIGHT CONTAINER
   FOR UP TO 1 WEEK

½ cup (1 stick/100 g) unsalted butter
1⅓ cups (300 g) superfine sugar
⅓ cup (50 g) all-purpose (plain) flour,
   sifted
1 cup (250 ml) whipping cream
5¼ cups (400 g) flaked almonds
2¾ cups (200 g) candied orange peel,
   chopped
1 cup (200 g) candied cherries, chopped
9 oz (150 g) dark chocolate, tempered
   (see page 11)

1 Preheat the oven to 325°F (160°C). Line a 8-in × 12-in (20-cm x 30-cm) brownie pan with parchment baking paper.
2 Combine the butter and sugar in a saucepan over low heat, stirring until melted. Mix in the sifted flour. Stir in the cream, then add the almonds, candied orange peel and cherries, and mix well. Press the mixture into the prepared pan.
3 Bake the brownies for 45 minutes, until golden. Allow to cool completely in the pan, then refrigerate for about 2 hours, until firm.
4 Spread a thin layer of melted chocolate over the top of the brownies. Allow to set, then cut into squares.

Walnut, Rum and Raisin Brownies

MAKES 12 SQUARES
PREPARATION TIME: 50 MINS + 2 HRS
  CHILLING TIME + 1 HR FRUIT SOAK-
  ING TIME
COOKING TIME: 1 HR
STORE IN AN AIRTIGHT CONTAINER
  FOR UP TO 3 DAYS

**1 quantity Sweet Shortcrust Pastry (page
  175)**
$^2/_3$ cup (100 g) raisins
3 tablespoons dark rum
6$^1/_2$ oz (180 g) dark chocolate
**$^3/_4$ cup (1$^2/_3$ sticks/180 g) unsalted
  butter, diced**
1$^1/_3$ cups (300 g) superfine sugar
3 eggs
1$^1/_4$ cups (180 g) all-purpose (plain) flour
1$^3/_4$ cups (225 g) walnuts, chopped

1 Make the Sweet Shortcrust Pastry by
following the recipe on page 175.
2 Preheat the oven to 325°F (160°C).
Line a 8-in × 12-in (20-cm x 30-cm)
brownie pan with parchment baking paper.
3 On a lightly floured surface, roll out
the sweet pastry to a thickness of $^1/_8$ in
(3 mm), then cut it to fit the base of the
pan. Place the pastry into the pan and
refrigerate until the filling is ready.
4 Combine the raisins and rum, and
stand for at least 1 hour. Melt the chocolate and butter together in the microwave
or over a double boiler until smooth.
5 Whisk together the sugar and eggs
in a separate bowl, then pour this into
the chocolate mixture and stir well to
combine. Sift in the flour and whisk until
smooth, then add the rum-soaked raisins
and the walnuts. Pour the mixture over the
pastry base.
6 Bake the brownies for 1 hour, until firm
to the touch. Allow to cool completely in
the pan, then cut into rectangles.

Pastries

Shortcrust Pastry

This recipe makes the most beautiful melt-in-the-mouth pastry; ideal for pies, tarts and quiches. It is also very easy to work with, so lining pie and tart pans is a breeze. Be sure to chill the dough well after mixing and again before baking to stop the pastry from shrinking in the oven.

MAKES 1⅛ LB (500 G)
PREPARATION TIME: 20 MINS + 2 HRS
    CHILLING TIME
STORE IN THE REFRIGERATOR FOR UP TO
    3 DAYS OR FREEZE FOR UP TO 1 MONTH

1⅔ cups (250 g) all-purpose (plain) flour
¾ cup (1¾ sticks/200 g) unsalted butter, diced
2 teaspoons superfine sugar
2 teaspoons fine sea salt
3½ tablespoons milk
1 egg yolk

1 Combine the sifted flour with the butter, sugar and salt in the bowl of an electric mixer fitted with the paddle attachment. Mix on low speed for 5 minutes, or until pieces of butter are no longer visible. Add the milk and egg yolk, and mix on low speed until a dough forms.
2 Alternatively, you can make the dough by hand (see photos at right). Sift the flour onto a work surface or into a large bowl. Add the sugar, salt and butter (1). Using your fingertips, rub the butter into the flour until there are no lumps of butter visible (2 and 3). Make a well in the center (4), add the milk and egg yolk, and mix together with your hands (5) until a dough forms (6).
3 Wrap the dough in plastic wrap. Refrigerate for at least 2 hours before using.

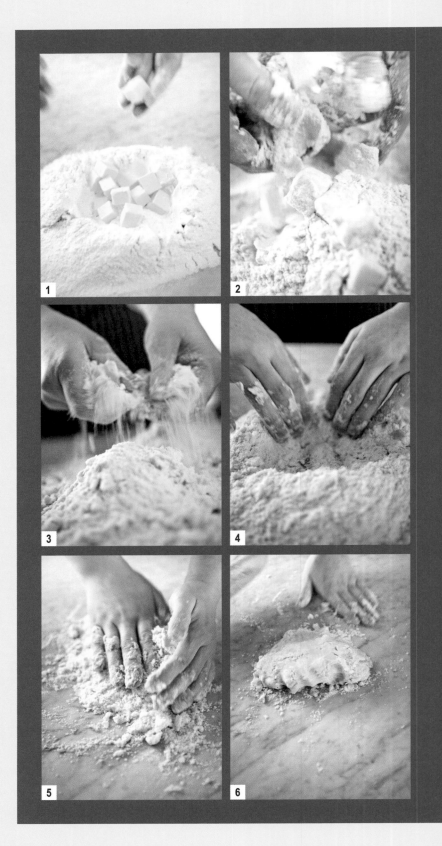

Smoked Salmon and Dill Quiche

When cooking quiches, be sure to cook only until the filling is just set—it should wobble like jelly. To make cutting easier, allow the quiche to cool at room temperature for at least 15 minutes before serving.

SERVES 8
PREPARATION TIME1 HR 50 MINS +
  2 HRS 30 MINS CHILLING TIME
COOKING TIME: 45 MINS
BEST SERVED ON THE DAY OF BAKING

**1 quantity Shortcrust Pastry (page 164)
  or Sour Cream Pastry (page 21)**
14 oz (400 g) smoked salmon
2½ cups (250 g) tasty cheese, grated
1 cup (250 ml) milk
1 cup (250 ml) whipping cream
4 eggs
2 tablespoons chopped fresh dill
1 teaspoon fine sea salt
Freshly-ground black pepper

1 Make the Shortcrust Pastry or Sour Cream Pastry by following their respective recipes on pages 164 or 21.
2 Place a 1½ in (4 cm) deep 8½ in (22 cm) tart ring on a baking sheet lined with parchment baking paper. Roll out the pastry on a lightly floured work surface, then use it to line the tart ring. Refrigerate for at least 30 minutes.
3 Preheat the oven to 325°F (160°C).
4 Cut the smoked salmon into large pieces and place in the base of the pastry case, then cover evenly with the grated cheese.
5 Whisk together the milk, cream, eggs and chopped dill in a bowl, and season with the salt and some freshly-ground pepper. Pour the mixture over the other ingredients in the pastry case.
6 Bake the quiche for 45 minutes, until it is golden and the filling is set. Serve hot or cold with a salad.

Goat's Cheese and Pea Quiche

This quiche is delicious served for lunch with a crisp side salad. Use fresh peas when they are in season.

SERVES 8
PREPARATION TIME: 1 HR 20 MINS +
  2 HRS 30 MINS CHILLING TIME
COOKING TIME: 45 MINS
BEST SERVED ON THE DAY OF BAKING

1 quantity Shortcrust Pastry (page 164)
  or Sour Cream Pastry (page 21)
¼ cup (60 ml) extra-virgin olive oil
1 onion, finely chopped
2 cloves garlic, finely chopped
1 cup (250 ml) whipping cream
1 cup (250 ml) milk
4 eggs
1 teaspoon fine sea salt
Freshly-ground black pepper

7 oz (200 g) soft goat's cheese, broken
  into pieces
2 cups (300 g) fresh or frozen (defrosted)
  peas
1½ cups (150 g) grated tasty cheese

1 Make the Shortcrust Pastry or Sour Cream Pastry by following their respective recipes on pages 164 or 21.
2 Place a 1½ in (4 cm) deep 8½ in (22 cm) tart ring on a baking sheet lined with parchment baking paper. Roll out the pastry on a lightly floured work surface, then use it to line the tart ring. Refrigerate for at least 30 minutes.

3 Preheat the oven to 325°F (160°C).
4 Meanwhile, heat the olive oil in a skillet and sauté the onion and garlic over medium heat for 10 minutes, until the onions are soft. Remove from the skillet and set aside to cool.
5 Whisk together the cream, milk and eggs in a bowl, and season with the salt and some freshly-ground pepper. Combine the goat's cheese, peas, tasty cheese and cooked onion and place in the pastry case, then pour the egg mixture over.
6 Bake the quiche for 45 minutes, until it is golden and the filling is set. Serve hot or cold with a salad.

Bacon and Caramelized Onion Quiche

Making caramelized onions takes some time and patience. Allow them to cook slowly until they are sweet and nicely caramelized—if the heat is too high they will burn and become bitter.

SERVES 8
PREPARATION TIME: 1 HR 20 MINS +
  2 HRS 30 MINS CHILLING TIME
COOKING TIME: 45 MINS
BEST SERVED ON THE DAY OF BAKING

1 quantity Shortcrust Pastry (page 164)
  or Sour Cream Pastry (page 21)
¼ cup (60 ml) extra-virgin olive oil
¼ cup (½ stick/60 g) butter
1¼ lb (600 g) onion, finely sliced
1 bay leaf
1 sprig fresh thyme
Fine sea salt
Freshly-ground black pepper
¾ cup (150 g) diced bacon
1½ cups (150 g) grated tasty cheese
1 cup (250 ml) milk
1 cup (250 ml) whipping cream
4 eggs

1 Make the Shortcrust Pastry or Sour Cream Pastry by following their respective recipes on pages 164 or 21.

2 Place a 1½ in (4 cm) deep 8½ in (22 cm) tart ring on a baking sheet lined with parchment baking paper. Roll out the pastry on a lightly floured work surface, then use it to line the tart ring. Refrigerate for at least 30 minutes.

3 Meanwhile, heat the olive oil and butter in a large saucepan, add the onions, bay leaf and thyme, and season with salt and pepper. Cover and cook over medium heat, stirring regularly, for 20 minutes or until the onions are very soft. Remove the lid and continue to cook for 20–30 minutes, until the onions are soft, sweet and caramelized. Remove the onions from the saucepan and set aside to cool.

4 Preheat the oven to 325°F (160°C).

5 Spread the cooled onions over the base of the pastry case, add the bacon and then sprinkle the grated cheese over.

6 Whisk together the milk, cream and eggs in a bowl, and season with 1 teaspoon of salt and some freshly-ground pepper. Pour the mixture over the other ingredients in the pastry case.

7 Bake the quiche for 45 minutes, until it is golden and the filling is set. Serve hot or cold with a salad.

Cornish Pasties

I remember making pasties as a child with my father on cold winter's days. We always served them with my great-grandmother's home-made tomato chutney.

MAKES 4
PREPARATION TIME: 1 HR 5 MINS +
  2 HRS CHILLING TIME
COOKING TIME: 40 MINS

**1 quantity Shortcrust Pastry (page 164)
  or Sour Cream Pastry (page 21)**
**⅛ cup (¼ stick/20 g) butter, cut into four
  pieces**
1 egg, beaten

FILLING
**11 oz (300 g) lean rump steak, finely
  diced**
1 onion, finely chopped
1 potato, cut into small dice
1 swede, cut into small dice
Salt and freshly-ground black pepper

1 Make the Shortcrust Pastry or Sour Cream Pastry by following their respective recipes on pages 164 or 21.
2 To make the Filling, combine the rump steak with the onion, potato and swede, and season with salt and pepper.
3 Divide the pastry into four equal pieces. On a lightly floured work surface, roll out each piece to a 6 in (15 cm) round.
4 Divide the Filling between the four rounds, place a piece of butter on top of the meat, and brush the edges of the pastry with beaten egg. Fold up the sides of the pastry to meet at the top and pinch together with your fingertips to seal. Place the pasties on a baking sheet lined with parchment baking paper and brush with the beaten egg. Refrigerate for 30 minutes before baking.

5 Preheat the oven to 340°F (170°C).
6 Bake the pasties for 40 minutes, until golden. Serve hot with chutney or tomato sauce.

Trout and Asparagus Tart

SERVES 6
PREPARATION TIME: 1 HR 20 MINS +
   2 HRS 30 MINS CHILLING TIME
COOKING TIME: 25 MINS
BEST SERVED ON THE DAY OF BAKING

1 quantity Shortcrust Pastry (page 164)
  or Sour Cream Pastry (page 21)
One × 11 oz (300 g) smoked trout
1 cup (100 g) tasty cheese, grated
30 asparagus spears
½ cup (125 ml) whipping cream
½ cup (125 ml) milk
2 eggs
½ teaspoon fine sea salt
Freshly-ground black pepper

1 Make the Shortcrust Pastry or Sour Cream Pastry by following their respective recipes on pages 164 or 21.
2 Roll out the pastry on a lightly floured work surface, then use it to line a 14-in × 4½-in (35-cm × 11-cm) tart pan. Refrigerate for at least 30 minutes.
3 Preheat the oven to 325°F (160°C).
4 Prebake the pastry case for 10 minutes, then remove the prebaking weights and cook for a further 10 minutes, until the pastry is lightly colored. Set aside to cool while preparing the filling.
5 Carefully remove the skin from the trout and discard. Use a fork or knife to flake the flesh away from the bones. Make sure there are no small bones remaining in the trout flesh. Place the flaked fish in the base of the tart case, then cover evenly with the grated cheese.
6 Cook the asparagus in boiling water for 2 minutes, drain, then refresh in cold water and drain well again. Trim the asparagus spears so they are all the same length—just the right size to fit in the tart pan—then line the spears up next to each other on top of the trout and cheese.
7 Whisk together the cream, milk and eggs in a bowl, and season with the salt and some freshly-ground black pepper. Pour the mixture evenly over the asparagus spears.
8 Bake the tart for 25 minutes, until it is golden and the filling is set. Serve hot or cold with a salad.

Lamb and Rosemary Pies

The traditional pairing of lamb and rosemary works wonderfully in this delicious, rich pie filling.

MAKES 8
PREPARATION TIME: 1 HR 30 MINS +
30 MINS CHILLING TIME + TIME TO
MAKE THE SHORTCRUST PASTRY,
AND PUFF PASTRY
COOKING TIME: 3 HRS

**1 quantity Shortcrust Pastry (page 164)
or Sour Cream Pastry (page 21)**
½ quantity Puff Pastry (page 212)
1 egg, beaten

FILLING
6 tablespoons extra-virgin olive oil
**1¼ lb (600 g) lamb shoulder, trimmed
of fat and sinew, cut into ⅜-in (1-cm)
dice**
2 onions, finely diced
4 cloves garlic, finely chopped
1 carrot, peeled and cut into small dice
3 sticks celery, cut into small dice
½ cup (100 g) tomato paste
1 cup (250 ml) dry white wine
1 cup (200 g) canned tomatoes
2 cups (500 ml) beef stock
**1 tablespoon finely chopped fresh
rosemary**
1 tablespoon finely chopped fresh sage
3 tablespoons all-purpose (plain) flour
⅓ cup (80 ml) water
Salt and freshly-ground black pepper

1 Make the Shortcrust Pastry or Sour Cream Pastry by following their respective recipes on pages 164 or 21. Make the Puff Pastry by following the recipe on page 212.

2 Preheat the oven to 300°F (150°C).

3 To make the Filling, heat ¼ cup (60 ml) of the oil in a large ovenproof saucepan or flameproof casserole dish. Add the lamb and cook over high heat until the meat is sealed. Remove the lamb from the pot and set aside. Add the remaining 2 tablespoons oil to the pot and add the onions, garlic, carrot and celery. Cook over medium heat until the vegetables are colored and softened. Return the lamb to the pot, add the tomato paste and white wine, and cook for 2 minutes. Add the tomatoes, beef stock, rosemary and sage, mix well and cover with a lid. Bake in the oven for 2–2½ hours, until the lamb is tender. Place the pot back on the stove over low heat. Whisk together the flour and water, stir it into the stew, then simmer, stirring continuously, for 5 minutes. Season to taste with salt and freshly-ground black pepper. Allow the Filling to cool, then chill in the refrigerator.

4 Roll out the Shortcrust Pastry on a lightly floured work surface, then use it to line eight 5 in (12 cm) pie pans. Refrigerate for at least 30 minutes.

5 Preheat the oven to 340°F (170°C).

6 On a lightly floured surface, roll out the Puff Pastry to a thickness of ⅛ in (3 mm). Cut out eight rounds slightly larger than the pie pans.

7 Spoon the pie Filling into the pastry cases, filling them right to the top. Brush the edges of each pastry case with beaten egg and place a Puff Pastry round on top. Press firmly around the edges to seal. Cut a small hole in the center of each pastry lid to allow steam to escape during baking. Brush the tops of the pies with the beaten egg.

8 Bake the pies for 25–30 minutes, until golden. Serve hot.

Rabbit and Pancetta Pies

Ask your butcher to grind the rabbit meat if you don't have the equipment at home to do it yourself.

MAKES 8
PREPARATION TIME: 1 HR 30 MINS +
   30 MINS CHILLING TIME + TIME
   TO MAKE THE SHORTCRUSTY
   PASTRY, AND PUFF PASTRY
COOKING TIME: 1 HR 15 MINS

1 quantity Shortcrust Pastry (page 164)
   or Sour Cream Pastry (page 21)
½ quantity Puff Pastry (page 212)
1 egg, beaten

FILLING
¼ cup (60 ml) extra-virgin olive oil
1 onion, finely diced
4 cloves garlic, finely chopped
1⅛ lb (500 g) rabbit meat, coarsely
   ground
½ cup (100 g) smoked pancetta, finely
   chopped
7 tablespoons red wine
2 tablespoons finely chopped fresh sage
½ cup (100 g) tomato paste
One × 14-oz (400-g) can tomatoes
2 cups (500 ml) chicken stock
⅓ cup (50 g) all-purpose (plain) flour
7 tablespoons water
Salt and freshly-ground black pepper

1 Make the Shortcrust Pastry or Sour Cream Pastry by following their respective recipes on pages 164 or 21. Make the Puff Pastry by following the recipe on page 212.

2 To make the Filling, heat half the olive oil in a large saucepan and sauté the onion and garlic over medium heat until soft. Remove from the saucepan and set aside. Heat the remaining olive oil in the saucepan, add the ground rabbit meat and pancetta, and cook, stirring continuously, until the meat is cooked through (about 5 minutes). Return the onion and garlic to the pan, pour in the red wine and cook for 2 minutes. Add the sage, tomato paste and tomatoes, and simmer for 10 minutes until reduced. Add the chicken stock to the pan and simmer, uncovered, for 45 minutes, stirring regularly. Whisk together the flour and water, stir it quickly into the rabbit mixture, then simmer, stirring continuously, for 5 minutes. Season to taste with salt and pepper. Allow the Filling to cool, then chill in the refrigerator.

3 Roll out the Shortcrust Pastry on a lightly floured work surface, then use it to line eight 5 in (12 cm) pie pans. Refrigerate for at least 30 minutes.

4 Preheat the oven to 340°F (170°C).

5 On a lightly floured surface, roll out the Puff Pastry to a thickness of ⅛ in (3 mm). Cut out eight rounds slightly larger than the pie pans.

6 Spoon the pie Filling into the pastry cases, filling them right to the top. Brush the edges of each pastry case with the beaten egg and place a Puff Pastry round on top. Press firmly around the edges to seal. Cut a small hole in the center of each pastry lid to allow steam to escape during baking. Brush the tops of the pies with the beaten egg.

7 Bake the pies for 25–30 minutes, until golden. Serve hot.

Vegetable Puffs

1 Make the Shortcrust Pastry or Sour Cream Pastry by following their respective recipes on pages 164 or 21.

2 To make the Filling, heat the olive oil in a saucepan and sauté the onion and garlic over medium heat until soft. Add the potatoes, parsnip, pumpkin and vegetable stock, and cook for 10 minutes over medium heat, until the vegetables are tender. Stir in the peas and butter, and season to taste with salt and pepper. Set aside to cool.

3 Divide the pastry into four equal pieces. On a lightly floured work surface, roll out each piece to a 6 in (15 cm) round.

4 Divide the Filling between the four rounds. Brush the edges of the pastry with the beaten egg, then fold up the sides of the pastry to meet at the top and pinch together with your fingertips to seal. Place the puffs on a baking sheet lined with parchment baking paper and brush with the beaten egg. Refrigerate for 30 minutes before baking.

5 Preheat the oven to 340°F (170°C).

6 Bake the puffs for 40 minutes, until golden. Serve hot with chutney or tomato sauce.

MAKES 4
PREPARATION TIME: 1 HR 20 MINS +
    2 HRS CHILLING TIME
COOKING TIME: 40 MINS

1 quantity Shortcrust Pastry (page 164)
    or Sour Cream Pastry (page 21)
1 egg, beaten

FILLING
2 tablespoons extra-virgin olive oil
1 onion, finely chopped
2 cloves garlic, finely chopped
2 potatoes, peeled and cut into small
    dice
1 parsnip, peeled and cut into small dice
7 oz (200 g) pumpkin, peeled and cut
    into small dice
3/4 cup (200 ml) vegetable stock
1 cup (150 g) peas
1/8 cup (1/4 stick/20 g) butter
Salt and freshly-ground black pepper

VARIATION
Curried Vegetable Puffs: Add 1 tablespoon curry powder to the onion and garlic while cooking.

Sweet Shortcrust Pastry

A good sweet shortcrust pastry recipe is indispensable; you will use this one over and over again for all of your tart and pie recipes.

MAKES 1 LB (450 G)
PREPARATION TIME: 20 MINS+ 2 HRS
  CHILLING TIME
STORE IN THE REFRIGERATOR FOR UP TO
  3 DAYS OR FREEZE FOR UP TO 1 MONTH

1½ cups (225 g) all-purpose (plain) flour
Pinch of salt
½ cup (60 g) confectioner's (icing) sugar
½ cup (1 stick/110 g) unsalted butter, diced
2 egg yolks

1 Combine the sifted flour with the salt, icing sugar and butter in the bowl of an electric mixer fitted with the paddle attachment. Mix on low speed until no lumps of butter are visible. Add the egg yolks and mix on low speed until the mixture comes together to form a dough.
2 Alternatively, you can make the dough by hand (see photos on right). Sift the flour onto a work surface or into a large bowl. Add the sugar, salt and butter (1). Using your fingertips, rub the butter into the flour (2) until there are no lumps of butter visible (3). Make a well in the center, add the egg yolks (4), and mix together with your hands (5) until a dough forms (6).
3 Wrap the dough in plastic wrap and refrigerate for at least 2 hours before using.

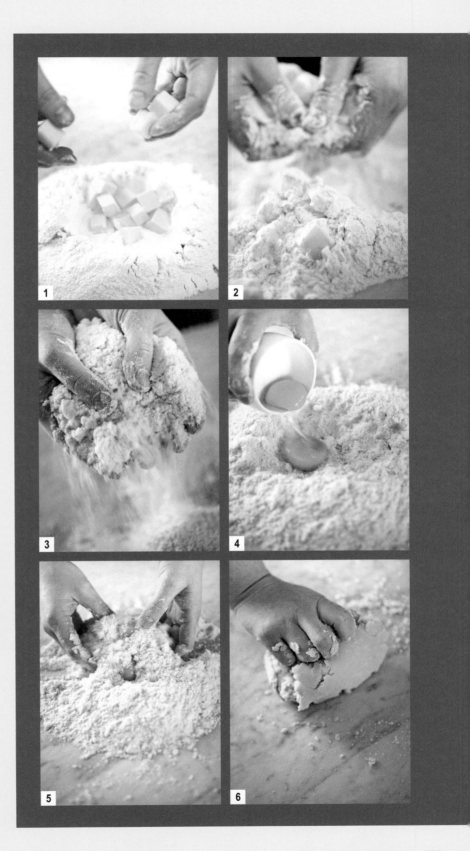

Apple Crumble Tart

Try replacing some of the apple with other ingredients: golden raisins, blackberries and diced rhubarb all work well.

SERVES 12
PREPARATION TIME: 1 HR 35 MINS +
  2 HRS 30 MINS CHILLING TIME
COOKING TIME: 50 MINS
BEST SERVED ON THE DAY OF BAKING

1 quantity Sweet Shortcrust Pastry (page
  175)
10 green apples, peeled, cored
  and diced
1 teaspoon ground cinnamon
²/₃ cup (150 g) superfine sugar
3½ tablespoons water
½ quantity Almond Cream (page 20)

TOPPING
½ cup (1 stick/100 g) unsalted butter,
  softened
3½ tablespoons superfine sugar

¼ cup (50 g) soft brown sugar
¾ cup (100 g) almond flour
¾ cup (110 g) all-purpose (plain) flour
1 cup (100 g) desiccated coconut

1 Make the Sweet Shortcrust Pastry and Almond Cream by following their respective recipes on pages 175 and 20.
2 Place a 1½ in (4 cm) deep 8½ in (22 cm) tart ring on a baking sheet lined with parchment baking paper. Roll out the pastry on a lightly floured work surface, then use it to line the tart ring. Refrigerate for at least 30 minutes.
3 Preheat the oven to 340°F (170°C).
4 Prebake the tart case for 15 minutes, then lift out the prebaking weights and bake the case for a further 10 minutes,

until golden. (Leave the oven on.)
5 Combine the chopped apple, cinnamon, sugar and water in a saucepan. Cook over medium heat for about 10 minutes, until the apples are soft. Cool, then drain off any excess liquid.
6 Spread the Almond Cream over the base of the tart case, then scatter the cooked apple evenly on top.
7 To make the Topping, beat the butter and sugars in the bowl of an electric mixer fitted with the paddle attachment on high speed for 5 minutes until pale and creamy. Add the almond flour, sifted flour and coconut, and mix well.
8 Sprinkle the Topping over the apple. Bake the tart for 25 minutes, until golden. Serve hot with cream or ice-cream.

Caramel Walnut Tart

Try using a different type of nut, or even a mixture of nuts, in this tart.

SERVES 8
PREPARATION TIME: 1 HR 5 MINS +
  2 HRS 30 MINS CHILLING TIME
COOKING TIME: 55 MINS
BEST SERVED ON THE DAY OF BAKING

1 quantity Sweet Shortcrust Pastry
** (page 175)**
2½ cups (250 g) walnuts
1 quantity Apricot Glaze (page 21)

FILLING
½ cup (125 g) soft brown sugar
½ cup (1 stick/125 g) unsalted butter,
** diced**

½ cup (150 g) honey
3 eggs

1 Make the Sweet Shortcrust Pastry and Apricot Glaze by following their respective recipes on pages 175 and 21.
2 Roll out the pastry on a lightly floured work surface, then use it to line a 10-in (25-cm) tart pan. Refrigerate for at least 30 minutes.
3 Preheat the oven to 340°F (170°C).
4 Prebake the tart case for 15 minutes, then lift out the prebaking weights and bake the case for a further 10 minutes, until golden. (Leave the oven on.)
5 To make the Filling, place the soft brown sugar, butter and honey in a saucepan. Bring to a boil over medium heat, stirring continuously. Pour the mixture into a heatproof bowl and set aside to cool to lukewarm. Whisk in the eggs.
6 Spread the walnuts over the base of the tart case, then pour the Filling over the walnuts.
7 Bake the tart for 25–30 minutes, until golden and set. Allow to cool slightly, then brush with the Apricot Glaze. Serve hot or cold with whipped cream.

Baked Custard Tart

This tart is great served with seasonal fruit; the crisp pastry and creamy filling go well with fresh berries, pitted fruits such as peaches, plums or apricots, or even stewed rhubarb.

SERVES 8
PREPARATION TIME: 50 MINS + 2 HRS
  30 MINS CHILLING TIME
COOKING TIME: 1 HR 25 MINS
BEST SERVED ON THE DAY OF BAKING

**1 quantity Sweet Shortcrust Pastry
  (page 175)**
1 egg yolk, beaten
Freshly-grated nutmeg

FILLING
4 eggs
3 egg yolks
³⁄₄ cup (180 g) superfine sugar
2¼ cups (550 ml) whipping cream

1 Make the Sweet Shortcrust Pastry by following the recipe on page 175.
2 Place a 1½ in (4 cm) deep 8½ in (22 cm) tart ring on a baking sheet lined with parchment baking paper. Roll out the pastry on a lightly floured work surface, then use it to line the tart ring. (Reserve leftover pastry.) Refrigerate the pastry case for at least 30 minutes.
3 Preheat the oven to 340°F (170°C).
4 Prebake the tart case for 15 minutes, then lift out the prebaking weights and bake the case for a further 10 minutes, until golden. If there are any cracks or holes in the case, repair them with some of the raw pastry, then return the case to the oven briefly to set. As soon as it comes out of the oven, brush the inside of the tart case with the beaten egg yolk to seal the pastry. (Reduce oven temperature to 285°F/140°C.)
5 To make the Filling, whisk together the whole eggs, egg yolks and sugar. Add the cream and mix well. Pour the Filling into a jug.
6 Place the tart case on the middle shelf of the oven, then pour in the filling and sprinkle the grated nutmeg over the top. Bake for 50 minutes to 1 hour, until the custard is set. Remove from the oven and allow to cool at room temperature for 2 hours before serving.

Baked Lemon Tart

This is the ultimate lemon tart recipe. Make sure your tart case does not have any cracks or holes in it before adding the filling, or it will leak out while baking.

SERVES 8
PREPARATION TIME: 1 HR 5 MINS +
  2 HRS 30 MINS CHILLING TIME
COOKING TIME: 1 HR 10 MINS
BEST SERVED ON THE DAY OF BAKING

1 quantity Sweet Shortcrust Pastry (page 175)
1 egg yolk, beaten
½ cup (50 g) confectioner's (icing) sugar,
  for dusting

FILLING
Finely grated zest of 4 lemons
1¼ cups (280 g) superfine sugar
9 eggs
1 cup (250 ml) freshly-squeezed lemon juice
1 cup (250 ml) whipping cream

1 Make the Sweet Shortcrust Pastry by following the recipe on page 175.

2 Place a 1½ in (4 cm) deep 8½ in (22 cm) tart ring on a baking sheet lined with parchment baking paper. Roll out the pastry on a lightly floured work surface, then use it to line the tart ring. (Reserve leftover pastry.) Refrigerate the pastry case for at least 30 minutes.

3 Preheat the oven to 340°F (170°C).

4 Prebake the tart case for 15 minutes, then lift out the prebaking weights and bake the case for a further 10 minutes, until golden. If there are any cracks or holes in the case, repair them with some of the raw pastry, then return to the oven briefly to set. As soon as it comes out of the oven, brush the inside of the tart case with the beaten egg yolk to seal the pastry. (Reduce oven temperature to 265°F/130°C.)

5 To make the Filling, combine the lemon zest and sugar in a bowl, mixing well. Whisk in the eggs, then pour in the lemon juice and combine. Finally, stir in the cream. Strain the Filling into a jug.

6 Place the tart case on the middle shelf of the oven, then pour in the Filling. Bake for 45 minutes, until the Filling is set. Remove from the oven and allow to cool at room temperature for 2 hours, then dust with icing sugar.

Chocolate Ganache and Raspberry Tart

Use a good-quality dark chocolate (preferably 60 per cent cocoa or higher) for this recipe.

SERVES 8
PREPARATION TIME: 50 MINS + 2 HRS
   30 MINS CHILLING TIME
COOKING TIME: 25 MINS
BEST SERVED ON THE DAY OF BAKING

1 quantity Sweet Shortcrust Pastry (page 175)
3¼ cups (400 g) fresh raspberries

GANACHE
1⅔ cups (400 ml) whipping cream
2¾ cups (350 g) dark chocolate, chopped
2 tablespoons corn syrup (liquid glucose)
2 tablespoons unsalted butter, diced, softened

1 Make the Sweet Shortcrust Pastry by following the recipe on page 175.
2 Roll out the pastry on a lightly floured work surface, then use it to line a 10-in (25-cm) tart pan. Refrigerate for at least 30 minutes.
3 Preheat the oven to 340°F (170°C).
4 Prebake the tart case for 15 minutes, then lift out the prebaking weights and bake the case for a further 10 minutes, until golden. Set aside to cool.
5 To make the Ganache, bring the cream to a boil, then pour it over the chocolate,add the glucose and butter, and stir until smooth.
6 Pour the chocolate Ganache into the tart case, and chill for 2 hours. Pile the fresh raspberries onto the top of the tart to serve.

Peach and Mascarpone Tart

This tart should be made with good-quality mascarpone to ensure a creamy texture and rich flavor.

SERVES 10
PREPARATION TIME: 1 HR 5 MINS +
  2 HRS 30 MINS CHILLING TIME
COOKING TIME: 1 HR 25 MINS
BEST SERVED ON THE DAY OF BAKING

1 quantity Sweet Shortcrust Pastry (page 175)
2¼ cups (500 g) thinly-sliced pitted fresh or canned pitted peaches
1 quantity Apricot Glaze (page 21)

FILLING
1¼ lb (600 g) mascarpone cheese
4 eggs
4 egg yolks
⅔ cup (150 g) superfine sugar
2 teaspoons vanilla extract

1 Make the Sweet Shortcrust Pastry and the Apricot Glaze by following their respective recipes on pages 175 and 21.
2 Place a 1½ in (4 cm) deep 8½ in (22 cm) tart ring on a baking sheet lined with parchment baking paper. Roll out the pastry on a lightly floured work surface, then use it to line the tart ring. Refrigerate for at least 30 minutes.
3 Preheat the oven to 340°F (170°C).
4 Prebake the tart case for 15 minutes, then lift out the prebaking weights and bake the case for a further 10 minutes, until golden. (Reduce oven temperature to 285°F/140°C.)
5 To make the Filling, place the mascarpone, whole eggs, egg yolks, sugar and vanilla in a bowl and whisk until smooth.
6 Pour the Filling into the tart case. Bake the tart for 1 hour, until the Filling is set. Remove from the oven and allow to cool at room temperature for 2 hours before serving.
7 Arrange the peach slices decoratively on top of the tart. Brush with the Apricot Glaze before serving.

Lattice Jam Tart

As a child I would often pick blackberries at my grandparents' farm, and we would then make them into jam. A keen baker from a young age, I tried every recipe I could find that used jam—this was one of my favorites.

SERVES 8
PREPARATION TIME: 50 MINS + 2 HRS
   30 MINS CHILLING TIME
COOKING TIME: 35 MINS
BEST SERVED ON THE DAY OF BAKING

1½ quantities Sweet Shortcrust Pastry (page 175)
1½ cups (500 g) blackberry jam (preferably homemade)
1 egg, beaten

1 Make the Sweet Shortcrust Pastry by following the recipe on page 175.
2 Roll out two-thirds of the pastry on a lightly floured work surface, then use it to line a 10-in (25-cm) tart pan. Refrigerate for at least 30 minutes.
3 Preheat the oven to 340°F (170°C).
4 Prebake the tart case for 15 minutes, then lift out the prebaking weights and bake the case for a further 5 minutes, until lightly colored. (Leave oven on.)
5 Fill the tart case with the jam.
6 Roll out the remaining pastry and cut it into strips ¼ in (5 mm) wide. Brush the edge of the tart case with a little of the beaten egg, then arrange the pastry strips over the top of the jam to make a lattice pattern, trimming off any excess pastry around the edges. Gently press the ends of each strip into the edge of the pastry case.
7 Bake the tart for 10–15 minutes, until the pastry is golden. Serve warm or cold with cream.

Drunken Prune, Chocolate and Walnut Tart

This tart is beautifully rich. The combined texture of the crisp pastry, soft filling and crunchy walnuts is magnificent.

SERVES 12
PREPARATION TIME: 1 HR 5 MINS +
   2 HRS 30 MINS CHILLING + 1 HOUR
   FRUIT SOAKING TIME
COOKING TIME: 50 MINS
BEST SERVED ON THE   OF BAKING

1¼ cups (200 g) prunes, pitted
7 tablespoons port
1 quantity Sweet Shortcrust Pastry (page
  175)

FILLING
6½ oz (180 g) dark chocolate
¾ cup (1²/₃ sticks/180 g) unsalted butter,
  diced
3 eggs
1¹/₃ cups (300 g) superfine sugar
1 tablespoon instant coffee granules dissolved in 4 teaspoons boiling water
1¼ cups (180 g) all-purpose (plain) flour
1³/₄ cups (225 g) walnuts, coarsely
  chopped

1 Make the Sweet Shortcrust Pastry by following the recipe on page 175.
2 Soak the prunes in the port for at least 1 hour (or overnight).
3 Place a 1½ in (4 cm) deep 8½ in (22 cm) tart ring on a baking sheet lined with parchment baking paper. Roll out the pastry on a lightly floured work surface, then use it to line the tart ring. Refrigerate for at least 30 minutes.
4 Preheat the oven to 340°F (170°C).
5 To make the Filling, melt the chocolate and butter together in a double boiler or in the microwave until smooth. In another bowl, whisk together the eggs and sugar, then stir in the chocolate mixture. Add the coffee, sift in the flour, and whisk to combine.

Stir in the walnuts.
6 Pour half the Filling into the pastry case. Arrange the prunes on top, then pour the remaining Filling over.

7 Bake the tart for 50 minutes, until the Filling is firm to the touch and the pastry is golden. Serve warm or cold with whipped cream.

Coconut and Lime Tart

This is a lovely tart to serve for dessert in summer.

SERVES 10
PREPARATION TIME: 1 HR 5 MINS +
  2 HRS 30 MINS CHILLING TIME
COOKING TIME: 55 MINS
BEST SERVED ON THE DAY OF BAKING

**1 quantity Sweet Shortcrust Pastry (page
175)**
1 egg yolk, beaten

FILLING
1 cup (225 g) superfine sugar
Finely grated zest and juice of 1 lemon
Finely grated zest and juice of 3 limes
4 eggs
¾ cup (180 ml) coconut cream

1 Make the Sweet Shortcrust Pastry by following the recipe on page 175.

2 Roll out the pastry on a lightly floured work surface, then use it to line a 25-cm (10-in) tart pan. (Reserve leftover pastry.) Refrigerate the pastry case for at least 30 minutes.

3 Preheat the oven to 340°F (170°C).

4 Prebake the tart case for 15 minutes, then lift out the prebaking weights and bake the case for a further 10 minutes, until golden. If there are any cracks or holes in the case, repair them with some of the raw pastry, then return to the oven briefly to set. As soon as it comes out of the oven, brush the inside of the tart case with the beaten egg yolk to seal the pastry. (Reduce oven temperature to 285°F/140°C.)

5 To make the Filling, combine the sugar, lemon zest and lime zest in a bowl, rubbing the mixture between your hands to release the flavor of the zest into the sugar. Add the lemon and lime juice, the eggs and coconut cream, and whisk well. Strain the mixture through a fine sieve into a jug.

6 Place the pastry case on the middle shelf of the oven, then pour in the Filling. Bake for 30 minutes, until the Filling is just set. Remove from the oven and allow to cool at room temperature for 2 hours before serving with whipped cream.

Fruit Mince Pies

Be sure the fruit mince is made at least a week in advance to allow the flavors to develop.

MAKES 12

PREPARATION TIME: 1 HR 5 MINS +
 2 HRS CHILLING TIME + 1–2 WKS
 FRUIT SOAKING TIME
COOKING TIME: 25 MINS
STORE IN AN AIRTIGHT CONTAINER
 FOR UP TO 3 DAYS

2 quantities Sweet Shortcrust Pastry
 (page 175)
Egg wash: 2 egg yolks whisked with 2
 tablespoons milk
$\frac{1}{3}$ cup (90 g) superfine sugar

FRUIT MINCE
1$\frac{2}{3}$ cups (250 g) golden raisins (sultanas)
$\frac{2}{3}$ cup (90 g) currants
$\frac{1}{2}$ cup (90 g) raisins
$\frac{1}{2}$ cup (60 g) dried dates, pitted and
 chopped
$\frac{1}{3}$ cup (60 g) prunes, pitted and
 chopped
$\frac{1}{3}$ cup (90 g) candied cherries, chopped
2 tablespoons candied ginger, chopped
2 tablespoons candied pineapple,
 chopped
1 green apple, peeled and grated
3 tablespoons apricot jam
1 teaspoon mixed spice
Finely grated zest and juice of 1 lemon
Finely grated zest of 2 oranges and juice
 of 1 orange
7 tablespoons port
$\frac{3}{8}$ cup (100 g) soft brown sugar

VARIATION
Mini Mince Pies: To make 24 small mince
pies, use mini-muffin trays or small tart pans,
and bake for 15 minutes.

1 Make the Sweet Shortcrust Pastry by following the recipe on page 175.

2 To make the Fruit Mince, combine all the ingredients in a large bowl and mix well. Transfer to an airtight container and refrigerate for 1–2 weeks to allow the flavors to develop.

3 Preheat the oven to 325°F (160°C).

4 Roll out the pastry on a lightly floured work surface, then use it to line twelve 4 in (10 cm) individual tart pans. (Reserve leftover pastry.) Spoon the Fruit Mince into the cases. Roll out the remaining pastry to a thickness of $\frac{1}{8}$ in (3mm). Cut out rounds the same size as the top of the tart pans. Brush the edges of the pastry cases with the egg wash, place a pastry round on top and gently press the edges together to seal.

5 Brush the tops of the pies with the egg wash. Make a small incision in the center of each pastry lid to allow steam to escape during baking. Sprinkle the pies liberally with the superfine sugar.

6 Bake the pies for 25 minutes, until golden. Cool for 10 minutes in the pans, then turn out and transfer to a wire rack to cool completely.

Chocolate Pecan Tarts

MAKES 8
PREPARATION TIME: 1 HR 5 MINS +
  2 HRS 30 MINS CHILLING TIME
COOKING TIME: 35 MINS
BEST SERVED ON THE DAY OF BAKING

1 quantity Sweet Shortcrust Pastry (page 175)
8 pecan halves, to decorate

FILLING
3 tablespoons all-purpose (plain) flour, sifted
$1/3$ cup (30 g) cocoa (unsweetened)
$3/4$ cup (200 g) superfine sugar
1 egg
3 tablespoons unsalted butter, melted
1 teaspoon vanilla extract
$2/3$ cup (140 ml) milk
1 cup (125 g) pecans, chopped

1 Make the Sweet Shortcrust Pastry by following the recipe on page 175.
2 Divide the pastry into eight equal portions. Roll out each piece on a lightly floured work surface, then use to line eight 4 in (10 cm) individual tart pans. Refrigerate for at least 30 minutes.
3 Preheat the oven to 340°F (170°C).
4 Prebake the tart cases for 15 minutes, then lift out the prebaking weights and bake the cases for a further 10 minutes, until golden. (Leave the oven on.)
5 To make the Filling, combine the sifted flour and cocoa, and sugar in a bowl. Add the egg, butter, vanilla and milk, and stir well to combine. Stir in the chopped pecans.
6 Divide the Filling between the eight pastry cases, and top each tart with a pecan half. Bake for 10 minutes, until the Filling is set. Serve hot or cold with cream.

Treacle Tart

This English dessert is best served hot with cream or ice-cream.

SERVES 8
PREPARATION TIME: 50 MINS + 2
  HRS 30 MINS CHILLING TIME
COOKING TIME: 55 MINS

**1 quantity Sweet Shortcrust Pastry
  (page 175)**
1³/₄ cups (550 g) golden syrup
**1³/₄ cups (100 g) fresh white bread-
  crumbs**
Finely grated zest and juice of 1 lemon
1 teaspoon ground ginger
1 egg, beaten

1 Make the Sweet Shortcrust Pastry by following the recipe on page 175.
2 Roll out the pastry on a lightly floured work surface, then use it to line a 10-in (25-cm) tart pan. Refrigerate for at least 30 minutes.
3 Preheat the oven to 340°F (170°C).
4 Prebake the tart case for 15 minutes, then lift out the prebaking weights and bake the case for a further 10 minutes, until golden. (Reduce oven temperature to 325°F/160°C.)
5 Warm the golden syrup in a saucepan, then stir in the breadcrumbs, lemon juice, zest and ginger. Allow to cool for 5 minutes, then whisk in the egg.
6 Pour the filling into the tart case. Bake for 30 minutes, until the filling is set. Serve hot with whipped cream or ice-cream.

Cherry Coconut Tart

I like to toast coconut in a skillet rather than in the oven, as a more even result is achieved. Be sure to remove it from the skillet as soon as it is ready, to stop the cooking process.

SERVES 8
PREPARATION TIME: 1 HR 5 MINS + 2
  HRS 30 MINS CHILLING TIME
COOKING TIME: 1 HR 5 MINS
BEST SERVED ON THE DAY OF BAKING

**1 quantity Sweet Shortcrust Pastry (page
  175)**
1 cup (100 g) desiccated coconut
½ cup (125 g) superfine sugar
**3 tablespoons all-purpose (plain) flour,
  sifted**
1¼ cups (300 ml) whipping cream
3 eggs
3 egg yolks
2¼ cups (300 g) cherries, pitted

1 Make the Sweet Shortcrust Pastry by
following the recipe on page 175.
2 Place a 1½ in (4 cm) deep 8½ in (22 cm)
tart ring on a baking sheet lined with parchment baking paper. Roll out the pastry on a
lightly floured work surface, then use it to line
the tart ring. Refrigerate for at least 30 minutes.
3 Preheat the oven to 340°F (170°C).
4 Prebake the tart case for 15 minutes, then
lift out the prebaking weights and bake the
case for a further 10 minutes, until golden.
(Reduce oven temperature to 325°F/160°C.)
5 Toast the coconut in a skillet over low heat,
stirring continuously until golden. Remove from
the skillet and set aside to cool.
6 Combine the sugar, sifted flour and coconut in a bowl. Add the cream, whole eggs
and egg yolks, and mix well with a whisk
until smooth.
7 Scatter the cherries evenly over the base
of the tart case, then pour the coconut filling
over.
8 Bake the tart for 40 minutes, until the filling is set. Serve hot or cold.

Pear and Frangipane Tart

Frangipane is a filling made from almonds. Try using fruits such as raspberries, peaches or plums in place of the pears in this tart.

SERVES 8
PREPARATION TIME: 1 HR 5 MINS + 2 HRS
   30 MINS CHILLING TIME
COOKING TIME: 50 MINS
BEST SERVED ON THE DAY OF BAKING

1 quantity Sweet Shortcrust Pastry (page 175)
6 canned or poached pear halves
¼ cup (30 g) confectioner's (icing) sugar, for dusting

FILLING
¾ cup (1¾ sticks/200 g) unsalted butter, softened
¾ cup (200 g) superfine sugar
1 egg
1 egg yolk
1⅓ cups (200 g) almond flour

1 Make the Sweet Shortcrust Pastry by following the recipe on page 175.
2 Roll out the pastry on a lightly floured work surface, then use it to line a 10-in (25-cm) tart pan. Refrigerate for at least 30 minutes.
3 Preheat the oven to 340°F (170°C).
4 Prebake the tart case for 15 minutes, then lift out the prebaking weights and bake the case for a further 10 minutes, until golden. (Leave the oven on.)
5 To make the Filling, beat the butter and sugar in the bowl of an electric mixer fitted with the paddle attachment, on medium speed until smooth. Add the whole egg and egg yolk, and beat again until combined. Add the almond flour and mix well on low speed to combine.
6 Spread the Filling into the tart case and arrange the pears on top.
7 Bake the tart for 20–25 minutes, until golden. Allow to cool, then dust with icing sugar.

Summer Fruit Tart

For a great variation of this recipe, use slices of fresh mango instead of the berries and drizzle with fresh passionfruit pulp to serve.

SERVES 8
PREPARATION TIME: 50 MINS + 2 HRS
   30 MINS CHILLING TIME
COOKING TIME: 25 MINS
BEST SERVED ON THE DAY OF BAKING

1 quantity Sweet Shortcrust Pastry (page 175)
2 oz (60 g) white chocolate, melted
2 cups (250 g) fresh strawberries, hulled and quartered
1$\frac{2}{3}$ cups (200 g) fresh raspberries
1$\frac{2}{3}$ cups (200 g) fresh blueberries
1$\frac{2}{3}$ cups (200 g) fresh blackberries
Fresh mint leaves, to garnish

FILLING
1$\frac{1}{8}$ lb (500 g) mascarpone cheese
$\frac{3}{4}$ cup (100 g) confectioner's (icing) sugar
1 vanilla bean, split and seeds scraped

1 Make the Sweet Shortcrust Pastry by following the recipe on page 175.
2 Roll out the pastry on a lightly floured work surface, then use it to line a 14-in × 4$\frac{1}{2}$-in (35-cm × 11-cm) tart pan. Refrigerate for at least 30 minutes.
3 Preheat the oven to 340°F (170°C).
4 Prebake the tart case for 15 minutes, then lift out the prebaking weights and bake the case for a further 10 minutes, until golden. Allow to cool.
5 Brush the inside of the cooled tart case with the melted white chocolate, then chill for 2–3 minutes until the chocolate is set.
6 To make the Filling, whisk together the mascarpone, icing sugar and vanilla seeds.
7 Spread the Filling into the base of the tart case, then pile all the berries on top and garnish with fresh mint leaves.

Rhubarb and Apple Pie

If you are a bit apprehensive about working with pastry, this is a great pie to begin with as the end result is supposed to look rustic.

SERVES 6
PREPARATION TIME: 1 HR 20 MINS +
   2 HRS CHILLING TIME
COOKING TIME: 1 HR 10 MINS

$1\frac{1}{2}$ **quantities Sweet Shortcrust Pastry**
  (page 175)
Egg wash: 1 egg yolk whisked with 3
  teaspoons milk

FILLING
$1\frac{1}{8}$ **lb (500 g) rhubarb, chopped**
$1\frac{5}{8}$ **lb (700 g) green apples, peeled,**
  cored and diced
$\frac{3}{4}$ **cup (200 g) superfine sugar**
$3\frac{1}{2}$ **tablespoons water**

1 Make the Sweet Shortcrust Pastry by following the recipe on page 175.
2 Preheat the oven to 325°F (160°C).
3 To make the Filling, combine the rhubarb, apple, sugar and water in a large saucepan and cook over medium heat for 10 minutes, or until the rhubarb is tender but still holding its shape. Allow the Filling to cool, then drain off any excess liquid.
4 On a lightly floured work surface, roll out the pastry to a 16-in (40-cm) round. Lift the pastry into a 10-in (25-cm) pie dish. Place the Filling in the center and fold the edges of the pastry over the fruit to cover loosely. Don't worry if the pastry breaks while you are folding it over, as it is not meant to look perfect.
5 Brush the pastry with the egg wash and bake for 1 hour, until golden. Serve hot with vanilla ice-cream.

Cherry Pie

Cherries are in season for such a short time that when they are available I like to make as many different recipes with them as I can. This is one of the easiest options; just be sure to rest the pie in the fridge before baking so the pastry doesn't shrink.

SERVES 8
PREPARATION TIME: 50 MINS + 2 HRS
  30 MINS CHILLING TIME
COOKING TIME: 35 MINS

¾ cup (200 g) superfine sugar
2 tablespoons cornstarch
4½ cups (1 kg) cherries, pitted
1 quantity Sweet Shortcrust Pastry (page 175)
Egg wash: 1 egg yolk whisked with 3 teaspoons milk
2 tablespoons superfine sugar, extra

1 Make the Sweet Shortcrust Pastry by following the recipe on page 175.
2 Combine the sugar and cornstarch in a bowl, add the cherries and mix well. Place the cherry filling in a 10-in (25-cm) pie dish.
3 On a lightly floured work surface, roll out the pastry until slightly larger than the pie dish. Brush the edge of the pie dish with a little egg wash, then place the pastry lid on top. Press around the edges to seal, and trim off any excess pastry with a small knife. Use leftover pastry to make decorations for the top of the pie. Refrigerate for at least 30 minutes before baking.
4 Preheat the oven to 360°F (180°C).
5 Brush the pie with the remaining egg wash and sprinkle with the extra sugar. Bake for 35 minutes, until golden. Serve hot with vanilla ice-cream.

Classic Apple Pie

So satisfying yet simple to make, an apple pie will always be well received.

SERVES 8
PREPARATION TIME: 1 HR 5 MINS + 2 HRS
   30 MINS CHILLING TIME
COOKING TIME: 40 MINS
BEST SERVED ON THE DAY OF BAKING

2 quantities Sweet Shortcrust Pastry (page 175)
2¼ lb (1 kg) green apples, peeled, cored and sliced
½ cup (125 g) soft brown sugar
1 teaspoon ground cinnamon
1 tablespoon cornstarch
Egg wash: 1 egg yolk whisked with 3 teaspoons milk
2 tablespoons superfine sugar

1 Make the Sweet Shortcrust Pastry by following the recipe on page 175.
2 Roll out half the pastry on a lightly floured work surface, then use it to line a 10-in (25-cm) pie dish or tart pan. Refrigerate for at least 30 minutes.
3 Preheat the oven to 360°F (180°C).
4 Combine the sliced apple, sugar, cinnamon and cornstarch in a bowl, and mix well. Place the apple mixture into the pastry case.
5 Roll out the remaining pastry until it is slightly larger than the pie dish or pan. Brush the edges of the pastry case with the egg wash, then lift the top piece of pastry onto the pie. Press the edges together to seal, then use a sharp knife to trim away the excess pastry. Brush the top of the pie with the remaining egg wash and sprinkle liberally with superfine sugar. Cut a small hole in the center of the pastry lid to allow steam to escape during baking.
6 Bake the pie for 35–40 minutes, until golden. Serve hot or cold with cream and ice-cream.

Pumpkin Pie

This is a traditional American pie served at Thanksgiving and Christmas time. The pumpkin custard filling is spiced with cinnamon, ginger and cloves.

SERVES 6
PREPARATION TIME: 50 MINS + 2 HRS 30
  MINS CHILLING TIME
COOKING TIME:1 HR 40 MINS

1 quantity Sweet Shortcrust Pastry (page 175)

FILLING
**2¼ lb (1 kg) pumpkin, peeled and cut into small
  pieces**
½ cup (125 ml) whipping cream
3 eggs
¼ cup (60 g) soft brown sugar
¼ cup (60 g) superfine sugar
1 teaspoon ground cinnamon
½ teaspoon ground ginger
Pinch of ground cloves
¼ teaspoon fine sea salt

1 Make the Sweet Shortcrust Pastry by following the recipe on page 175.
2 Roll out the pastry on a lightly floured work surface, then use it to line a 10-in (25-cm) pie dish or a 14-in × 4½-in (35-cm × 11-cm) tart pan. Refrigerate for at least 30 minutes.
3 Preheat the oven to 340°F (170°C).
4 To make the Filling, spread the pumpkin on a baking sheet and cover with aluminum foil. Bake for 1 hour, until the pumpkin is very soft. Remove the pumpkin from the oven and increase oven temperature to 360°F (180°C). Purée the pumpkin in a food processor or with a hand-held blender until smooth. Measure out 2 cups (500 ml) of the pumpkin purée and pour it into a mixing bowl. Whisk in the cream, then the eggs, soft brown sugar, superfine sugar, cinnamon, ginger, cloves and salt.
5 Pour the Filling into the tart case. Bake the tart for 40 minutes, until the Filling is set and the pastry is golden. Serve warm with whipped cream.

Lemon Meringue Tarts

SERVES 8
PREPARATION TIME: 1 HR 25 MINS + 2 HRS
  30 MINS CHILLING TIME
COOKING TIME: 25 MINS
BEST SERVED ON THE DAY OF BAKING

1 quantity Sweet Shortcrust Pastry (page 175)
1 quantity Lemon Curd (page 20), chilled

MERINGUE
3 egg whites
½ cup (120 g) superfine sugar

1 Make the Sweet Shortcrust Pastry and the
Lemon Curd by following their respective recipes
on pages 175 and 20.
2 Divide the pastry into eight equal portions. Roll
out each piece on a lightly floured work surface,
then use to line eight 4-in (10-cm) individual tart
pans. Refrigerate for at least 30 minutes.
3 Preheat the oven to 340°F (170°C).
4 Prebake the tart cases for 15 minutes, then lift
out the prebaking weights and bake the cases
for a further 10 minutes, until golden. Set aside
to cool.
5 Remove the cooled tart cases from the pans
and fill with the Lemon Curd. Refrigerate while
preparing the meringue.
6 To make the Meringue, heat the egg whites
and sugar over a double boiler until the sugar is
dissolved and the mixture is blood temperature
(about 105°F/40°C)—check with a sugar thermometer if possible. Whip the meringue mixture
in the bowl of an electric mixer fitted with the
whisk attachment, on high speed for 10 minutes,
until thick and glossy.
7 Place the Meringue into a piping bag fitted with
a ⅜ in (10 mm) plain nozzle and pipe it onto the
lemon tarts. Use a cooking blowtorch to lightly
brown the Meringue. (Alternatively, place the pies
under a very hot preheated grill for 1 minute.) Keep
the pies refrigerated if not serving immediately.

Phyllo Pastry

Homemade phyllo pastry is very easy to make and has slightly more texture than the store-bought version.

MAKES 2¼ LB/1 KG (16 SHEETS)
PREPARATION TIME: 45 MINS + 2 HRS
    RESTING TIME
USE IMMEDIATELY, OR WRAP TIGHTLY IN
    PLASTIC WRAP AND STORE IN THE
    REFRIGERATOR FOR UP TO 24 HOURS,
    OR FREEZE FOR UP TO 2 WEEKS.

3¾ cups (550 g) all-purpose (plain) flour
1½ teaspoons fine sea salt
1⅔ cups (400 ml) warm water
2¾ tablespoons extra-virgin olive oil
Cornstarch, for dusting

1 Combine the sifted flour with the salt, water and olive oil in the bowl of an electric mixer fitted with the dough hook attachment. Mix on low speed until the dough begins to come together. Scrape down the sides of the bowl, then mix on medium speed for 5 minutes, until the dough begins to come away from the sides of the bowl.

2 Turn the dough out onto a work surface that has been lightly dusted with cornstarch, see photos on right (1). Divide into 16 equal pieces and roll each into a ball. Place the balls on a baking sheet that has been dusted with corn-starch, cover with plastic wrap and rest at room temperature for at least 2 hours.

3 On a work surface that has been lightly dust-ed with cornstarch, roll out each piece of pastry to ⅛ in (2 mm) in thickness (2). Carefully lift each sheet onto a clean cotton tea towel and gently stretch out until transparent, being careful not to tear it (3). The finished sheet should be about 10 in × 16 in (25 cm × 40 cm).

4 Dust each sheet of pastry with a little corn-starch and keep covered with a damp cloth to prevent it from drying out.

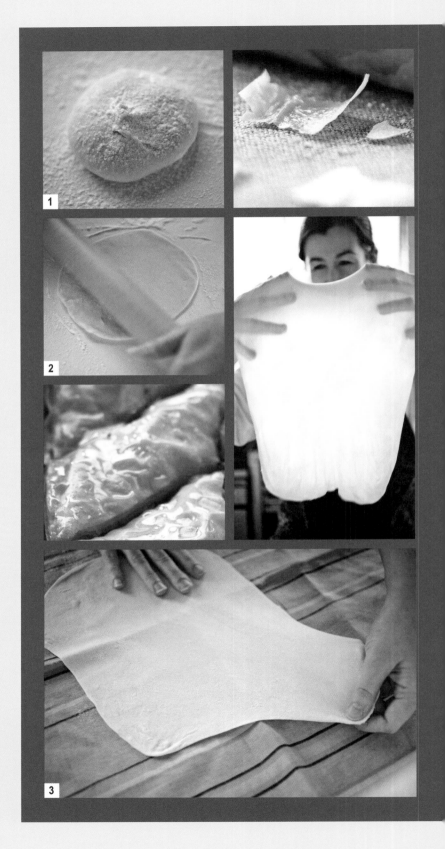

Bacon and Egg Phyllo Tarts

These tarts are a great alternative to fried eggs and bacon for breakfast. Omit the bacon and add some cooked spinach for a vegetarian version.

MAKES 6
PREPARATION TIME: 1 HR 15 MINS +
  2 HRS RESTING TIME
COOKING TIME: 10 MINS

**6 sheets Phyllo Pastry (page 196) or
  ready-made phyllo**
**½ cup (1 stick/100 g) unsalted butter,
  melted**
6 eggs
½ cup (120 g) finely chopped bacon

FILLING
⅓ cup (70 ml) milk
⅓ cup (70 ml) whipping cream
2 eggs
1 egg yolk
1 teaspoon salt
1 tablespoon finely chopped fresh parsley

1 Make the Phyllo Pastry by following the recipe on page 196.
2 Preheat the oven to 360°F (180°C). Grease six 4-in (10-cm) tart pans with melted butter.
3 Layer the six sheets of phyllo on top of each other, brushing each sheet with melted butter before adding the next. Using a round pastry cutter (or an upside-down saucer and a knife), cut out six 5 in (12 cm) rounds. Press the phyllo rounds into the tart pans.
4 To make the Filling, whisk together the milk, cream, whole eggs, egg yolk, salt and parsley in a mixing bowl.
5 Crack an egg into each tart case, divide the bacon between the tart cases, then pour in the Filling.
6 Bake the tarts for 10 minutes, until the Filling is set and the pastry is golden. Serve immediately.

Baklava

This classic Greek pastry is traditionally served with coffee. Be sure not to press the pastry down as you layer it, as this will result in a less flaky baklava.

MAKES 24
PREPARATION TIME:1 HR 30 MINS +
   2 HRS RESTING TIME
COOKING TIME: 30 MINS
STORE IN AN AIRTIGHT CONTAINER
   FOR UP TO 1 WEEK

**15 sheets Phyllo Pastry (page 196) or
   ready-made phyllo**
**3/4 cup (1 3/4 sticks/200 g) unsalted but-
   ter, melted**

SYRUP
1 1/2 cups (350 g) superfine sugar
7/8 cup (225 ml) water
2 tablespoons rosewater

FILLING
**1 1/3 cups (200 g) blanched whole
   almonds, finely chopped**

2 cups (200 g) walnuts, finely chopped
**1 1/4 cups (150 g) confectioner's (icing)
   sugar**

1 Make the Phyllo Pastry by following the recipe on page 196.

2 Preheat the oven to 360°F (180°C). Grease a 8-in × 12-in (20-cm × 30-cm) brownie pan with melted butter.

3 To make the Syrup, bring the sugar and water to a boil in a small saucepan. Simmer for 5–7 minutes, until slightly reduced and thickened. Pour the Syrup into a bowl and allow to cool, then add the rosewater.

4 To make the Filling, mix together the almonds, walnuts and icing sugar in a bowl.

5 Place a sheet of phyllo in the base of the prepared pan and brush with the melted butter. Repeat with four more sheets of phyllo, brushing each sheet with melted butter. Spread half of the Filling over the phyllo, then layer in another five sheets of phyllo, brushing each with melted butter. Spread the remaining Filling evenly over the top, then layer on the last five sheets of phyllo, brushing each with melted butter. Trim away excess pastry from the edges with a sharp knife, then cut the baklava into diamond shapes. Brush the remaining butter over the top of the baklava.

6 Bake the baklava for 30 minutes, until golden. Pour the Syrup over the top while it's still hot, then allow to cool completely in the pan.

Spanakopita

This classic cheese and spinach pie is best served for a summer lunch, with a Greek salad alongside.

SERVES 8
PREPARATION TIME: 1 HR 45
 MINS + 2 HRS RESTING TIME
COOKING TIME: 1 HR
BEST SERVED ON THE DAY OF
 BAKING

¾ cup (1¾ sticks/200 g) unsalted
 butter, melted
10 sheets Phyllo Pastry (page 196)
 or ready-made phyllo

FILLING
¼ cup (60 ml) extra-virgin olive oil
2 onions, finely chopped
2 cloves garlic, finely chopped
3⅓ cups (250 g) baby spinach
 leaves
1 tablespoon finely chopped fresh
 mint
1 tablespoon finely chopped fresh
 basil
1 tablespoon finely chopped fresh
 parsley
3 eggs
2 cups (200 g) finely crumbled feta
 cheese
9 oz (250 g) ricotta cheese
½ cup (50 g) finely grated pecorino
 or parmesan cheese
¼ teaspoon ground nutmeg
Salt and freshly-ground black
 pepper

1 Make the Phyllo Pastry by following the recipe on page 196.
2 Preheat the oven to 360°F (180°C). Grease a 8-in × 12-in (20-cm × 30-cm) brownie pan or baking dish with melted butter.
3 To make the Filling, heat the oil in a large skillet and sauté the onion and garlic over medium heat until soft. Add the spinach leaves and cook until wilted, then transfer the spinach mix to a sieve to drain and cool. Combine the herbs, eggs and cheeses in a large bowl. Add the cooled spinach mix and stir to combine. Add the nutmeg, and season with salt and pepper.
4 Layer four sheets of phyllo in the prepared baking sheet, brushing each sheet with melted butter before adding the next. Spread the Filling evenly over the pastry, then layer the remaining six sheets of phyllo on top, brushing each sheet with melted butter. Brush melted butter over the top. Trim away excess pastry from the edges with a knife, then score the top layers of pastry into serving-sized portions.
5 Bake the spanakopita for 45 minutes to 1 hour, until golden. Serve hot or cold with a salad.

Turkish Delight Fingers

These fingers of molten Turkish delight encased by crisp pastry are lovely served with coffee.

MAKES 12
PREPARATION TIME: 1 HR 15 MINS +
  2 HRS RESTING TIME
COOKING TIME: 12 MINS

12 oz (350 g) rose Turkish delight
6 sheets Phyllo Pastry (page 196) or ready-made phyllo
½ cup (1 stick/100 g) unsalted butter, melted
2 teaspoons sesame seeds
¼ cup (30 g) confectioner's (icing) sugar, for dusting

1 Make the Phyllo Pastry by following the recipe on page 196.
2 Preheat the oven to 360°F (180°C). Grease a baking sheet with melted butter.
3 Cut the Turkish delight into 12 strips, each about 4 in (10 cm) long. Cut the stack of phyllo sheets in half to make two squares. Brush a piece of phyllo with melted butter and place a strip of Turkish delight along one side. Begin to roll up the Turkish delight in the pastry, then fold in the ends and continue to roll up to make a long finger. Brush the finger with melted butter and sprinkle with sesame seeds, then place on the prepared baking sheet. Repeat the process to make 11 more fingers.
4 Bake the fingers for 10–12 minutes, until golden. Allow to cool for 5 minutes, then dust with icing sugar and serve.

Honey, Nougat and Chocolate Rolls

Serve these tasty little parcels with vanilla ice-cream for dessert.

MAKES 16
PREPARATION TIME: 1 HR 15 MINS +
  2 HRS RESTING TIME
COOKING TIME: 15 MINS

8 sheets Phyllo Pastry (page 196) or
  ready-made phyllo
$^2/_3$ cup (1$^1/_3$ sticks/150 g) unsalted
  butter, melted
11$^1/_4$ oz (320 g) almond nougat, cut into
  16 equal rectangles
1 tablespoon honey
$^3/_4$ cup (90 g) grated dark chocolate
$^1/_2$ cup (30 g) flaked almonds

1 Make the Phyllo Pastry by following
the recipe on page 196.
2 Preheat the oven to 360°F (180°C).
Grease a baking sheet with melted butter.
3 Cut the stack of phyllo sheets into
two long rectangles. Brush one piece of
phyllo with melted butter, place a piece
of nougat across one of the short ends
and drizzle with a small amount of honey,
then sprinkle with about 2 teaspoons of
grated chocolate. Begin to roll up the
nougat in the pastry, then fold in the ends
and continue to roll up. Repeat this process to make 15 more rolls.
4 Place the nougat rolls on the prepared baking sheet, brush them with
melted butter and sprinkle with the flaked
almonds.
5 Bake the rolls for 15 minutes, until
golden. Serve immediately, with ice-
cream.

Apple and Raisins Strudel

Sprinkling almond flour between the sheets of phyllo helps to keep the layers separate, making the pastry extra crisp when baked.

SERVES 8
PREPARATION TIME: 1 HR 30 MINS + 2 HRS
    RESTING TIME
COOKING TIME: 40 MINS

8 sheets Phyllo Pastry (page 196) or ready-
    made phyllo
½ cup (1 stick/100 g) unsalted butter, melted
⅓ cup (60 g) almond flour
2 tablespoons superfine sugar
1 teaspoon ground cinnamon

FILLING
6 green apples, peeled, cored and diced
3½ tablespoons water
1 teaspoon ground cinnamon
½ cup (100 g) superfine sugar
⅔ cup (100 g) golden raisins (sultanas)

1 Make the Phyllo Pastry by following the recipe on page 196.
2 To make the Filling, combine the apple, water, cinnamon, sugar and golden raisins in a saucepan. Cook over medium heat for about 10 minutes, stirring regularly, until the apples are softened. Transfer to a bowl and set aside to cool.
3 Preheat the oven to 360°F (180°C). Grease a baking sheet with melted butter.
4 Place a sheet of phyllo on your work surface, brush all over with the melted butter, then sprinkle with a little almond flour. Layer the remaining phyllo sheets on top, brushing with butter and sprinkling with almond flour between each layer. Place the Filling along the long edge of the pastry stack and then roll up into a log, folding in the ends as you go.
5 Carefully lift the strudel onto the prepared baking sheet and brush with melted butter. Combine the superfine sugar and ground cinnamon, and sprinkle it on top of the strudel.
6 Bake the strudel for 35–40 minutes, until golden. Serve immediately, with cream or ice-cream.

Ricotta, Lemon and Blueberry Strudel

Try to source good-quality ricotta cheese for this recipe—an Italian or Greek deli is the best place to find it.

MAKES 12
PREPARATION TIME: 1 HR 15 MINS + 2
  HRS RESTING TIME
COOKING TIME: 20 MINS
BEST SERVED ON THE DAY OF BAKING

12 sheets Phyllo Pastry (page 196) or ready-made phyllo
2/3 cup (1 1/3 sticks/150 g) unsalted butter, melted
1/4 cup (60 g) superfine sugar

FILLING
14 oz (400 g) ricotta cheese
Finely grated zest of 2 lemons
2 teaspoons vanilla extract
2/3 cup (150 g) superfine sugar
1/3 cup (60 g) almond flour
1 egg
1 egg yolk
1 1/4 cups (150 g) blueberries

1 Make the Phyllo Pastry by following the recipe on page 196.
2 Preheat the oven to 360°F (180°C). Grease a baking sheet with melted butter.
3 To make the Filling, mix together the ricotta, lemon zest, vanilla, sugar, almond flour, whole egg, egg yolk and blueberries in a large bowl.
4 Place a sheet of phyllo on your work surface and brush with butter, then fold it in half to make a long rectangle. Place a spoonful of the Filling at one end and fold the phyllo over the filling to make a triangle. Continue to fold the triangle over and over until the end of the pastry strip. Place the triangle on the prepared baking sheet, brush with melted butter and sprinkle with a little superfine sugar. Repeat the process to make another 11 triangles.
5 Bake the strudel for 20 minutes, until golden. Serve hot or cold with ice-cream.

Choux Pastry

Choux pastry is really very easy to make—if you follow the guidelines in this recipe to ensure your pastry is the right consistency, you can't go wrong.

MAKES 1¼ LB (600 G)
PREPARATION TIME: 30 MINS
USE THE FINISHED PASTRY IMMEDIATELY,
   AS REQUIRED

7 tablespoons milk
⅔ cup (150 ml) water
⅖ cup (¾ stick/90 g) unsalted butter, diced
½ teaspoon fine sea salt
1 teaspoon superfine sugar
1 cup (150 g) all-purpose (plain) flour, sifted
3–4 eggs

1 Combine the milk, water, butter, salt and sugar in a saucepan, and bring to a boil over medium heat, see photos on right (1). Immediately remove from the heat and add the sifted flour (2). Stir with a wooden spoon until the mixture is smooth and comes away from the sides of the pan. Return the pan to the heat and continue mixing over low heat for 2 minutes (3).
2 Transfer the mixture to a mixing bowl. (Alternatively, this step can be done in an electric mixer fitted with the paddle attachment.) Add the eggs to the bowl one at a time (4), beating well with a wooden spoon between each addition—all of the eggs may not be required. After adding the third egg, check to see if the mixture is thick, smooth and shiny; if it is, it may be ready. To test if the pastry is ready, dip a clean finger into the mixture and pull it out, then point your finger upwards. If the peak of pastry stands up straight, the mixture is too stiff and requires another egg. If the peak folds over slowly, the pastry is ready. (If the peaks flop over completely, the pastry is too wet and will not rise properly.)

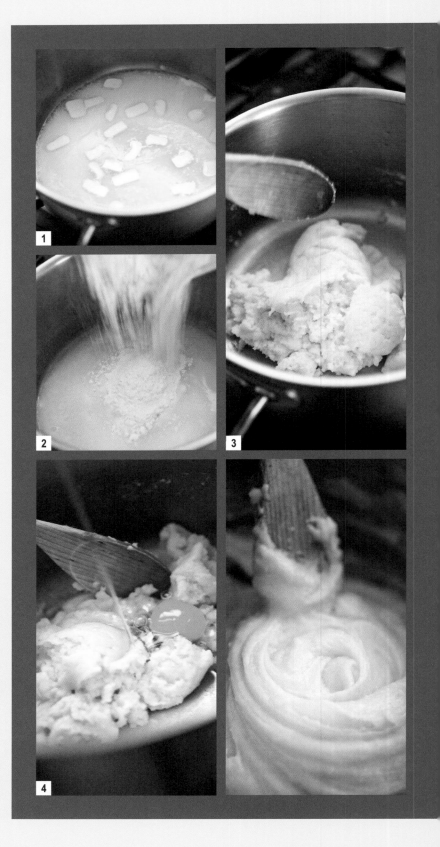

Gougères

Gougères are traditionally made with gruyère cheese, but any strong cheese will work well.

MAKES 30
PREPARATION TIME: 45 MINS
COOKING TIME: 25 MINS

1 quantity Choux Pastry (page 204)
1½ cups (150 g) grated gruyère cheese
Pinch of cayenne pepper
Egg wash: 1 egg yolk whisked with 3
**   teaspoons milk**
1 teaspoon paprika

1 Make the Choux Pastry by following the recipe on page 204.
2 Preheat the oven to 360°F (180°C). Grease two baking sheets.
3 Mix together the Choux Pastry, 1 cup (100 g) of the gruyère cheese and a pinch of cayenne pepper in a bowl. Place this mixture into a piping bag fitted with a ⅜ in (10 mm) plain nozzle.
4 Pipe 1¼ in (3 cm) mounds of the pastry mixture onto the prepared baking sheets. Brush with the egg wash, then sprinkle lightly with paprika and the remaining gruyère cheese.
5 Bake the gougères for 25 minutes, until golden and crisp. Allow to cool on a wire rack for 5 minutes before serving.

Coffee Éclairs

These are the ultimate treat for coffee lovers. Be sure to cook your éclairs until they are golden and crisp to avoid soggy pastry.

MAKES 16
PREPARATION TIME: 1 HR 20 MINS
COOKING TIME: 30 MINS
BEST SERVED ON THE DAY OF BAKING

1 quantity Choux Pastry (page 204)
Egg wash: 1 egg yolk whisked with 3
   teaspoons milk
2³/₄ tablespoons water
2¹/₂ tablespoons superfine sugar
2 tablespoons instant coffee granules
2 quantities Vanilla Custard (page 21)
2 cups (250 g) confectioner's (icing)
   sugar
2 tablespoons unsalted butter, melted
1 oz (30 g) dark chocolate, melted

1 Make the Choux Pastry and the Vanilla Custard by following their respective recipes on pages 204 and 21.
2 Preheat the oven to 360°F (180°C). Line two baking sheets with parchment baking paper.
3 Place the Choux Pastry into a piping bag fitted with a ⁵/₈ in (15 mm) plain nozzle. Pipe 16 éclairs, each 4 in (10 cm) long, onto the prepared sheets.
4 Brush the éclairs with the egg wash and bake for 25–30 minutes, until golden and crisp. Transfer to a wire rack to cool.
5 Combine the water and sugar in a small saucepan over low heat, stirring to dissolve the sugar. Add the coffee granules and stir to dissolve. Set aside to cool.
6 Place the Vanilla Custard in a bowl and whisk in half the coffee syrup. Transfer the custard to a clean piping bag fitted with a ¹/₄ in (5 mm) plain nozzle. Pierce the center of the bottom of each éclair with the nozzle and fill with the custard.
7 Sift the icing sugar into a bowl and add the melted butter. Stir in the remaining coffee syrup a teaspoon at a time until a thick icing forms (add a little warm water if needed).
8 Spread the top of each éclair with the coffee icing and drizzle with the melted chocolate, then leave to set for 15 minutes. Keep refrigerated if not serving immediately.

Chocolate Éclairs

I love the flavor of the whipped cream in a chocolate éclair. If you would like a more chocolaty version, fill them with Chocolate Custard (page 21) instead.

MAKES 16
PREPARATION TIME: 1 HR
COOKING TIME: 30 MINS
BEST SERVED ON THE DAY OF BAKING

1 quantity Choux Pastry (page 204)
Egg wash: 1 egg yolk whisked with 3 teaspoons milk

VANILLA CREAM
1²⁄₃ cups (400 ml) whipping cream
¼ cup (60 g) superfine sugar
2 teaspoons vanilla extract

GANACHE
²⁄₃ cup (150 ml) whipping cream
1²⁄₃ cups (200 g) chopped dark chocolate

1 Make the Choux Pastry by following the recipe on page 204.
2 Preheat the oven to 360°F (180°C). Line two baking sheets with parchment baking paper.
3 Place the Choux Pastry into a piping bag fitted with a ⅝ in (15 mm) plain nozzle. Pipe 16 éclairs, each 4 in (10 cm) long, onto the prepared sheets.
4 Brush the éclairs with the egg wash and bake for 25–30 minutes, until golden and crisp. Transfer to a wire rack to cool.
5 To make the Vanilla Cream, whip the cream, sugar and vanilla in the bowl of an electric mixer fitted with the whisk attachment, on high speed until thick.
6 Place the Vanilla Cream into a clean piping bag fitted with a ¼ in (5 mm) plain nozzle, pierce the center of the bottom

of each éclair with the nozzle and fill with the Vanilla Cream.
7 To make the Ganache, bring the whipping cream to a boil, then pour it over the chocolate and stir until smooth.

8 Dip the top of each éclair into the Ganache, then leave to set for 15 minutes. Keep refrigerated if not serving immediately.

Gateau Saint Honoré

This cake is named after the French patron saint of bakers.

MAKES 16

PREPARATION TIME: 3 HRS 20 MINS +
6 HRS 30 MINS CHILLING/RESTING
TIME

COOKING TIME: 1 HR

BEST SERVED ON THE DAY OF BAKING

½ quantity Puff Pastry (page 212)

1 quantity Choux Pastry (page 204)

Egg wash: 1 egg yolk whisked with 3
teaspoons milk

2 quantities Chocolate Custard (page 21)

1 teaspoon cocoa (unsweetened), for
dusting

CARAMEL

1⅓ cups (300 g) superfine sugar

7 tablespoons water

VANILLA CREAM

2 cups (500 ml) whipping cream

¼ cup (60 g) superfine sugar

1 teaspoon vanilla extract

1 Make the Puff Pastry, the Choux Pastry and the Chocolate Custard by following their respective recipes on pages 212, 204 and 21.

2 On a lightly floured work surface, roll out the Puff Pastry to a thickness of ⅛ in (3 mm). Cut out a 10 in (25 cm) round (you can cut around an upturned dinner plate). Transfer the Puff Pastry round to a baking sheet lined with parchment baking paper. Prick the pastry all over with a fork, then refrigerate for 30 minutes.

3 Preheat the oven to 360°F (180°C).

4 Place two-thirds of the Choux Pastry into a piping bag fitted with a ⅜ in (10 mm) plain nozzle. Pipe a spiral of Choux Pastry onto the Puff Pastry round, starting in the center and finishing with a thicker border around the edge. Brush with the egg wash and bake for 35 minutes, until golden. Transfer to a wire rack to cool.

5 Pipe sixteen 1¼ in (3 cm) mounds of choux onto a greased baking sheet. Brush with the egg wash and bake for 25 minutes, until golden. Cool on a wire rack.

6 Place the Chocolate Custard into a clean piping bag fitted with a 5 mm (¼ in) plain nozzle. Pierce the bottom of each choux puff with the nozzle and fill with the custard. (Reserve leftover custard.)

7 To make the Caramel, place the sugar and water in a small saucepan and bring to a boil over medium heat. Clean the sides of the pot using a pastry brush dipped in cold water, to prevent the sugar from crystallizing. Continue to cook the syrup over medium heat until it changes to a pale caramel color. Remove the pan from the heat and use the Caramel immediately.

8 Being careful not to burn yourself, dip the top of each choux puff into the hot Caramel, then place on a clean baking sheet to set. Dip the base of each choux puff into the remaining caramel and immediately place around the edge of the Puff Pastry and choux base (the caramel will adhere the puffs to the base as it sets).

9 Spread the remaining Chocolate Custard in the center of the gateau.

10 To make the Vanilla Cream, whip the cream, sugar and vanilla in the bowl of an electric mixer fitted with the whisk attachment, on high speed until thick.

11 Place the Vanilla Cream into a clean piping bag fitted with a large plain nozzle and pipe it decoratively into the center of the gateau. Dust the Vanilla Cream with a little cocoa to finish. Keep the gateau refrigerated if not serving immediately.

Paris-Brest Pastry Wheels

Created in honor of a bicycle race from Paris to Brest in France, this pastry resembles a bicycle wheel.

MAKES 16
PREPARATION TIME: 1 HR 20 MINS
COOKING TIME: 35 MINS
BEST SERVED ON THE DAY OF BAKING

1 quantity Choux Pastry (page 204)
Egg wash: 1 egg yolk whisked with 3
    tablespoons milk
1½ cups (100 g) flaked almonds
¼ cup (60 g) honey
¼ cup (30 g) confectioner's (icing) sugar,
    for dusting

FILLING
1¼ cups (300 ml) whipping cream
¼ cup (60 g) superfine sugar
1 teaspoon vanilla extract
1 quantity Vanilla Custard (page 21)

1 Make the Choux Pastry and the Vanilla Custard by following their respective recipes on pages 204 and 21.

2 Preheat the oven to 360°F (180°C). Grease a baking sheet.

3 Place the Choux Pastry into a piping bag fitted with a ⅝ in (15 mm) plain nozzle. Pipe 12 circles, each 4 in (10 cm) in diameter, leaving a hole in the center, onto the prepared baking sheet.

4 Brush the circles with the egg wash, then bake for 35 minutes, until golden and crisp. Transfer to a wire rack to cool.

5 Reduce the oven temperature to 325°F (160°C). Spread the flaked almonds on a baking sheet and bake for 5 minutes, until light golden brown.

6 To make the Filling, whip the cream, sugar and vanilla in the bowl of an electric mixer fitted with the whisk attachment, on high speed until thick. Fold the whipped cream into the Vanilla Custard.

7 Cut the pastries in half horizontally and use a piping bag or dessert spoon to fill the bottom half with the custard filling. Place the top back on. Warm the honey until it is runny, then brush it over the tops of the pastries. Sprinkle the flaked almonds over and dust with icing sugar. Keep pastries refrigerated if not serving immediately.

Traditional Puff Pastry

It's important to make sure the butter is pliable before placing it inside the dough—if it is too hard you will have difficulty rolling; too soft and it will ooze out of any gaps in the pastry. To ensure the right texture, remove the butter from the fridge an hour before use, and give it a good thump with a rolling pin just before adding it to the pastry.

MAKES 2½ LB (1.1 KG)
PREPARATION TIME: 1 HR 15 MINS + 6 HRS CHILLING/RESTING TIME
STORE IN THE REFRIGERATOR FOR UP TO 3 DAYS OR FREEZE FOR UP TO 1 MONTH

3⅓ cups (500 g) all-purpose (plain) flour
⅞ cup (220 ml) water
2 teaspoons fine sea salt
3½ tablespoons unsalted butter, melted
1¾ cups (3½ sticks/400 g) unsalted butter, at room temperature

1 Combine the sifted flour with the water, salt and melted butter in the bowl of an electric mixer fitted with the dough hook attachment. Mix on low speed for 5 minutes, until the dough is smooth and elastic.
2 Alternatively, you can make the dough by hand (see photos on facing page). Sift the flour into a bowl, make a well in the center and add the water (1), salt and melted butter (2). Mix by hand (3) until a dough forms (4). Then knead on a work surface (5) for 5 minutes, or until the dough is smooth and elastic.
3 Remove the dough from the bowl and knead into a ball. Cut a ¾ in (2 cm) deep cross in the top of the dough (6), then wrap in plastic wrap. Refrigerate for at least 1 hour (or overnight).
4 Use the rolling pin to bash the room-temperature butter into a rectangle to make it pliable (7). On a lightly floured work surface, press out the four corners of the dough with the heel of your hand. Using a rolling pin, roll out the four sides to make flaps about ¼ in (5mm) thick (8). Place the butter in the center of the dough and fold the flaps over to cover it completely (9).
5 **FIRST TURN** On a lightly floured work surface, roll out the dough to approximately 8 in × 16 in (20 cm x 40 cm). Fold the short ends of the dough over the middle to make three layers.
6 **SECOND TURN** Give the dough a quarter turn, then roll out to a rectangle as before, and again fold into thirds. Wrap in plastic wrap and refrigerate for at least 2 hours.
7 **THIRD AND FOURTH TURNS** Repeat the rolling and folding process twice more. Wrap, and refrigerate for 2 hours.
8 **FIFTH AND SIXTH TURNS** Repeat the rolling and folding process twice more. Wrap, and refrigerate again for at least 1 hour. The pastry is now ready to use.

Quick Puff Pastry

This recipe is easier and quicker than traditional puff pastry, and will still produce excellent results.

MAKES 2½ LB (1.1 KG)
PREPARATION TIME: 45 MIN + 1 HOUR 30 MIN CHILLING TIME
STORE IN THE REFRIGERATOR FOR UP TO 3 DAYS OR FREEZE FOR UP TO 1 MONTH

3 cups (450 g) all-purpose (plain) flour, sifted
2 cups (4 sticks/450 g) unsalted butter, very cold, diced
2 teaspoons fine sea salt
⅞ cup (225 ml) ice-cold water

1 Combine the sifted flour with the butter and salt in the bowl of an electric mixer fitted with the dough hook attachment. Mix on low speed until the butter is in small pieces and the mixture has started to become grainy. Gradually add the water and mix until combined; there should still be pieces of butter visible. Wrap in plastic wrap and refrigerate for 30 minutes.
2 On a lightly floured work surface, roll out the dough to a rectangle 8 in × 16 in (20 cm × 40 cm). Fold the short ends of the dough over the middle to make three layers, then give it a quarter turn and roll out again to the same size as before. Fold into thirds again, then wrap in plastic wrap and refrigerate for 30 minutes.
3 Roll out the pastry and fold as before, then repeat once more. Refrigerate for 30 minutes before use.

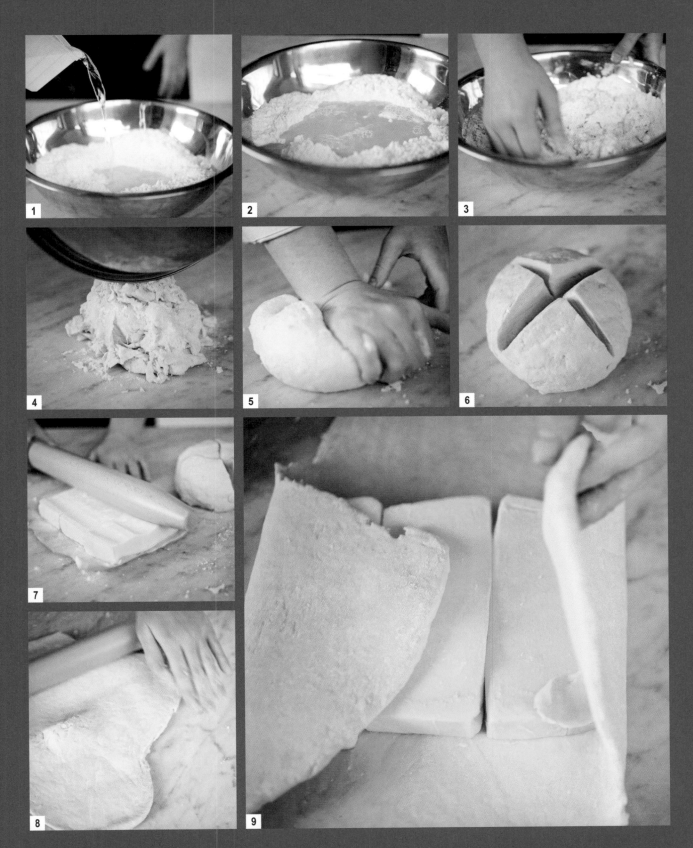

Pork, Veal and Sage Sausage Rolls

When I was 16 years old I worked in a bakery one night a week to gain experience. I loved watching the bakers making meters and meters of sausage rolls in just minutes.

MAKES 16

PREPARATION TIME: 45 MINS +
   TIME TO MAKE THE PUFF PASTRY
COOKING TIME: 30 MINS

²⁄₃ cups (60 g) dried breadcrumbs
½ cup (120 ml) milk
2½ cups (300 g) ground pork
2½ cups (300 g) ground veal
1 tablespoon finely chopped fresh
   sage
2 cloves garlic, finely chopped
1 teaspoon fine sea salt
Freshly-ground black pepper
½ quantity Puff Pastry (page 212)
2 egg yolks, beaten

1 Make the Puff Pastry by following the recipe on page 212.

2 Preheat the oven to 360°F (180°C). Line two baking sheets with parchment baking paper.

3 Combine the breadcrumbs and milk in a bowl, and allow to stand for 5 minutes. Add the ground pork and vea, sage, garlic, salt and pepper, and mix well.

4 On a lightly floured work surface, roll out the Puff Pastry to a rectangle 16 in × 24 in (40 cm x 60 cm) with a thickness of ⅛ in (3mm). Cut the pastry lengthwise into two long rectangles.

5 Place the meat mixture into a piping bag fitted with a ¾ in (20 mm) plain nozzle and pipe a line of filling along the center of one pastry rectangle. (Alternatively, shape half the meat mixture into a log with your hands and place on the pastry.) Brush one long edge of the pastry with the egg yolk, then fold the other long edge over the filling and join with the other side, pressing down firmly to seal. Place the roll join side down. Press down with a knife to mark out eight thick slices (rolls), but do not cut through the pastry. Repeat this process with the second rectangle of pastry and remaining meat mixture.

6 Place the logs on the prepared baking sheets and brush with the remaining egg yolk. Bake for 25–30 minutes, until golden brown. Serve hot.

Beef, Red Wine and Thyme Pie

This is a great meal to prepare ahead of time. The filling can be made up to 2 days in advance and the pie lid placed on 1 day before baking. Keep chilled until required, then it's only 35 minutes in the oven until you have a delicious pie on the table.

SERVES 8
PREPARATION TIME: 1 HR + 30 MINS CHILL-
  ING + TIME TO MAKE THE PUFF PASTRY
COOKING TIME: 2 HR 30 MINS

7 tablespoons extra-virgin olive oil

2 onions, cut into large dice

2 carrots, peeled and chopped into ³⁄₄ in
  (2 cm) pieces

2 sticks celery, cut into ³⁄₄ in (2 cm) pieces

2 cloves garlic, crushed

4 cups (800 g) diced stewing beef

½ cup (60 g) all-purpose (plain) flour

¼ cup (60 g) tomato paste

1 tablespoon fresh thyme leaves

2 cups (500 ml) red wine

2 cups (500 ml) beef stock

Salt and freshly-ground black pepper

½ quantity Puff Pastry (page 212)

1 egg, beaten

1 Make the Puff Pastry by following the recipe on page 212.

2 Heat half the olive oil in a large saucepan. Add the onions, carrots, celery and garlic, and sauté over medium heat for 5 minutes, until softened. Remove the vegetables from the saucepan and set aside. Dredge the beef in the flour. Heat the remaining olive oil in the pan and sauté the beef until lightly golden. Add the tomato paste, thyme and red wine to the saucepan, bring to a boil, then add the beef stock and return the vegetables to the pan. Simmer over low heat for 1½–2 hours, uncovered, until the beef is tender and the sauce has thickened and reduced. Stir regularly as the sauce thickens, to prevent burning. Season to taste with salt and pepper. Transfer the filling to a 10 in (25 cm) pie dish and set aside to cool.

3 On a lightly floured work surface, roll out the Puff Pastry to a thickness of ⅛ in (3 mm). The pastry should be large enough to fit the top of the pie dish. Brush the edge of the pie dish with egg, then place the pastry on top and press around the edges to seal. Use a sharp knife to trim off any excess pastry. Use offcuts of pastry to decorate the top of the pie, then brush the pastry with the remaining egg. Refrigerate the prepared pie for at least 30 minutes before baking to allow the pastry to rest.

4 Preheat the oven to 360°F (180°C).

5 Bake the pie for 35 minutes, until golden. Serve hot.

Cheese Twists

Serve these tasty twists with drinks before a meal. Experiment with different types of cheese until you find your favorite flavor.

MAKES 40
PREPARATION TIME: 30 MINS + TIME
   TO MAKE THE PUFF PASTRY
COOKING TIME: 15 MINS
BEST SERVED ON THE DAY OF BAKING

½ **quantity Puff Pastry (page 212)**
1 egg, beaten
2 cups (200 g) grated parmesan, gruyère
   or Emmental (Swiss) cheese
½ **teaspoon paprika**

1 Make the Puff Pastry by following the recipe on page 212.

2 Preheat the oven to 360°F (180°C). Line a baking sheet with parchment baking paper.

3 On a lightly floured work surface, roll out the Puff Pastry to a rectangle 8 in × 16 in (20 cm × 40 cm) with a thickness of ⅛ in (3 mm).

4 Brush the pastry with the beaten egg and sprinkle evenly with the grated cheese and paprika. Cut the pastry into strips ⅜ in (1 cm) wide, then twist the strips several times and place on the prepared baking sheet.

5 Bake the twists for 12–15 minutes, until golden. Cool on a wire rack.

Apricot Strudel

Serve this strudel hot with ice-cream for dessert, or cold for afternoon tea. Plums or peaches would also work well in this recipe.

SERVES 8
PREPARATION TIME: 45 MINS + TIME
  TO MAKE THE PUFF PASTRY
COOKING TIME: 40 MINS
BEST SERVED ON THE DAY OF BAKING

½ quantity Puff Pastry (page 212)
1 quantity Almond Cream (page 20)
12 canned apricot halves
2 egg yolks, beaten

1 Make the Puff Pastry and the Almond Cream by following their respective recipes on pages 212 and 20.
2 Preheat the oven to 375°F (190°C). Line a baking sheet with parchment baking paper.
3 On a lightly floured work surface, roll out the Puff Pastry to a rectangle 10 in × 12 in (25 cm × 30 cm). Cut the pastry lengthwise into two long rectangles.
4 Place one rectangle of pastry on the prepared baking sheet. Spread the Almond Cream over the rectangle, leaving a ¾ in (2 cm) border around the edge. Arrange the apricot halves cut side down on top of the Almond Cream.
5 Using a sharp knife, cut decorative slits, ¼ in (5 mm) apart, across the second (top) piece of pastry, leaving a ¾ in (2 cm) border around the edge. Brush the border of the pastry base with egg yolk, then place the top pastry piece on top. Use a fork to press around the edges of the strudel to seal, then brush the top with the egg yolk.
6 Bake the strudel for 35–40 minutes, until golden. Serve hot or cold with cream or ice-cream.

Chicken and Leek Pies

Pie fillings are generally made using the same technique; once you have mastered the recipes in this book, you can start to create your own flavors with other combinations of meat, vegetables and spices.

MAKES 8
PREPARATION TIME: 45 MINS + 30
  MINS CHILLING TIME + TIME TO
  MAKE THE PUFF PASTRY
COOKING TIME: 55 MINS

¼ cup (60 ml) extra-virgin olive oil

1 onion, finely chopped

2 cloves garlic, crushed

2 leeks, cut into large dice

2 teaspoons fresh thyme leaves

2 carrots, peeled and chopped

1¼ lb (600 g) skinless chicken thigh
  fillets, diced

¼ cup (½ stick/60 g) unsalted butter

½ cup (60 g) all-purpose (plain) flour

2 cups (500 ml) hot chicken stock

1 cup (250 ml) whipping cream

Salt and freshly-ground black pepper

½ quantity Puff Pastry (page 212)

1 egg, beaten

1 Make the Puff Pastry by following the recipe on page 212.

2 Heat half the olive oil in a large saucepan. Add the onion, garlic, leeks, thyme and carrots, and sauté over medium heat for 5 minutes, until softened. Remove the vegetables from the saucepan and set aside. Heat the remaining olive oil in the pan, then add the diced chicken and cook for 2–3 minutes over high heat to seal. Remove the chicken from the pan and set aside. Melt the butter in the pan, then add the flour and stir to make a paste. Pour in the hot chicken stock and stir until smooth, then return the vegetables and chicken to the pan. Pour in the cream and simmer for 30 minutes, stirring regularly. Season to taste with salt and pepper.

3 Divide the chicken and leek filling between eight 8 fl oz (250 ml) individual pie dishes and set aside to cool.

4 On a lightly floured work surface, roll out the Puff Pastry to a thickness of ⅛ in (3 mm). Cut out rounds that are ¾ in (2 cm) larger than the pie dishes. Brush the edges of each pie dish with the beaten egg, then place a pastry round on top and press around the edges to seal. Use offcuts of pastry to decorate the tops of the pies, then brush them with the beaten egg. Refrigerate the prepared pies for at least 30 minutes before baking to allow the pastry to rest.

5 Preheat the oven to 360°F (180°C).

6 Bake the pies for 25 minutes, until golden. Serve hot.

French Apple Tart

This tart can be made with other sliced fruits, such as fresh figs, peaches or poached pears.

SERVES 8
PREPARATION TIME: 50 MINS + TIME
  TO MAKE THE PUFF PASTRY
COOKING TIME: 35 MINS
BEST SERVED ON THE DAY OF BAKING

½ quantity Puff Pastry (page 212)
½ quantity Almond Cream (page 20)
3 green apples, peeled, cored and thinly
  sliced
2 tablespoons unsalted butter, melted
2 tablespoons superfine sugar
1 quantity Apricot Glaze (page 21)

1 Make the Puff Pastry, the Almond Cream and the Apricot Glaze by following their respective recipes on pages 212, 20 and 21.
2 Preheat the oven to 360°F (180°C). Line a baking sheet with parchment baking paper.
3 On a lightly floured work surface, roll out the Puff Pastry to a thickness of ⅛ in (3 mm). Cut out a 12 in (30 cm) round (you can cut around an upturned dinner plate).
4 Prick the pastry all over with a fork. Pinch around the edges of the pastry to crimp. Slide the pastry onto the prepared baking sheet. Spread the Almond Cream evenly over the pastry base, then neatly arrange the apple slices in a circular pattern to completely cover the Almond Cream.
5 Brush the apple with the melted butter, then sprinkle with the superfine sugar.
6 Bake the tart for 30–35 minutes, until the pastry is golden. Brush with the Apricot Glaze. Serve warm or cold with vanilla ice-cream.

Galette Des Rois

In France this cake is made in January to celebrate Epiphany. Traditionally a trinket is baked inside the cake and whoever finds it in their piece is crowned king for the day.

SERVES 8
PREPARATION TIME: 30 MINS + 30
   MINS CHILLING TIME + TIME TO
   MAKE THE PUFF PASTRY
COOKING TIME: 45 MINS
BEST SERVED ON THE DAY OF BAKING

1 quantity Puff Pastry (page 212)
2 quantities Almond Cream (page 20)
4 teaspoons rum
2 egg yolks, beaten

1 Make the Puff Pastry and the Almond Cream by following their respective recipes on pages 212 and 20.
2 Divide the Puff Pastry into two equal pieces. On a lightly floured work surface, roll out each piece of pastry to a 12 in (30 cm) round.
3 Place one round on a baking sheet lined with parchment baking paper.

Combine the Almond Cream and rum, then spread this mixture evenly over the pastry round, leaving a 1 in (2.5 cm) border around the edge. Brush the edge of this round with the beaten egg yolk, then place the second round of pastry on top and press around the edges to seal. Use a knife to trim the edges neatly, then brush the top of the galette with the egg

yolk. Refrigerate for 30 minutes before baking.
4 Preheat the oven to 375°F (190°C).
5 To decorate, use a sharp knife to score the top of cake, being careful not to cut all the way through the pastry. Bake the galette for 40–45 minutes, until golden. Serve warm or cold with cream or ice-cream.

Chocolate and Hazelnut Pithiviers

A pithivier is a round, enclosed pie with a decorative top, usually with a sweet filling such as Almond Cream or fruit. This mini version is my favorite: chocolate and hazelnut is a winning combination.

MAKES 8
PREPARATION TIME: 1 HR + 30 MINS
CHILLING TIME + TIME TO MAKE THE PUFF PASTRY
COOKING TIME: 25 MINS
BEST SERVED ON THE DAY OF BAKING

¾ cup (100 g) hazelnuts
½ cup (⅞ stick/100 g)) unsalted butter, softened
½ cup (100 g) superfine sugar
1 egg
1 teaspoon vanilla extract
3 tablespoons all-purpose (plain) flour
¾ cup (90 g) grated dark chocolate
½ quantity Puff Pastry (page 212)
2 egg yolks, beaten

1 Make the Puff Pastry by following the recipe on page 212.

2 Preheat the oven to 325°F (160°C).

3 Place the hazelnuts on a baking sheet and bake for 10 minutes until the skins begin to loosen. Cool the hazelnuts slightly then rub them between the palms of your hands to remove the skins. Chop finely.

4 Beat the butter and sugar in the bowl of an electric mixer fitted with the paddle attachment, on high speed for 5 minutes until pale and creamy. Add the whole egg and vanilla, and beat again for 2 minutes. Add the hazelnuts, flour and grated chocolate, and mix well.

5 On a lightly floured work surface, roll out the Puff Pastry to a thickness of ⅛ in (3 mm). Cut out 16 rounds, each 4 in (10 cm) in diameter. Divide the filling into eight equal portions and place a portion in the center of half the pastry rounds. Brush the edges of these rounds with egg yolk and place the remaining pastry rounds on top. Press around the edges to seal, ensuring there is no air trapped inside. Place the pithiviers on a baking sheet lined with parchment baking paper and brush with egg yolk. Refrigerate for 30 minutes before baking.

6 Preheat the oven to 360°F (180°C).

7 To decorate, use a sharp knife to score the top of each pithivier, being careful not to cut all the way through the pastry. Bake for 25 minutes, until golden. Serve hot or cold with cream or ice-cream.

Vanilla Custard Mille Feuilles

This recipe brings back memories of my high school days, when vanilla brownies was my favorite treat from the canteen. Now that I'm a little older, I prefer this more sophisticated version, with layers of crisp caramelized puff pastry and rich custard.

SERVES 6
PREPARATION TIME: 1 HR 5 MINS
+ TIME TO MAKE THE PUFF
  PASTRY
COOKING TIME: 35 MINS
BEST SERVED ON THE DAY OF
  BAKING

½ quantity Puff Pastry (page 212)
½ cup (100 g) superfine sugar
2 quantities Vanilla Custard (page
  21), chilled
¼ cup (30 g) confectioner's (icing)
  sugar, for dusting

1 Make the Puff Pastry and the Vanilla Custard by following their respective recipes on pages 212 and 21.

2 Preheat the oven to 360°F (180°C). Line two baking sheets with parchment baking paper.

3 On a lightly floured work surface, roll out the Puff Pastry to a rectangle 20 in × 14 in (50 cm x 35 cm) with a thickness of ⅛ in (2 mm). Cut the pastry into three rectangles, each approximately 14 in × 6½ in (35 cm x 16 cm). Use a fork to prick holes all over the pastry pieces, then transfer them to the prepared baking sheets. Sprinkle the pastry liberally with the superfine sugar.

4 Bake the pastry for 5–7 minutes, until risen. Remove from the oven, lay a sheet of parchment baking paper on top of the pastry and place a baking sheet on top. Press down firmly and return the pastry to the oven (with the baking sheet still on top). Bake for 25–30 minutes, until golden. Cool on a wire rack.

5 Cut each piece of pastry into six equal-sized rectangles. Pipe the Vanilla Custard onto one piece of pastry, place another layer of pastry on top, pipe on more Vanilla Custard, then top with a third layer of pastry. Repeat with the remaining pastry rectangles to make five more stacks. Dust the top of each mille feuille with icing sugar. Keep refrigerated if not serving immediately.

Caramelized Apple Snail Pastries

These are called snail pastries because the puff pastry is rolled into a spiral shape before being rolled out and filled. Keep the pastry in the fridge in between cutting, rolling and filling, as it is much easier to work with cold.

MAKES 16
PREPARATION TIME: 1 HR + 2 HRS
   CHILLING TIME + TIME TO MAKE
   THE PUFF PASTRY
COOKING TIME: 25 MINS
BEST SERVED ON THE DAY OF BAKING

½ quantity Puff Pastry (page 212)
½ cup (1 stick/100 g) unsalted butter,
  melted
¾ cup (100 g) confectioner's (icing)
  sugar
½ cup (1 stick/100 g) unsalted butter,
  diced
8 green apples, peeled, cored and cut
  into small dice
½ cup (100 g) superfine sugar
½ quantity Almond Cream (page 20)
Egg wash: 2 egg yolks whisked with
  2 tablespoons milk
¼ cup (30 g) confectioner's (icing) sugar,
  for dusting

1 Make the Puff Pastry and the Almond Cream by following their respective recipes on pages 212 and 20.

2 On a lightly floured work surface, roll out the Puff Pastry to a square with a thickness of ⅛ in (2 mm). Brush the entire surface of the pastry with the melted butter and dust evenly with the icing sugar. Roll up the pastry firmly into a log. Wrap in plastic wrap and refrigerate for 2 hours.

3 Heat a large skillet, add the diced butter and apple, and cook over high heat until the apple starts to change color. Add the superfine sugar and continue to cook until caramelized. Transfer the apples to a heatproof dish and set aside to cool.

4 Preheat the oven to 360°F (180°C). Line two baking sheets with parchment baking paper.

5 Using a sharp knife, cut the pastry log into ⅜ in (1 cm) slices. Place each puff spiral cut side up on a lightly floured work surface and roll out to an oval shape with a thickness of ⅛ in (2 mm). Place 2 teaspoons of Almond Cream in the center and 3 tablespoonfuls of the caramelized apple mixture on top. Brush the edges of the pastry with egg wash and fold one side over to form a semicircle, then press edges together firmly to seal. Brush the pastries with the egg wash and place on the prepared baking sheets.

6 Bake the snail pastries for 20–25 minutes, until golden. Allow to cool for 5 minutes, then dust with icing sugar to serve.

Palmiers

You can never eat just one of these crisp caramelized pastries—they're so simple yet so divine.

MAKES 60
PREPARATION TIME: 15 MINS + 2 HR
   CHILLING TIME
COOKING TIME: 15 MINS
BEST SERVED ON THE DAY OF BAKING

½ quantity Puff Pastry (page 212)
1 cup (225 g) superfine sugar, for dusting
  and coating

1 Make the Puff Pastry by following the recipe on page 212.
2 Divide the pastry into two equal pieces. On a work surface that has been dusted with sugar, roll out each piece of pastry to a rectangle 8 in × 12 in (20 cm x 30 cm). Trim the edges to make even rectangles.
3 Take one piece of pastry and fold each long side over about 2 in (5 cm) towards the middle, then fold each long side in again. There should be a ⅜ in (1 cm) gap in the center. Now fold the pastry in half lengthwise to finish. Repeat with the second piece of pastry. Wrap in plastic wrap and refrigerate for 2 hours before using.
4 Preheat the oven to 360°F (180°C). Line two baking sheets with parchment baking paper.
5 Cut the pastry logs into ⅜ in (1 cm) slices. Dip both cut sides of each slice in superfine sugar. Place the palmiers cut side up on the prepared baking sheets.
6 Bake the palmiers for 12–15 minutes, until golden.

Pear and Chocolate Tarts

These tarts can also be made with other fillings—try Vanilla Custard (page 21) or Almond Cream (page 20).

SERVES 8
PREPARATION TIME: 50 MINS + TIME
  TO MAKE THE PUFF PASTRY
COOKING TIME: 25 MINS
BEST SERVED ON THE DAY OF BAKING

½ quantity Puff Pastry (page 212)

8 canned pear halves

½ quantity Chocolate Custard (page 21)

2 tablespoons unsalted butter, melted

2 tablespoons superfine sugar

1 oz (30 g) dark chocolate, melted

¼ cup (30 g) confectioner's (icing) sugar, for dusting

1 Make the Puff Pastry and the Chocolate Custard by following their respective recipes on pages 212 and 21.

2 Preheat the oven to 360°F (180°C). Line a baking sheet with parchment baking paper.

3 On a lightly floured work surface, roll out the pastry to a thickness of ⅛ in (3mm). Using one of the pear halves as a template, cut out eight pear shapes ¾ in (2 cm) larger than the pear half.

4 Place the eight pear-shaped pastry pieces on the prepared baking sheet. Prick each pastry shape all over with a fork, then place a tablespoonful of Chocolate Custard in the center. Cut the pear halves into thin slices, holding the pear in its original shape as you slice, then place on top of the custard and fan slightly. Brush the pears with melted butter then sprinkle with the superfine sugar.

5 Bake the pastries for 25 minutes, until golden. Allow to cool for 5 minutes, then drizzle with the melted chocolate and dust with icing sugar.

Croissants, Brioches and Doughnuts

Croissants

Similar to puff pastry, croissant dough has the addition of yeast to help it rise. Any extra croissants can be frozen, uncooked, so you can enjoy them freshly-baked another day, without all the work.

MAKES 16

PREPARATION TIME: 1 HR 30 MINS +
  3 HRS FOR THE DOUGH TO RISE + 5
  HRS 30 MINS CHILLING TIME

COOKING TIME: 15 MINS

BEST SERVED ON THE DAY OF BAKING

8 teaspoons (40 g) fresh yeast

⅞ cup (225 ml) warm milk

3⅓ cups (500 g) all-purpose (plain) flour, sifted

2 teaspoons fine sea salt

2½ tablespoons superfine sugar

1 tablespoons unsalted butter, diced, at room temperature

1 cup (2 sticks/250 g) unsalted butter, at room temperature (but not too soft), extra

Egg wash: 2 egg yolks whisked with 2 tablespoons milk

SYRUP

¼ cup (60 g) superfine sugar

¼ cup (60 ml) water

1 Place the yeast and milk in the bowl of an electric mixer, and stir to dissolve. Add the sifted flour, salt, sugar and diced butter to the bowl. Using the dough hook attachment, mix on low speed for 3–5 minutes, until the dough is well combined. Do not overmix.

2 Remove the dough hook, leaving the dough in the bowl. Cover the bowl with plastic wrap. Leave to rise in a warm place for approximately 1 hour, until the dough has doubled in size. Turn the dough over in the bowl and punch down to its original volume. Cover the bowl with plastic wrap again and refrigerate for at least 3 hours, or up to 24 hours.

3 Turn the dough out onto a lightly floured work surface and knead into a ball. Refer to illustrated steps on facing page. Cut a ¾ in (2 cm) deep cross in the top of the dough (1), then press out the four corners of the dough with the heel of your hand. Using a rolling pin, roll out the four sides to make flaps about ¼ in (5mm) thick (2). Use the rolling pin to bash the extra butter into a rectangle to make it pliable (3), then place it in the center of the dough (4). Fold the flaps over the butter to cover it completely (5).

4 **FIRST TURN** On a lightly floured work surface, roll out the dough to a 8 in × 16 in (20 cm x 40 cm) rectangle (6). Fold the short ends over the middle to make three layers (7), then wrap in plastic wrap and refrigerate for 1–2 hours.

5 **SECOND TURN** Give the dough a quarter turn, then roll out to a rectangle as before, and again fold into thirds. Wrap in plastic wrap and refrigerate for 1–2 hours.

6 **THIRD TURN** Repeat the rolling and folding process, then wrap the dough in plastic wrap and refrigerate for at least 30 minutes before using.

7 Unwrap the finished dough and place on a lightly floured work surface. Roll out to a thickness of ¼ in (5mm). Using parchment baking paper, make a triangle template that is 4 in (10 cm) across the base and 7 in (18 cm) long. Use the template to cut out 16 triangles from the pastry.

8 To roll each croissant, position a triangle of dough with the base closest to you and cut a ⅜ in (1 cm) slit in the center of the base. Roll up the triangle, starting from the base (8). (Croissants can be frozen for up to a week at this stage; thaw in the refrigerator prior to the next step.)

9 Place the croissants on a baking sheet lined with parchment baking paper and brush with the egg wash. (Reserve leftover egg wash.) Leave to rise in a warm place for approximately 2 hours, until they have doubled in size.

10 Preheat the oven to 375°F (190°C).

11 Lightly brush the croissants with the egg wash again. Bake for 12–15 minutes, until golden. (Make the Syrup while the croissants are baking.)

12 To make the Syrup, bring the sugar and water to a boil in a small saucepan.

13 Brush the croissants with the Syrup as soon as they come out of the oven.

14 Serve the croissants warm or cold, spread with jam or butter, or filled with cheese and ham and toasted.

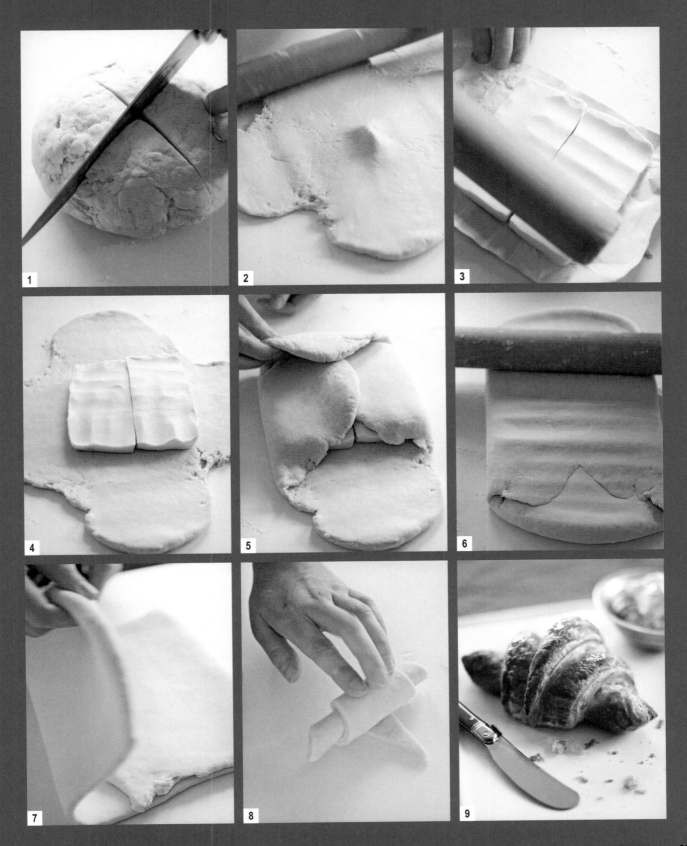

Cheese Croissants

Serve these croissants as part of a cooked breakfast.

MAKES 16
PREPARATION TIME: 2 HRS + 2 HRS FOR
    THE DOUGH TO RISE + TIME TO MAKE
    THE CROISSANT DOUGH
COOKING TIME: 15 MINS

1 quantity Croissant dough (page 230)
2 cups (200 g) grated Emmental (Swiss) or
    gruyère cheese (or other strong-flavored
    cheese)
Egg wash: 2 egg yolks whisked with 2 table-
    spoons milk

1 Make the Croissant dough by following the recipe on page 230.
2 On a lightly floured work surface, roll out the Croissant dough to a thickness of ¼ in (5 mm). Using parchment baking paper, make a triangle template that is 4 in (10 cm) across the base and 7 in (18 cm) long. Use the template to cut out 16 triangles from the pastry.
3 To roll each croissant, position a triangle of dough with the base closest to you and cut a ⅜ in (1 cm) slit in the center of the base. Place about a tablespoon of grated cheese in a pile at the top of the slit, then roll up the triangle, starting from the base. (Croissants can be frozen for up to 1 week at this stage; thaw in the refrigerator prior to the next step.)
4 Place the croissants on a baking sheet lined with parchment baking paper and brush with the egg wash. (Reserve leftover egg wash.) Leave to rise in a warm place for 2 hours, or until they have doubled in size.
5 Preheat the oven to 375°F (190°C).
6 Lightly brush the croissants with the egg wash again and sprinkle with more grated cheese. Bake for 12–15 minutes, until golden. Serve warm.

Almond Croissants

Sweet and crunchy with a soft almond filling, this is my favorite croissant.

MAKES 16
PREPARATION TIME: 2 HRS 5 MINS + 2 HRS
  FOR THE DOUGH TO RISE + TIME TO MAKE
  THE CROISSANT DOUGH
COOKING TIME: 15 MINS
BEST SERVED ON THE DAY OF BAKING

1 quantity Croissant dough (page 230)
1 quantity Almond Cream (page 20)
Egg wash: 2 egg yolks whisked with 2 table-
  spoons milk
1 cup (60 g) flaked raw almonds
¼ cup (30 g) confectioner's (icing) sugar, for
  dusting

1 Make the Croissant dough and the Almond Cream by following their respective recipes on pages 230 and 20.
2 On a lightly floured work surface, roll out the Croissant dough to a thickness of ¼ in (5 mm). Using parchment baking paper, make a triangle template that is 4 in (10 cm) across the base and 7 in (18 cm) long. Use the template to cut out 16 triangles from the pastry.
3 To roll each croissant, position a triangle of dough with the base closest to you and cut a ⅜ in (1 cm) slit in the center of the base. Place a spoonful of the Almond Cream at the top of the slit, then roll up the triangle, starting from the base. (Croissants can be frozen for up to 1 week at this stage; thaw in the refrigerator prior to the next step.)
4 Place the croissants on a baking sheet lined with parchment baking paper and brush with the egg wash. (Reserve leftover egg wash.) Leave to rise in a warm place for 2 hours, or until they have doubled in size.
5 Preheat the oven to 375°F (190°C).
6 Lightly brush the croissants with the egg wash again and sprinkle with the flaked almonds. Bake for 12–15 minutes, until golden. Cool the croissants for 15 minutes before dusting with icing sugar.

Apricot and Almond Pastries

Try using different fruits in place of the apricots: plums, cherries, peaches and berries all work well with this recipe.

MAKES 16
PREPARATION TIME: 2 HRS 40 MINS + 2
   HRS FOR THE DOUGH TO RISE + TIME
   TO MAKE THE CROISSANT DOUGH
COOKING TIME: 15 MINS
BEST SERVED ON THE DAY OF BAKING

1 quantity Croissant dough (page 230)
Egg wash: 2 egg yolks whisked with 2
   tablespoons milk
½ quantity Almond Cream (page 20)
½ quantity Vanilla Custard (page 21)
32 canned apricot halves, drained
1 quantity Apricot Glaze (page 21)
¼ cup (30 g) confectioner's (icing) sugar,
   for dusting

1 Make the Croissant dough, the Almond Cream, the Vanilla Custard and the Apricot Glaze by following their respective recipes on pages 230, 20 and 21.
2 On a lightly floured work surface, roll out the croissant dough to a thickness of ¼ in (5 mm). Cut the dough into 4 in (10 cm) squares and place on baking sheets lined with parchment baking paper. Fold in two opposite corners of each square to meet in the center and press gently to secure. Leave to rise in a warm place for 2 hours, or until the dough has doubled in size.
3 Preheat the oven to 375°F (190°C).
4 Brush the pastries with the egg wash. Combine the Almond Cream and Vanilla Custard in a bowl. Place a spoonful of this mixture in the center of each pastry, then put two apricot halves on top, cut side down.
5 Bake the pastries for 12–15 minutes, until golden. Allow to cool for 15 minutes, then brush the apricots with Apricot Glaze and dust the pastries with the icing sugar.

Blueberry Custard Pastries

Any berries can be used for these custard-filled pastries. Use frozen berries when fresh berries are not in season.

MAKES 16
PREPARATION TIME: 1 HR 25 MINS +
   2 HRS FOR THE DOUGH TO RISE
COOKING TIME: 15 MINS
BEST SERVED ON THE DAY OF BAKING

1 quantity Croissant dough (page 230)
Egg wash: 2 egg yolks whisked with 2
   tablespoons milk
1 quantity Vanilla Custard (page 21)
1¼ cups (150 g) blueberries
1 quantity Apricot Glaze (page 21)
¼ cup (30 g) confectioner's (icing)
   sugar, for dusting

1 Make the Croissant dough, the Vanilla Custard, and the Apricot Glaze by following their respective recipes on pages 230 and 21.

2 On a lightly floured work surface, roll out the croissant dough to a thickness of ¼ in (5 mm). Cut the dough into 4 in (10 cm) squares and place on baking sheets lined with parchment baking paper. Fold in all four corners of each square to meet in the center and press gently to secure. Leave to rise in a warm place for 2 hours, or until the dough has doubled in size.

3 Preheat the oven to 375°F (190°C).

4 Brush the pastries with the egg wash. Place a spoonful of the Vanilla Custard in the center of each pastry and top with about six blueberries.

5 Bake the pastries for 12–15 minutes, until golden. Allow to cool for 15 minutes, then brush the blueberries with the Apricot Glaze and dust the pastries lightly with the icing sugar.

Chocolate Croissants

Known as pain au chocolat *in France, these ever-popular croissants are great dipped in coffee.*

MAKES 16
PREPARATION TIME: 2 HRS + 2 HRS
  FOR THE DOUGH TO RISE
COOKING TIME: 15 MINS

1 quantity Croissant dough (page 230)
11¼ oz (320 g) dark chocolate, cut into baton ⅜ in × 3 in (1 cm x 8 cm)
Egg wash: 2 egg yolks whisked with 2 tablespoons milk

SYRUP
¼ cup (60 g) superfine sugar
¼ cup (60 ml) water

1 Make the Croissant dough by following the recipe on page 230.
2 On a lightly floured work surface, roll out the croissant dough to a thickness of ¼ in (5 mm). Cut the dough into 16 rectangles, each 5 in × 3 in (12 cm x 8 cm).
3 Allowing ¾ oz (20 g) chocolate per croissant, arrange pieces of dark chocolate in two lines, 1¼ in (3 cm) in from each short end of a rectangle. Fold the short ends of the rectangle over the chocolate to meet in the middle and press to seal. Turn the croissant over so the seams face down, then press the two sides together to enclose the seams. Place the croissants, 2 in (5 cm) apart, on a baking sheet lined with parchment baking paper. Leave to rise in a warm place for 2 hours, or until they have doubled in size.
4 Preheat the oven to 375°F (190°C).
5 Brush the croissants with the egg wash, then bake for 12–15 minutes, until golden. (Make the Syrup while the croissants are in the oven.)
6 To make the Syrup, bring the sugar and water to a boil in a small saucepan.
7 Brush the croissants with the Syrup as soon as they come out of the oven. Serve warm.

Snails (Escargots)

Consisting of a spiral of croissant dough filled with Vanilla Custard and rum-soaked raisins, this resembles a snail's (escargot in French) shell once baked.

MAKES 16
PREPARATION TIME: 2 HRS 25 MINS +
  2 HRS FOR THE DOUGH TO RISE
COOKING TIME: 15 MINS
BEST SERVED ON THE DAY OF BAKING

1²⁄₃ cups (250 g) golden raisins (sultanas)
¼ cup (60 ml) water
2 tablespoons rum
1 quantity Croissant dough (page 230)
1 quantity Vanilla Custard (page 21)
Egg wash: 2 egg yolks whisked with 2
  tablespoons milk
1 quantity Apricot Glaze (page 21)

1 Make the Croissant dough, the Vanilla Custard and the Apricot Glaze by following their respective recipes on pages 230 and 21.

2 Place the golden raisins and water in a small saucepan and cook over low heat for 5 minutes to soften the golden raisins. Add the rum to the golden raisins and set aside to cool.

3 On a lightly floured work surface, roll out the croissant dough to a rectangle 16 in × 24 in (40 cm x 60 cm). Spread a thin layer of Vanilla Custard evenly over the dough, then sprinkle with the golden raisins. Starting from a long side, roll up the dough into a log, then cut into 16 equal slices. (Snails can be frozen for up to a week at this stage; thaw in the refrigerator prior to the next step.)

4 Place the pastries cut side up on a baking sheet lined with parchment baking paper. Leave to rise in a warm place for 2 hours, or until they are doubled in size.

5 Preheat the oven to 375°F (190°C).

6 Brush the pastries with the egg wash, then bake for 12–15 minutes, until golden. Cool on the baking sheet for 15 minutes, then brush with Apricot Glaze. Serve warm or cold.

Brioche

Brioche dough is very sticky at room temperature, so make sure it is well chilled before you try to work with it. Add a teaspoon of cinnamon to the dry ingredients to make a brioche that's a great match for pâté.

MAKES 2 LOAVES
PREPARATION TIME: 45 MINS +
   3 HRS 30 MINS FOR THE DOUGH
   TO RISE + 3 HRS CHILLING TIME
COOKING TIME: 40 MINS
BEST SERVED ON THE DAY OF BAKING

1 tablespoon (15 g) fresh yeast
$^2\!/_3$ cup (140 ml) warm water
3$^1\!/_3$ cups (500 g) all-purpose (plain) flour
$^1\!/_4$ cup (60 g) superfine sugar
2 teaspoons fine sea salt
4 eggs
1 cup (2 sticks/250 g) unsalted butter,
**   diced, softened**
Egg wash: 1 egg yolk whisked with 3
**   teaspoons milk**

1 Place the yeast and water in the bowl of an electric mixer, and stir to dissolve. Add the flour, sugar, salt and eggs to the bowl. Using the dough hook attachment, mix on medium speed for 10 minutes, until the dough is smooth and elastic. With the mixer running on low speed, add the diced butter to the bowl a piece at a time. Then mix on medium speed for 5 minutes, until the dough is smooth, elastic and shiny.

2 Remove the dough hook, leaving the dough in the bowl. Cover the bowl with plastic wrap. Leave to rise in a warm place for 1–1$^1\!/_2$ hours, until the dough has doubled in size. Punch down the dough and cover the bowl with plastic wrap again. Refrigerate for at least 3 hours, or up to 24 hours, before use.

3 Grease two fluted brioche molds or two 8$^1\!/_2$-in × 4$^1\!/_2$-in (22-cm × 11-cm) loaf pans with melted butter. Turn the dough out onto a lightly floured surface.

4 If using brioche molds, divide the dough into two equal pieces, then break off a third of each piece. Shape the two larger pieces into balls and place one in the bottom of each greased mold. Press your fingers through the center of each ball to form a hole. Roll the two smaller pieces of dough into log shapes and press one into the center of each ball, leaving only about a quarter of the center piece visible. If using loaf pans, divide the dough into two equal pieces and roll each into a log shape, then place in the loaf pans.

5 Brush the brioches with the egg wash. (Reserve leftover egg wash.) Leave to rise in a warm place for approximately 2 hours, until the dough has doubled in size.

6 Preheat the oven to 360°F (180°C).

7 Brush the brioches with the egg wash again, then bake for 40 minutes, until golden. Cool in the pan for 10 minutes, then turn out onto a wire rack to cool completely.

Rum Babas

I once waited in line for more than 30 minutes at a famous French patisserie for a rum baba—it was worth the wait, and so are these. They make an impressive dinner party dessert and can be prepared ahead of time.

MAKES 16

PREPARATION TIME: 2 HRS + 30 MINS
   FOR THE DOUGH TO RISE

COOKING TIME: 15 MINS

BAKED BABAS CAN BE FROZEN FOR
   UP TO 2 WEEKS; THAW FOR 2
   HOURS BEFORE SOAKING IN THE
   RUM SYRUP

Melted butter, for greasing
½ quantity Brioche dough (page 238), chilled
1 cup (250 ml) dark rum

SYRUP
6⅔ cups (1.5 kg) superfine sugar
5¼ cups (1.25 l) water

VANILLA CREAM
1¼ cups (300 ml) whipping cream
¼ cup (60 g) superfine sugar
1 vanilla bean, split and seeds scraped

1 Make the Brioche dough by following the recipe on page 238.

2 Grease sixteen 5-in (12-cm) individual baba molds with melted butter. If you do not have baba molds, use two 12-hole muffin tray.

3 To make the Syrup, combine the sugar and water in a large saucepan. Bring to a boil over medium heat and boil for 2 minutes. Set aside to cool.

4 Turn the brioche dough out onto a lightly floured work surface, divide into 16 equal portions and roll into balls. If using baba molds, press a finger through the center of each ball to make a hole, then press the dough into the baba molds. (If using muffin trays, you don't need to make a hole in the balls.) Place the baba molds on a baking sheet and leave to rise in a warm place for 30 minutes, or until the dough has risen slightly.

5 Preheat the oven to 360°F (180°C).

6 Bake the babas for 10–15 minutes, until golden. Remove from the oven and immediately turn out onto a wire rack.

7 Warm the sugar syrup to 122°F (50°C)—check the temperature using a sugar thermometer—then stir in the rum and remove from the heat. Soak the babas in the Syrup for 10 minutes on each side. Remove the babas from the Syrup with a slotted spoon and place on a wire rack set over a tray to drain.

8 To make the Vanilla Cream, whip the cream, sugar and vanilla seeds in the bowl of an electric mixer fitted with the whisk attachment on high speed until thick.

9 Serve the rum babas immediately, with the Vanilla Cream alongside.

Olive and Pancetta Brioche

These are great served warm with eggs for breakfast. Make the brioche dough the day before and chill it in the refrigerator overnight so you can sleep in a little longer.

MAKES 12
PREPARATION TIME: 1 HR + 45 MINS
FOR THE DOUGH TO RISE
COOKING TIME: 12 MINS

½ **quantity Brioche dough (page 238), chilled**
¾ **cup (100 g) black olives, pitted and chopped**
12 slices smoked pancetta
Egg wash: 1 egg yolk whisked with 3 teaspoons milk

1 Make the Brioche dough by following the recipe on page 238.
2 On a lightly floured work surface, knead the chopped olives into the Brioche dough. Divide the dough into 12 equal pieces and roll into 4 in (10 cm) logs. Wrap a piece of pancetta around the center of each.
3 Place the brioches on a baking sheet lined with parchment baking paper. Leave to rise in a warm place for 45 minutes, until doubled in size.
4 Preheat the oven to 360°F (180°C).
5 Brush the brioches with the egg wash, then bake for 12 minutes, until golden. Serve immediately.

Vanilla Custard and Raspberry Brioche

This recipe has endless variations; I have chosen a favorite of mine and included a few other suggestions for you to try.

MAKES 16
PREPARATION TIME: 1 HR 15 MINS +
  2 HRS FOR THE DOUGH TO RISE
COOKING TIME: 15 MINS
BEST SERVED ON THE DAY OF BAKING

1 quantity Sweet Brioche dough (page 242), chilled
Egg wash: 1 egg yolk whisked with 3 teaspoons milk
1 quantity Vanilla Custard (page 21)
1¼ cups (150 g) fresh or frozen (defrosted) raspberries
¼ cup (30 g) confectioner's (icing) sugar, for dusting

VARIATIONS

Vanilla and Blueberry Brioche: Fill with Vanilla Custard and top with blueberries.
Chocolate and Pear Brioche: Fill with Chocolate Custard and top with canned pear pieces.
Vanilla Apple Crumble Brioche: Fill with Vanilla Custard and top with diced cooked apple, then sprinkle with crushed plain sweet biscuits.
Vanilla, Apricot and Almond Brioche: Fill with Vanilla Custard and top with diced canned apricot halves, then sprinkle with flaked almonds.

1 Make the Sweet Brioche dough, and the Vanilla Custard by following their respective recipes on page 242 and 21. Chill before using.
2 Turn the brioche dough out onto a lightly floured work surface, divide into 16 equal pieces and roll into balls. Place the balls, 2 in (5 cm) apart, on a baking sheet lined with parchment baking paper. Leave to rise in a warm place for 2 hours, or until the dough has doubled in size.
3 Preheat the oven to 360°F (180°C).
4 Brush the brioches with the egg wash, then use two fingers to press a hole through the center of each ball, nearly to the bottom. Place the custard into a piping bag fitted with a narrow nozzle and pipe it into the hole. Press 3–4 raspberries into the custard.
5 Bake the brioches for 15 minutes, until golden. Cool on the baking sheet, then dust with the icing sugar.

Sweet Brioche

This brioche is delicious toasted for breakfast, or pan-fried with a little butter and served with fruit and ice-cream for dessert.

MAKES 2 LOAVES OR 12 MINI BRIOCHES
PREPARATION TIME: 45 MINS + 3 HRS
   30 MINS FOR THE DOUGH TO RISE +
   3 HRS CHILLING TIME
COOKING TIME: 40 MINS
BEST SERVED ON THE DAY OF BAKING

4 teaspoons (20 g) fresh yeast

³/₄ cup (180 ml) warm water

3¹/₃ cups (500 g) all-purpose (plain) flour

½ cup (125 g) superfine sugar

1 teaspoon fine sea salt

3 eggs

Finely grated zest of 1 orange

Finely grated zest of 1 lemon

²/₃ cup (1¹/₃ sticks/150 g) unsalted butter, diced, softened

Egg wash: 1 egg yolk whisked with 3 teaspoons milk

¼ cup (30 g) confectioner's (icing) sugar, for dusting

1 Place the yeast and water in the bowl of an electric mixer, and stir to dissolve. Add the flour, sugar, salt, eggs, and lemon and orange zests to the bowl. Using the dough hook attachment, mix on medium speed for 10 minutes, until the dough is smooth and elastic. With the mixer running on low speed, add the diced butter to the bowl a piece at a time. Mix on medium speed for 5 minutes, until the dough is smooth, elastic and shiny.

2 Remove the dough hook, leaving the dough in the bowl. Cover the bowl with plastic wrap. Leave to rise in a warm place for 1–1½ hours, until the dough has doubled in size. Punch down the dough and cover the bowl with plastic wrap again. Refrigerate for at least 3 hours, or up to 24 hours, before use.

3 Brush two large fluted brioche molds, two 8½-in × 4½-in (22-cm × 11-cm) loaf pans or twelve 4-in (10-cm) brioche molds with melted butter. Turn the dough out onto a lightly floured work surface.

4 If using large brioche molds, divide the dough into two equal pieces, then break off a third of each piece. Shape the two larger pieces into balls and place one in the bottom of each greased mold. Press your fingers through the center of each ball to form a hole. Roll the two smaller pieces of dough into log shapes and press one into the center of each ball, leaving only about a quarter of the center piece visible. Use the same method for mini brioche molds, but start by dividing the dough into 12 equal portions. If using loaf pans, divide the dough into two equal pieces and roll each into a log shape, then place in the loaf pans.

5 Brush the brioches with the egg wash. (Reserve leftover egg wash.) Leave to rise in a warm place for approximately 2 hours, until the dough has doubled in size.

6 Preheat the oven to 360°F (180°C).

7 Brush the brioches with the egg wash again. Bake large brioches for 40 minutes or mini brioches for 20 minutes, until golden. Cool in the pan for 10 minutes, then turn out onto a wire rack to cool completely. Dust with the icing sugar to serve.

Strawberry and Vanilla Doughnuts

MAKES 8
PREPARATION TIME: 1 HR 15 MINS +
2 HRS FOR THE DOUGH TO RISE
COOKING TIME: 25 MINS
BEST SERVED ON THE DAY OF BAKING

½ quantity Sweet Brioche dough (page 242), chilled
Oil, for frying
½ cup (150 g) strawberry jam

VANILLA SUGAR
1 cup (250 g) superfine sugar
1 vanilla bean, coarsely chopped

1 Make the Sweet Brioche dough by following the recipe on page 242. Chill before using.

2 Turn the brioche dough out onto a lightly floured work surface, divide into eight equal pieces and roll into balls. Place the balls, 2 in (5 cm) apart, on a baking sheet lined with parchment baking paper. Leave to rise in a warm place for 2 hours, or until the dough has doubled in size.

3 To make the Vanilla Sugar, place the sugar and vanilla bean in a food processor, and process for 1 minute. Sift the sugar to remove any chunks of vanilla bean.

4 Heat the oil to 325°F (160°C) in a deep fryer or large saucepan.

5 Carefully place the doughnuts into the oil 2–3 at a time (depending on the size of your fryer). Cook for 3 minutes on each side, turning using a slotted spoon. Remove the doughnuts from the oil using the slotted spoon, and dredge them immediately in the Vanilla Sugar. Allow to cool for 10 minutes.

6 Pierce a hole in each doughnut with a small knife. Place the strawberry jam into a piping bag fitted with a narrow nozzle, and pipe the jam into the doughnuts.

VARIATIONS
- Instead of strawberry jam, use your favorite jam flavor.
- For a special treat, fill the doughnuts with Vanilla or Chocolate Custard (page 21).

Chocolate-Orange Ravioli

I prefer to use a 70 per cent dark chocolate for this recipe—the bitterness of the chocolate balances well with the orange and sugar coating.

SERVES 6
PREPARATION TIME: 1 HR 30 MINS +
  2 HRS CHILLING TIME
COOKING TIME: 20 MINS

1 quantity Sweet Brioche dough (page 242), chilled
1 egg yolk, beaten
$1\frac{1}{8}$ cups (250 g) superfine sugar
Finely grated zest of 1 orange
Oil, for frying

FILLING
$\frac{2}{3}$ cup (150 ml) whipping cream
$1\frac{2}{3}$ cups (200 g) dark chocolate, chopped
4 teaspoons orange liqueur

1 Make the Sweet Brioche dough by following the recipe on page 242. Chill before using.

2 To make the Filling, bring the cream to a boil, then pour it over the chopped chocolate and orange liqueur. Allow to stand for 1 minute, then stir until smooth. Refrigerate the Filling for 2 hours, until firm. Using a small metal scoop or melon baller that has been heated in hot water, scoop out 32 balls and place on a tray. Chill until required.

3 On a lightly floured work surface, roll out the Sweet Brioche dough to a thickness of $\frac{1}{4}$ in (5 mm). Using a 3-in (8-cm) round biscuit cutter, cut out 32 rounds. Place a chocolate ball in the center of each round, brush the edges of the dough with the egg yolk, then fold one side over to form a semicircle. Press the edges together

firmly to seal. Chill in the refrigerator for at least 30 minutes before frying.

4 Combine the superfine sugar and orange zest in a bowl, rubbing the mixture between your fingertips until the zest is mixed in well.

5 Heat the oil to 325°F (160°C) in a deep fryer or large saucepan.

6 Using a slotted spoon, carefully place the ravioli into the hot oil a few at a time. Cook the ravioli for 2 minutes on each side, then remove with a slotted spoon and toss them in the orange zest sugar. Serve immediately, with ice-cream.

Gluten-free Baking

Gluten-free Bread

Gluten-free dough can be very soft to work with; shape it quickly then place straight onto the baking sheet.

MAKES 1 LOAF
PREPARATION TIME: 30 MINS
  + 2 HRS 30 MINS FOR THE
  DOUGH TO RISE
COOKING TIME: 25 MINS
BEST SERVED ON THE DAY OF
  BAKING

1$\frac{1}{3}$ cups (325 ml) warm water

4 teaspoons (20 g) fresh yeast

2$\frac{2}{3}$ cups (400 g) gluten-free
  plain flour, sifted

1 tablespoon fine sea salt

4 teaspoons extra-virgin olive oil

TOPPING

1 teaspoon sesame seeds

1 teaspoon poppy seeds

1 teaspoon caraway seeds

1 teaspoon sea salt flakes

1 Place the water and yeast in the bowl of an electric mixer, and stir to dissolve. Add the sifted flour and salt. Using the dough hook attachment, mix on low speed for 1 minute, then mix on medium speed for 5 minutes.

2 Remove the dough hook, leaving the dough in the bowl. Cover the bowl with plastic wrap. Leave to rise in a warm place for 2 hours, or until the dough has doubled in size.

3 Grease a baking sheet. Remove the dough from the bowl and place on a lightly floured work surface. Quickly shape the dough into a loaf and place on the baking sheet. Leave to rise again in a warm place for 30 minutes, until risen slightly.

4 Preheat the oven to 460°F (240°C).

5 To make the Topping, combine all the ingredients in a bowl.

6 Drizzle the loaf with the olive oil and scatter with the Topping. Place in the oven and immediately turn the temperature down to 360°F (180°C). Bake for 25 minutes, until the loaf sounds hollow when tapped. Cool on a wire rack.

Gluten-free Pizza Dough

This dough creates a nice crisp pizza crust. Simply add your favorite toppings for a quick gluten-free dinner.

MAKES 2 PIZZA BASES
PREPARATION TIME: 15 MINS
   + 2 HRS FOR THE DOUGH
   TO RISE
COOKING TIME: 12 MINS
REFRIGERATE UNCOOKED
   BASES (WELL WRAPPED, ON
   THEIR BAKING SHEETS) FOR
   UP TO 1 DAY OR FREEZE FOR
   1 WEEK. ALWAYS BRING
   BASES BACK TO ROOM TEM-
   PERATURE BEFORE BAKING

1 tablespoon (15 g) fresh yeast
3/4 cup (200 ml) warm water
2 cups (300 g) gluten-free plain
   flour, sifted
1 teaspoon fine sea salt
4 teaspoons extra-virgin olive oil

1 Place the yeast and water in the bowl of an electric mixer, and stir to dissolve. Add the sifted flour, salt and olive oil. Using the dough hook attachment, mix on low speed for 5 minutes, until the dough is smooth.

2 Remove the dough hook, leaving the dough in the bowl. Cover the bowl with plastic wrap. Leave to rise in a warm place for 2 hours, or until the dough has doubled in size.

3 Grease two 12-in (30-cm) pizza trays or two baking sheets. Turn the dough out onto a lightly floured work surface and divide into two equal pieces. Roll each portion into a ball and place on the prepared baking sheets. Use your fingers to press the dough out to a round approximately 10 in (25 cm) in diameter.

4 Preheat the oven to 390°F (200°C).

5 Top the pizza bases with your favorite toppings.

6 Bake the pizzas for 10–12 minutes, until the crust is golden. Serve immediately.

Passionfruit Sponge

A good alternative to a regular sponge cake, this cake can also be used to make lamingtons (see page 84 for the Chocolate Icing recipe).

SERVES 8
PREPARATION TIME: 45 MINS
COOKING TIME: 40 MINS
BEST SERVED ON THE DAY OF BAKING

4 eggs
¾ cup (170 g) superfine sugar
½ cup (60 g) cornstarch
5 tablespoons custard powder
1 teaspoon cream of tartar
½ teaspoon baking soda

VANILLA CREAM
2 cups (500 ml) whipping cream
½ cup (100 g) superfine sugar
1 teaspoon vanilla extract

PASSIONFRUIT ICING
2 cups (250 g) confectioner's (icing) sugar
Pulp of 4 passionfruits

1 Preheat the oven to 325°F (160°C). Line a 8-in (20-cm) round cake pan with parchment baking paper.
2 Beat the eggs and sugar in the bowl of an electric mixer fitted with the whisk attachment, on high speed for 10 minutes until pale and creamy. Sift the dry ingredients together twice, then fold into the egg mixture.
3 Pour the mixture into the prepared pan. Bake for 40 minutes, until the sponge springs back when pressed gently in the center. Cool in the pan for 5 minutes, then turn out onto a wire rack to cool completely.
4 To make the Vanilla Cream, whip the cream, superfine sugar and vanilla In the bowl of an electric mixer fitted with the whisk attachment, until thick.
5 Split the sponge in half using a serrated knife and fill with the cream.
6 To make the Passionfruit Icing, mix together the sugar and passionfruit pulp, adding a little water if necessary to make a smooth icing.
7 Pour the Passionfruit Icing over the top of the sponge.

Date Cake with Lemon Icing

You can replace the dates in this cake with other dried fruits, such as apricots, cherries, golden raisins or figs.

SERVES 10
PREPARATION TIME: 45 MINS
COOKING TIME: 40 MINS
STORE IN AN AIRTIGHT CON-
    TAINER FOR UP TO 3 DAYS

3³/₄ cups (375 g) dried dates, pitted
    and finely chopped

2 cups (300 g) almond flour

2 tablespoons honey

²/₃ cup (150 g) superfine sugar

¹/₃ cup (³/₄ stick/90 g) unsalted but-
    ter, melted

6 eggs, separated

2 teaspoons vanilla extract

Finely grated zest and juice of 2
    oranges

⁵/₈ cup (75 g) cornstarch

LEMON ICING

1¹/₂ cups (200 g) confectioner's
    (icing) sugar

Juice of 1 lemon

1¹/₂ tablespoons unsalted butter,
    melted

1 Preheat the oven to 325°F (160°C). Line a 8-in (20-cm) round cake pan with parchment baking paper.

2 Combine the dates, almond flour, honey, sugar and butter in a mixing bowl. Whisk the egg yolks with the vanilla, orange juice, orange zest and cornstarch in another bowl. Combine the two mixtures.

3 Whip the egg whites in the bowl of an electric mixer fitted with the whisk attachment, on high speed until firm peaks form. Fold the egg whites into the cake mixture.

4 Pour the mixture into the prepared pan. Bake for 40 minutes, or until a skewer inserted into the center of the cake comes out clean. Cool in the pan for 10 minutes, then turn out onto a wire rack to cool completely.

5 To make the Lemon Icing, combine the icing sugar, lemon juice and melted butter in a bowl. Mix until smooth, adding a little water if needed to make the icing of a spreadable consistency.

6 Use a palette knife to spread the Lemon Icing evenly over the top of the cooled cake.

Orange and Almond Cake

Even if you are not gluten intolerant you should try this recipe—it's unbelievably moist.

SERVES 10
PREPARATION TIME: 45 MINS
COOKING TIME: 1 HR
STORE IN AN AIRTIGHT CONTAINER
   FOR UP TO 3 DAYS

3 oranges
9 eggs
1½ cups (330 g) superfine sugar
2¾ cups (400 g) almond flour
1½ teaspoons baking powder

1 Place the whole oranges in a large saucepan and cover with water. Bring to a boil and simmer for 20 minutes, until the oranges are soft. Remove the oranges from the water with a slotted spoon, cut into quarters and set aside to cool. Remove any pips.
2 Preheat the oven to 300°F (150°C). Line a 8-in (20-cm) round springform cake pan with parchment baking paper.
3 Place the oranges into a food processor or blender and process until smooth, then add the eggs and purée for 1 minute.
4 Combine the sugar, almond flour and baking powder in a large bowl. Pour in the orange mixture and fold together.
5 Pour the mixture into the prepared pan. Bake for 1 hour, or until a skewer inserted into the center of the cake comes out clean. Cool in the pan for 10 minutes, then remove the sides of the pan and leave to cool completely. Serve with whipped cream if desired.

Apple and Cinnamon Cake

Wonderful for afternoon tea, served with whipped cream.

SERVES 8
PREPARATION TIME: 40 MINS
COOKING TIME: 45 MINS
STORE IN AN AIRTIGHT CONTAINER
  FOR UP TO 2 DAYS

3 green apples
Juice of 1 lemon
³⁄₄ cup (1²⁄₃ sticks/180 g) unsalted butter, softened
1¹⁄₈ cups (250 g) superfine sugar
3 eggs
1¹⁄₄ cups (180 g) soy flour
1¹⁄₂ cups (250 g) rice flour
3 teaspoons baking powder
3 teaspoons ground cinnamon
³⁄₄ cup (200 ml) milk
¹⁄₃ cup (²⁄₃ stick/75 g) unsalted butter, melted

1 Preheat the oven to 325°F (160°C). Line a 8-in (20-cm) round springform cake pan with parchment baking paper.
2 Peel, core and quarter the apples. Cut into thin slices, then squeeze the lemon juice over.
3 Beat the softened butter and sugar in the bowl of an electric mixer fitted with the paddle attachment, on high speed for 5 minutes, until pale and creamy. Add the eggs one at a time, beating well after each addition. Sift in the flours, baking powder and cinnamon, and add the milk. Mix on low speed until combined.
4 Spread the batter into the prepared pan and arrange the sliced apple decoratively on top. Brush with the melted butter. Bake for 45 minutes, or until a skewer inserted into the center of the cake comes out clean. Cool in the pan.

Chocolate, Date and Almond Torte

I have been making this cake for 15 years. It is so simple and quick, and the flavor is delicious. Be sure to use a good-quality dark chocolate.

SERVES 8
PREPARATION TIME: 45 MINS
COOKING TIME: 45 MINS
BEST SERVED ON THE DAY OF
   BAKING

1½ cups (250 g) whole blanched
   almonds, coarsely chopped
2 cups (250 g) chopped dark
   chocolate
2½ cups (250 g) dried dates, pitted
   and chopped
6 egg whites
½ cup (100 g) superfine sugar
1¾ oz (50 g) dark chocolate, extra,
   in a block

VANILLA CREAM
1 cup (250 ml) whipping cream
3½ tablespoons superfine sugar
1 teaspoon vanilla extract

1 Preheat the oven to 325°F (160°C). Line a 8-in (20-cm) round springform cake pan with parchment baking paper.
2 Combine the almonds, chopped chocolate and dates in a large bowl.
3 Whip the egg whites in the bowl of an electric mixer fitted with the whisk attachment, on high speed until firm peaks form. With the mixer on medium speed, gradually add the sugar to the whites, then beat for a further 2 minutes on high speed.
4 Add the egg whites to the almonds, chocolate and dates, and fold together until well combined.
5 Pour the mixture into the prepared pan. Bake for 45 minutes, until firm to the touch. Cool in the pan for 10 minutes, then remove the sides of the pan and leave to cool completely.
6 To make the Vanilla Cream, whip the cream, sugar and vanilla in the bowl of an electric mixer fitted with the whisk attachment, on high speed until thick.
7 Spread the Vanilla Cream over the top of the cooled cake.
8 Use a vegetable peeler to make chocolate curls from the extra chocolate. Sprinkle the curls over the top of the cake to decorate. Keep refrigerated until ready to serve.

Carrot Cake with Cream Cheese Frosting

This cake is so good no one will ever guess it's gluten-free.

SERVES 12
PREPARATION TIME: 45 MINS
COOKING TIME: 45 MINS
STORE THE UN-ICED CAKE IN AN
AIRTIGHT CONTAINER FOR UP
TO 3 DAYS

1½ cups (180 g) cornstarch
1½ cups (180 g) gluten-free self-
rising flour
1½ teaspoons ground nutmeg
1½ teaspoons ground cinnamon
⅞ cup (220 g) soft brown sugar
1 cup (140 g) golden raisins
(sultanas)
2 medium-sized carrots, peeled and
grated
1½ cups (140 g) chopped walnuts
3 eggs
¾ cup (200 ml) vegetable oil
1 quantity Cream Cheese Frosting
(page 20)
1 teaspoon ground cinnamon,
extra, for sprinkling

1 Make the Cream Cheese Frosting by following the recipe on page 20.

2 Preheat the oven to 325°F (160°C). Line a 8-in (20-cm) round cake pan with parchment baking paper.

3 Sift the cornstarch, self-rising flour, nutmeg and cinnamon into a mixing bowl. Add the soft brown sugar, golden raisins, carrot and walnuts, and mix well. Add the eggs and oil, and mix until combined.

4 Pour the mixture into the prepared pan. Bake for 40–45 minutes, or until a skewer inserted into the center of the cake comes out clean. Cool in the pan for 10 minutes, then turn out onto a wire rack to cool completely.

5 Use a palette knife to spread the Cream Cheese Frosting over the cooled cake, then sprinkle with the cinnamon.

Chocolate Cake with Strawberries and Cream

Strawberries and cream make a fantastic addition to this light chocolate cake. Raspberries can also be used when in season.

SERVES 8
PREPARATION TIME: 45 MINS
COOKING TIME: 30 MINS
BEST SERVED ON THE DAY OF BAKING

2¼ cups (280 g) chopped dark chocolate
¾ cup (1¾ sticks/200 g) unsalted butter, diced
6 eggs, separated
1¾ cups (280 g) almond flour
¾ cup (200 g) superfine sugar
2½ cups (500 g) strawberries, hulled and quartered
¼ cup (30 g) confectioner's (icing) sugar, for dusting

VANILLA CREAM
2 cups (500 ml) whipping cream
½ cup (100 g) superfine sugar
1 teaspoon vanilla extract

1 Preheat the oven to 325°F (160°C). Line two 8-in (20-cm) round cake pans with parchment baking paper.
2 Melt the chocolate and butter together in a double boiler or in the microwave until smooth. Whisk the egg yolks into the chocolate mixture, then stir in the almond flour.
3 Whip the egg whites in the bowl of an electric mixer fitted with the whisk attachment, on medium speed until soft peaks form. With the mixer running on medium speed, gradually add the sugar, then whip until firm peaks form. Fold the eggs whites into the chocolate mixture until well combined.
4 Divide the mixture evenly between the prepared pans. Bake for 30 minutes, or until a skewer inserted into the center of

a cake comes out clean. Cool in the pan for 10 minutes, then turn out onto wire racks to cool completely.
5 Whip the cream, sugar and vanilla in the bowl of an electric mixer fitted with the whisk attachment, on high speed until thick.
6 Place one of the cakes on a serving plate and use a palette knife to spread with half the Vanilla Cream, then arrange half the strawberries on top. Place the second cake on top and spread with the remaining cream. Decorate the top of the cake with the remaining strawberries. Keep cake refrigerated until ready to serve. Dust with icing sugar before serving.

Banana Cake with Coconut Topping

The cake should be almost cooked before adding the coconut topping; if it looks undercooked, allow extra cooking time before adding the topping.

SERVES 10
PREPARATION TIME: 30 MINS
COOKING TIME: 1 HR 30 MINS
STORE IN AN AIRTIGHT CONTAINER
  FOR UP TO 2 DAYS

1¼ cups (180 g) gluten-free plain flour
¾ cup (90 g) cornstarch
1 teaspoon ground ginger
1 teaspoon ground cinnamon
1 teaspoon baking soda
1⅛ cups (250 g) superfine sugar
1¾ cups (225 g) walnuts, chopped
1¼ cups (300 ml) vegetable oil
4 very ripe bananas, mashed
5 eggs

TOPPING
1 cup (90 g) shredded coconut
¼ cup (60 g) honey
2 tablespoons unsalted butter, melted

1 Preheat the oven to 325°F (160°C). Line a 8-in (20-cm) round springform cake pan with parchment baking paper.
2 Sift the plain flour, cornstarch, ginger, cinnamon and baking soda into a mixing bowl, then stir in the sugar and walnuts. Make a well in the center of the dry ingredients. Add the oil, mashed banana and eggs to the well, and mix until thoroughly combined.

3 Spread the mixture into the prepared pan. Bake for 1 hour and 15 minutes.
4 To make the Topping, combine the coconut, honey and butter in a bowl.
5 Spread the Topping evenly over the top of the cake, then bake for a further 15 minutes, until the coconut is golden brown and a skewer inserted into the center of the cake comes out clean. Cool in the pan for 10 minutes, then remove from the pan and place on a wire rack to cool completely.

Pineapple Fruit Cake

This delicious cake can be served warm with custard and ice-cream for a winter dessert or in place of the traditional Christmas pudding.

SERVES 16
PREPARATION TIME: 45 MINS
COOKING TIME: 1 HR 30 MINS
STORE IN AN AIRTIGHT CON-
TAINER FOR UP TO 2 WEEKS

One × 1 lb 1 oz (470 g) can crushed
  pineapple
2 cups (300 g) golden raisins
  (sultanas)
³⁄₄ cup (100 g) currants
3¹⁄₂ oz (100 g) candied cherries
²⁄₃ cup (50 g) candied orange peel,
  finely chopped
¹⁄₂ cup (1 stick/125 g) unsalted
  butter
1 cup (225 g) sugar
1 teaspoon mixed spice
1 teaspoon baking soda
2 eggs
³⁄₄ cup (120 g) soy flour
¹⁄₂ cup (60 g) cornstarch
¹⁄₃ cup (60 g) rice flour
2 teaspoons baking powder

1 Preheat the oven to 325°F (160°C). Line a 8-in (20-cm) round cake pan with parchment baking paper.

2 Combine the (undrained) pineapple, golden raisins, currants, cherries, orange peel, butter, sugar, mixed spice and baking soda in a saucepan. Stir over low heat until the sugar is dissolved, then bring to a boil and simmer for 3 minutes. Transfer to a large bowl and set aside to cool.

3 Add the eggs to the pineapple mixture, then sift in the flours and baking powder. Mix well.

4 Pour the mixture into the prepared pan. Bake for 1¹⁄₂ hours, or until a skewer inserted into the center of the cake comes out clean. Cool in the pan for 10 minutes, then turn out and serve hot. Alternatively, allow to cool completely in the pan and serve cold.

Chocolate Caramel Brownies

Indulgent, rich and sweet, this is the ultimate gluten-free sweet treat.

SERVES 16

PREPARATION TIME: 45 MINS +
   2 HRS COOLING TIME

COOKING TIME: 12 MINS

STORE IN AN AIRTIGHT CON-
   TAINER FOR UP TO 3 DAYS

½ cup (60 g) cornstarch

⅓ cup (60 g) rice flour

¾ cup (200 g) soft brown sugar

½ cup (40 g) desiccated coconut

½ cup (1 stick/100 g) unsalted
   butter, melted

CARAMEL

1⅓ cups (400 g) sweetened condensed milk

2 tablespoons unsalted butter,
   diced

¼ cup (50 g) corn syrup (or golden
   syrup)

TOPPING

1¼ cups (150 g) chopped dark
   chocolate

3 tablespoons unsalted butter,
   diced

1 Preheat the oven to 325°F (160°C). Line a 8-in × 12-in (20-cm × 30-cm) brownie pan with parchment baking paper.

2 Sift the cornstarch and rice flour into a bowl, then mix in the soft brown sugar, coconut and melted butter until well combined.

3 Press the mixture firmly into the base of the prepared pan. Bake for 12 minutes. Allow to cool.

4 To make the Caramel, combine the condensed milk, diced butter and corn syrup in a small saucepan. Cook over low heat, stirring continuously, for about 10 minutes, until the mixture is light golden brown.

5 Pour the Caramel over the cooked base and spread out evenly. Cool at room temperature for about 2 hours, until set.

6 To make the Topping, melt the chocolate and butter together in a double boiler or in the microwave until smooth.

7 Spread the Topping evenly over the Caramel. Allow the topping to set, then cut the brownies into squares or rectangles to serve.

Chocolate Brownies

These rich brownies are delicious served warm with ice-cream for dessert.

MAKES 12
PREPARATION TIME: 30 MINS
COOKING TIME: 40 MINS
STORE IN AN AIRTIGHT CONTAINER
   FOR UP TO 3 DAYS

3/4 cup (1 3/4 sticks/200 g) unsalted butter, diced
2 1/2 cups (300 g) chopped dark chocolate
1/4 cup (60 ml) milk
3 eggs
1 cup (225 g) superfine sugar
1/2 cup (40 g) cocoa (unsweetened)
3/4 cup (120 g) gluten-free self-rising
   flour, sifted
3/4 cup (100 g) chopped walnuts

1 Preheat the oven to 325°F (160°C).
Line a 8-in × 12 in (20-cm × 30-cm)
brownie pan with parchment baking paper.
2 Heat the butter, chocolate and milk
in a double boiler or in the microwave
until melted and smooth. Whisk the eggs
into the chocolate mixture. Combine the
sugar and cocoa, then whisk it into the
mixture. Stir in the sifted flour and then the
chopped walnuts.
3 Pour the batter into the prepared pan.
Bake for 40 minutes, or until a skewer
inserted into the brownie comes out
clean. Cool in the pan. Cut into squares
and serve warm or cold.

Honey and Sesame Seed Brownies

Sweet, soft and chewy, this brownie is a great lunchbox addition for morning or afternoon tea.

MAKES 2 LOAVES
PREPARATION TIME: 20 MINS
COOKING TIME: 30 MINS
STORE IN AN AIRTIGHT CONTAINER FOR
  UP TO 1 WEEK

3¼ cups (375 g) sesame seeds
2 cups (200 g) desiccated coconut
¾ cup (180 g) smooth peanut butter
¾ cup (225 g) honey
¾ cup (180 g) superfine sugar
2 teaspoons vanilla extract

1 Preheat the oven to 325°F (160°C). Line a 8-in × 12-in (20-cm × 30-cm) brownie pan with parchment baking paper.
2 Combine the sesame seeds, coconut, peanut butter, honey, sugar and vanilla in the bowl of an electric mixer fitted with the paddle attachment. Mix on low speed until well combined. Press the mixture into the prepared pan and smooth the top with the back of a spoon.
3 Bake for 25–30 minutes, until light golden brown. Cut the brownies in the pan while still warm, then leave to cool completely in the pan.

Chocolate Chip Cookies

Choose polenta labeled 'fine' or 'instant' for the best texture.

MAKES 40
PREPARATION TIME: 30 MINS
COOKING TIME: 12 MINS
STORE IN AN AIRTIGHT CONTAINER FOR
 UP TO 1 WEEK

$^2/_3$ cup (1$^1/_3$ sticks/150 g) unsalted butter,
 softened
$^3/_8$ cup (80 g) soft brown sugar
$^1/_2$ cup (125 g) superfine sugar
2 eggs
2 teaspoons vanilla extract
1$^1/_3$ cups (200 g) rice flour, sifted
2 cups (300 g) instant polenta (cornmeal)
2 teaspoons baking powder
1$^1/_2$ cups (250 g) dark chocolate chips

1 Preheat the oven to 325°F (160°C). Line two baking sheets with parchment baking paper.
2 Beat the butter and sugars in the bowl of an electric mixer fitted with the paddle attachment, on high speed for 5 minutes, until pale and creamy. Add the eggs one at a time, beating well after each addition. Add the vanilla, sifted rice flour, polenta and baking powder, and mix on low speed until combined. Add the chocolate chips and mix well.
3 Roll the dough into walnut-sized balls and place, 2 in (5 cm) apart, on the prepared baking sheets. Bake the cookies for 10–12 minutes, until slightly golden. Cool on wire racks.

Peanut Butter Cookies

This is a fantastic recipe to get children involved in the kitchen, as it's so simple and quick to make. Kids also love to eat these cookies.

MAKES 26
PREPARATION TIME:20 MINS
COOKING TIME: 12 MINS
STORE IN AN AIRTIGHT CONTAINER
  FOR UP TO 1 WEEK

1¼ cups (400 g) crunchy peanut butter
1 egg
1 cup (225 g) sugar
1 cup (180 g) dark chocolate chips

1 Preheat the oven to 325°F (160°C). Line two baking sheets with parchment baking paper.
2 Combine the peanut butter, egg and sugar in the bowl of an electric mixer fitted with the paddle attachment, on low speed until well mixed. Mix in the chocolate chips.
3 Roll the mixture into walnut-sized balls and place, at least 1¼ in (3 cm) apart, on the prepared baking sheets. Flatten the balls slightly with the back of a fork. Bake the cookies for 12 minutes, until firm to the touch. Cool on wire racks.

Gingerbread House Plan

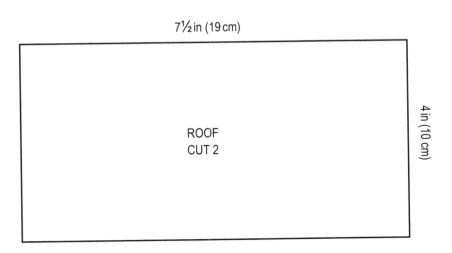

7½ in (19 cm)

ROOF
CUT 2

4 in (10 cm)

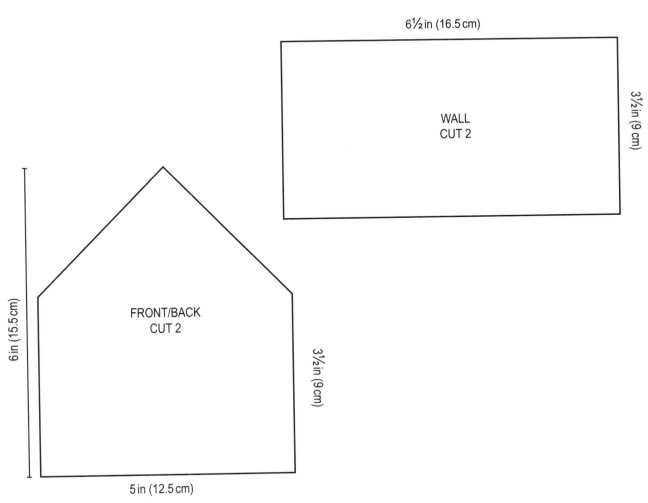

6½ in (16.5 cm)

WALL
CUT 2

3½ in (9 cm)

6 in (15.5 cm)

FRONT/BACK
CUT 2

3½ in (9 cm)

5 in (12.5 cm)

Index

Published by Tuttle Publishing, an imprint of Periplus Editions (HK) Ltd

www.tuttlepublishing.com

First published in 2011 by Penguin Group (Australia),
   250 Camberwell Road, Camberwell, Victoria 3124, Australia
   (a division of Pearson Australia Group Pty Ltd)

Text copyright © Alison Thompson 2011
Photographs copyright © Adrian Lander 2011
Cover photograph by Adrian Lander

ISBN: 978-0-8048-4302-7

Distributed by

North America, Latin America & Europe
Tuttle Publishing
364 Innovation Drive
North Clarendon, VT 05759-9436 U.S.A.
Tel: 1 (802) 773-8930; Fax: 1 (802) 773-6993
info@tuttlepublishing.com
www.tuttlepublishing.com

Japan
Tuttle Publishing
Yaekari Building, 3rd Floor
5-4-12 Osaki, Shinagawa-ku, Tokyo 141-0032
Tel: (81) 3 5437-0171; Fax: (81) 3 5437-0755
sales@tuttle.co.jp
www.tuttle.co.jp

Asia Pacific
Berkeley Books Pte. Ltd.
61 Tai Seng Avenue, #02-12, Singapore 534167
Tel: (65) 6280-1330; Fax: (65) 6280-6290
inquiries@periplus.com.sg
www.periplus.com

15 14 13 12   10 9 8 7 6 5 4 3 2 1
Printed in Singapore   1207TW

TUTTLE PUBLISHING® is a registered trademark of Tuttle Publishing, a division of Periplus Editions (HK) Ltd.

The Tuttle Story
"Books to Span the East and West"

Most people are surprised to learn that the world's largest publisher of books on Asia had its humble beginnings in the tiny American state of Vermont. The company's founder, Charles Tuttle, came from a New England family steeped in publishing, and his first love was books—especially old and rare editions.

Tuttle's father was a noted antiquarian dealer in Rutland, Vermont. Young Charles honed his knowledge of the trade working in the family bookstore, and later in the rare books section of Columbia University Library. His passion for beautiful books—old and new—never wavered through his long career as a bookseller and publisher.

After graduating from Harvard, Tuttle enlisted in the military and in 1945 was sent to Tokyo to work on General Douglas MacArthur's staff. He was tasked with helping to revive the Japanese publishing industry, which had been utterly devastated by the war. When his tour of duty was completed, he left the military, married a talented and beautiful singer, Reiko Chiba, and in 1948 began several successful business ventures.

To his astonishment, Tuttle discovered that postwar Tokyo was actually a book-lover's paradise. He befriended dealers in the Kanda district and began supplying rare Japanese editions to American libraries. He also imported American books to sell to the thousands of GIs stationed in Japan. By 1949, Tuttle's business was thriving, and he opened Tokyo's very first English-language bookstore in the Takashimaya Department Store in Ginza, to great success. Two years later, he began publishing books to fulfill the growing interest of foreigners in all things Asian.

Though a westerner, Tuttle was hugely instrumental in bringing a knowledge of Japan and Asia to a world hungry for information about the East. By the time of his death in 1993, he had published over 6,000 books on Asian culture, history and art—a legacy honored by Emperor Hirohito in 1983 with the "Order of the Sacred Treasure," the highest honor Japan bestows upon non-Japanese.

The Tuttle company today maintains an active backlist of some 1,500 titles, many of which have been continuously in print since the 1950s and 1960s—a great testament to Charles Tuttle's skill as a publisher. More than 60 years after its founding, Tuttle Publishing is more active today than at any time in its history, still inspired by Charles Tuttle's core mission—to publish fine books to span the East and West and provide a greater understanding of each.